KU-114-192

The Flaming Door

Influences of the Zodiac in the structure of the Human Body
(From Parcelsus)

Eleanor C Merry

The Flaming Door

The Mission of
the Celtic Folk-Soul

Floris Books

First published in 1936 by Rider & Co
Revised and enlarged edition published in 1962
by New Knowledge Books, East Grinstead.
Fifth edition published in 2008 by Floris Books
Second printing 2009

© Estate of Eleanor Merry 1962, 1983

All rights reserved. No part of this book may be
reproduced without the prior permission of Floris Books,
15 Harrison Gardens, Edinburgh, www.florisbooks.co.uk

British Library CIP Data available

ISBN 978-086315-644-1

Printed in Great Britain
by Bell & Bain Ltd, Glasgow

CONTENTS

INTRODUCTION

A quarter of a century has passed since the original publication of this book. Is there today a greater likelihood that it will be understood?

Interest in the study of the past, and particularly in civilisations that flourished before Greece or Rome, is much more widespread today; archaeology has perhaps become the most popular of all the sciences. In some directions there is abundant new evidence; and there are useful new methods, which can be applied almost everywhere. But whether progress has been made in interpreting the *mind* of the past, is more doubtful. That there is some kind of continuity between the mythologies of the ancient world and the deeper levels of our consciousness now, is fairly generally recognised; but this continuity can be interpreted in widely different ways. There are many who regard the development of the scientific consciousness, which concentrates on the measurable aspects of physical objects, as an unmixed gain. To them, the consciousness which was at home in myth and picture, rather than in the measurement of physical events, seems like a nightmare from which mankind was wholly fortunate to awake.

To others our position seems more complicated. They see our civilisation as a mixture of two cultures, which it has in no real sense reconciled, and which may in quite practical ways frustrate one another. We have the new scientific culture; and we have a religious and artistic culture which is really derived—though its exponents often fail to see this, or indeed hotly deny it—from the earlier dreamlike, participating consciousness. For some it seems almost self-evident that a kind of insight was possible in this earlier condition of man, which needs to be regained on fresh levels of consciousness today, and without which human existence would become meaningless. (Charles Davy has put this view very effectively in " Towards a Third Culture ".)

Eleanor Merry looked at the past with a mood of grateful

recognition. She did not regard herself as learned, though the tremendous width of her reading, and the retentiveness of her memory, are continually evident in this book. Nor did she regard herself as possessing the equipment of a scientist; though she had a mind capable of subtle distinctions, and of acute self-criticism. She felt that she could interpret the past, because so much in herself was closely akin to it. Her mind responded to the thoughts contained in the sermon of an early Christian Father, or to the sequence of pictures in the poem of an ancient Welsh Bard, more happily than to most of what she encountered as the products of the twentieth century. Need we believe that someone armed with all the instruments of scientific precision, but without this sense of kinship, would be better able to *interpret* the history of human beliefs?

Sometimes, indeed, outstanding academic abilities are found united with considerable imaginative insight. In their recent study of significant elements of ancient tradition in Ireland and Wales, " Celtic Heritage " (London, 1961), Dr. Alwyn Rees and Dr. Brinley Rees have approached the old legends and stories with reverence and love, aware that what has provided nourishment for so long must contain wisdom, however elusive it may be for us. " For countless ages men have found in these stories a support for their material and spiritual life . . . only through blind arrogance can all this testimony be dismissed as of little or no significance." They show in great detail how the traditional stories are always concerned with the frontiers between the world of our ordinary experience and another level of reality, which can only be described in terms of paradox. And yet only by reference to this other level of reality can the essentials of human life—birth, adolescence, marriage, social order, and death—perserve their true dignity. A story which at first sight may appear only an arbitrary sequence of fantastic adventures reveals itself as rich in meaning, and immediately concerned with the ways in which ordinary people can feel that the spiritual world touches their lives.

The Rees brothers amply confirm Eleanor Merry's fundamental theme: that Celtic tradition is dealing everywhere with " The Flaming Door "—the threshold between the physical and the spiritual worlds. But she is able to go further, in a sense, than they do; not only to point to the existence of a spiritual world in general, which presses upon human life with its mystery and summons man to adventure into

its depths—but to speak with confidence about the knowledge of that world.

Eleanor Merry had no doubt that throughout human
history there have been Mystery schools, through which men
and women, who wanted to know more about the ultimate
realities than the exoteric religion and culture of their age
could teach them, have been led further. If myth and legend
have their ultimate source in such Mysteries, it is through
knowledge of a similar kind that we will be helped toward
their interpretation. Eleanor Merry felt that she could
recognise traces of the work of the Mysteries in many
countries and periods; and she found in Rudolf Steiner a
twentieth-century personality who was able to speak with
authority on such matters. His teaching confirmed for her
a great deal which had accompanied her from early childhood, though she had not always been able to take hold of
it in fully conscious thought.

The reader of "*The Flaming Door*" will be able to find
his way through what seems at first its bewildering variety
of subject-matter if he sees what far-reaching illumination
Eleanor Merry derived from Rudolf Steiner's description of
the central act in the Hibernian Mysteries. The pupil
learned, not as a theoretical problem, but as a fundamental
tension in which his whole being was involved, the polarity
between knowledge and artistic creation. He was confronted
by two mighty figures, in whose characteristics he came to
recognise the cosmic significance of this polarity; and he
found it repeated in nature, in the alternation of winter and
summer. (The great part *this* alternation played in Celtic
culture, and the way that the human soul is torn between
the claims of these two, is well brought out by the brothers
Rees.) In "*The Flaming Door*" we can trace the wonderful
and complex variations through, which this problem has
passed in human history, right up to our present-day debate
about " the two cultures ".

When the pupil of the Hibernian Mysteries had felt deeply
enough the claims of knowledge upon the one hand, and of
the instinctive creative powers which bring happiness on
the other, and had come to experience the division in his
own nature as complete and apparently insuperable—then
he was led before the image of that Being, Whom we call
Christ. That this Being could be approached in the spirit
long before the Incarnation was a familiar fact to the early
Christians, and is explicit, for example, in St. John's Gospel.

The whole character and mood of Irish Christianity make evident that the Gospel was found in no way alien to the ancient tradition; in the story of Conchubar (illuminatingly interpreted in detail in Chapter III) a Druid describes to the King of Ireland the Crucifixion as it is happening in Palestine.

Through Christ, there can enter into the winter cold of knowledge a warmth which in no way obscures or corrupts it, but gives it life; and into the stormy creative chaos of the instinctive life He brings a light which does not lame it, but purifies and redeems it. In this experience is the source of Christian art; which constantly breaks through afresh, however often iconoclastic or puritan tendencies attempt to destroy it.

As early as the fourth century, exoteric Christianity began to deny its kinship with the Mysteries, under the influence of those who sought to continue the imperial power of Rome in another form; and esoteric Christianity was driven to follow hidden paths, some of which are wonderfully described in the later part of this book. It may be said that a tradition would not be esoteric, unless it chose secrecy. Yet secrecy is by no means the essential quality of esotericism; it is the warmth and humility of mind that fills the greatest versions of the Grail story.

Accounts of the ancient Mysteries, or of the esoteric stream in Christianity, are themselves valueless, unless they have something of this mood. And it is the same with the reader. The best will not be found in "*The Flaming Door*" if it is approached only as a storehouse of rare information; but only if it is taken slowly and meditatively, and perhaps compared where possible with some of the original texts (for example the easily accessible "*Life of St. Columba*" by St. Adamnan) or with modern writings in the same field, above all Rudolf Steiner's "*Mystery Centres*". Then this book will give of its honey.

ADAM BITTLESTON.

Michaelmas, 1961.

TO THE READER

WE shall, I believe, never fully understand our evolution, nor see in the glimmering light about us the sign-posts that point the way into the future, unless we recognise the greatness of our spiritual heritage. Innumerable books have been written and the most painstaking researches have been made for centuries past, and an enormous mass of material has been collected from the mythology, traditions, and legends of every country in the world, but it seems as though some vital link is missing. Fact is piled upon fact, old documents are deciphered, folk-lore is compared with folk-lore, archæologists dig, and astronomers calculate, and poets dream—but in the end the opinion is fostered that the ancient wisdom was as the babbling of childhood compared with the intellectual reasoning of grown men.

Seven hundred years ago there was a different outlook. John of Salisbury, who was Bishop of Chartres at the beginning of the thirteenth century, wrote:

" Our time is served by the beneficence of former days, and often knows more than the latter, but not, naturally, because the spirit of our time is the greater, but because it rests upon other powers and upon the ripe wisdom of our fathers." And he goes on to quote a saying of the great Bernard of Chartres: " He said we are like dwarfs who have climbed on to the shoulders of giants so that we may see more than they and further; but not because of the sharpness of our own eyesight or the tallness of our stature, because we have been lifted up and exalted by the greatness of the giants."

All myths and sagas and legends are like a shimmering veil of many colours, stirred now and then by the wind of our desires, but still hiding from most of us that Council of the Wise seated at the Round Table of the Stars, who once painted on the moving veil the bright pictures of fairy-tale and myth with the breath of their immortal Words. But between us and them lies the gulf of our arrogance and the mists of our unbelief.

He who would write history as some day it must be written should attend to the words of Wilhelm von Humboldt:

" Where two beings are separated from one another by a veritable abyss, no bridge of understanding can be created between them; if an understanding is ever to be reached, it must be because they have understood one another before—and in another way."

The writer of this book has tried to find that " other way ", confident that somewhere in the depths of the heart that *previous* understanding exists in all of us, but has been forgotten.

What else can it be that draws hundreds and thousands of people, as though by some ineradicable instinct, to search for the "fountain of Kunewara"? Our Grailsword is broken and it can only be mended, as the legend tells us, at the fountain of the Beginnings, whose waters are for ever murmuring in the secret recesses of every human soul. Not in external historical events do we find this fountain, but in the soul of the Human Being, whose quest has scattered over the whole world the traces of his many and ardent adventures, while he himself flees ever onward, his heart burning within him because he feels, but can no longer recognise, the glory of the Presence that goes with him on the way.

This book makes no pretence whatever of being " learned ". The author has brooded over these things for many years, painfully aware of the overshadowing mass of research and scholarship, compared with which her efforts are no more than little glow-worm lamps in the night. It is an attempt to reawaken in certain legends and myths, chiefly of Celtic origin, their slumbering secrets, which are without exception secrets of initiation: when men in the fullness of experience sought the Flaming Door without uncertainty, and passed through it into the company of the Wise, and could " go in and out and find pasture ".

Such a book, too, can have no " style ". It must all the time be struggling with the necessity to create a conversation between the accepted facts of history and the visions of the Hills of Dream, and it has to be a friendly conversation and not an argument. They are friends and brothers really, but they have been long estranged from one another. When silence falls at the end of these pages, which of the two voices will find its echo in the heart of the reader? Will there be peace between them?

Then there is a danger lest it should be thought that the Mysteries of Britain are singled out by the writer because—they are British. But every nation of the world has its Soul, and every nation can find it, if it will, and the Soul of every people—whose lineaments may be found, not in the mythical Gods themselves, but in what they *represent*—is destined each to find its altar, side by side with the altars of its brother Souls, in the Temple of the Grail—which is the World.

" There is no law set upon beauty ", says Fiona Macleod; " it has no geography. It is the domain of the spirit. And if, of those who enter there, peradventure any comes again, he is welcome for what he brings; nor do we demand if he be dark or fair, Latin or Teuton or Celt, or say of him that his tidings are lovelier or less lovely because he was born in the shadow of Gaelic hills or nurtured by Celtic shores. It is well that each should learn the mother-song of his land at the cradle-place of his birth. . . . But it is not well that because of the whistling of the wind in the heather one should imagine that nowhere else does the wind suddenly stir the reeds and the grasses in its incalculable hour."

Nevertheless, the Celtic Mysteries, as a whole, have a peculiar destiny, in that they contain—by reason of that destiny—an impulse of re-birth, not, of course, in their own original form, but as the bearers of a Light to lighten the way to a renewed, a nobler, Christianity —to a revelation of the spiritual origin and destiny of mankind on its journey from the Father, to the Son, and at last to the Holy Spirit who " brings together those that are separated ".

But the way is difficult, and every research into the ancient mythologies requires just that element of which Humboldt speaks, the sense of an understanding that is " pre-existent ".

This book deals chiefly—as a beginning—with ancient Hibernia and Wales. It is the author's deepest wish that other writers might attempt for Scotland, for Ireland, and for the Arthurian legends, what she has so inadequately and briefly outlined.

LONDON,
In the Spring of 1936.

PART I

BEFORE CHRIST

CHAPTER I

THE THREE AND THE SEVEN

" The letters of the Holy Name are called the three columns of truth, because there can be no knowledge of the truth but from the light thrown upon it; and the three columns of the sciences, because there can be no sciences, but from the light and truth."

(From the *Barddas*.)

AS everyone knows, there are conceptions of the world created by the human mind and recorded in ancient documents which point back to the most remote prehistoric times. But the art of writing or of making signs or hieroglyphs to represent these intuitive perceptions of the mystery of life on the earth, only came into existence thousands of years later than the events they seek to portray.

The soul of man has always had the characteristic of mobility. We know this when we observe our own emotional life; pleasure, pain, sympathy and antipathy, wonder and awe, give us a definite sense of inner movement, of soundless and invisible gesture. If the impressions that the outer world make upon us are strong, these inner movements break out into sound and visible gesture. We utter speech—we move—we cry Ah! or Oh! and when in fear we feel the darkness of the unknown in *U*. . . .

Speech makes a bond between man and man and between man and the world, which is divine. The universe speaks *in* us, and we utter its Word.

In the literature of Britain we are fortunate in possessing a written record of the way in which this wonderful relation between man and the world was experienced thousands of years ago. This history of the beginning of language is told to us in legendary form:

Menw, or Manu, the " Son of the Three Shouts ", beheld the original language, which began with the Name of God, in a vision, and his vision is recorded in the following words perhaps thousands of years later:*

" When God pronounced His Name, with the Word sprang the Light and Life; for previously there was no Life except God Himself. . . . His name was pronounced, and with the utterance was the springing of Light and vitality, and man, and every other living thing. And Menw beheld the springing of the light, and its form and appearance, not otherwise than thus, / | \ in three columns; and in the rays of light the vocalization—for one were the hearing and seeing, one unitedly the form and sound; and one unitedly with the form and sound was life, and one unitedly with these three was power, which power was God the Father. And since each of these was one unitedly, he understood that every voice, and hearing, and living, and being, and sight, and seeing, were one unitedly with God; nor is the least thing other than God. And by seeing the form, and in it hearing the voice—not otherwise —he knew what form and appearance voice should have.

" And having obtained Earth under him co-instantaneously with the Light, he drew the form of the voice and light on the Earth. And it was on hearing the sound of the voice, which had in it the kind and utterance of *three notes*, that he obtained the

* From *Barddas*.

three letters, and knew the sign that was suitable to one and other of them. . . . Thus was the voice that was heard, placed on record in the symbol, and meaning attached to each of the three notes: the sense of O was given to the first column, and the sense of I to the second or middle column, and the sense of W to the third; whence the word OIW.* That is to say it was by means of this word that God declared His existence, life, power, eternity, universality. And in the declaration was His love, that is, co-instantaneously with it sprang like lightning all the universe into life and existence, co-vocally and co-jubilantly with the uttered Name of God, in one united song of exultation and joy—then all the worlds to the extremities of Annwn. It was thus then that God made the worlds, namely, He declared His Name and existence / I \."

Then we are told that *Einigen the Giant* was the first to *understand* letters. Einigen, sometimes called Enigat, is the same designation as *Enoch* or *Hanokh*, and the word means a Seer or Initiate. *Enkidu*, the friend of the great Gilgamesh (Nimrod) of Babylon, was probably so called for the same reason. The " Book of Enoch " (an excluded Book of the Old Testament) is a history, written by an Initiate, of the wisdom known to the *Atlanteans* before the Deluge. But Enoch, or Einigen the Giant, is not the name of a single person, it is a designation applied to many who possessed the " inner eye ".

The Christian *Gnosis*, as given in the *Pistis Sophia*, is tinctured with the wisdom of Enoch; and has much to do with the mystery of the Divine Name and the descent of the Word into Flesh. St. Augustine indicates

* OIW. The " W " is our *U*, and pronounced as in " food."

that the reason why the Book of Enoch is not included in the Church canon is because of its great antiquity, not as a written document, but as to its contents.

According to Welsh tradition the *vision* of the Word appeared first; then came the *application* of the vision to letters or symbol; then came the *understanding* of sound and speech and the music of vocal song, and poetry. In this way the Three Rays of Light were found to contain all ART.

But Einigen the Giant perceived in them also " all the demonstrable SCIENCES that ever were ". These *two* pillars " Art " and " Science " were the whole wisdom of the ancient Mysteries. This wisdom was also found " inscribed on two pillars " by the great Hermes, teacher of the Egyptians. The Three Rays of Light included therefore two " opposites " that are to be united or harmonised in the third.

The realisation of the inherent truth in this ancient story is the very essence and core of any study of Celtic mythology—or indeed, of all the secrets of existence. There is everywhere a Triad. The human being can place himself in any relation—as the third—to the other two. They form, not an indivisible unity, but balance and harmony.

If we study the great culture-epochs of the past we find that they reveal that the world-creation was experienced in the depths of the human soul first in the form of Unity, then in a Duality, then in a Trinity of Divine Being, so that what was perceived in a single flash of vision by Menw the Son of the Three Shouts, is spread out through thousands of years as humanity begins to trace the meaning of evolution.

In the old Indian civilization the idea of Unity prevailed. Those magnificent scriptures of the primeval East which we now possess, were handed down for long ages only by word of mouth, the *Veda*—or Word; and from them we know how man felt himself entirely united with the spiritual origin of his existence. The three vowels of the sacred Word were experienced differently: as A, O, U, and they culminated in a fourth sound, M, which signifies *silence*—the closing of the mouth. So that the Three " Rays " were, in silence, brought back into a single One—enclosed; even as the Self of man is enclosed within his skin, so this Self was also enclosed within the whole Being of God.

In head, heart, and breath, the ancient Indian, though aware that these held for him a triad of experiences, felt himself completely identified with the Earth, the Sun, and the sun-impregnated atmosphere. He " looked toward the Self with *reverted* sight " (i.e. outwards, into the Cosmic All), " seeking deathlessness ".

In the old Persian civilisation, which is now known to have flourished six thousand years before Christ,[1] the idea of a Duality was present: the Darkness of matter was separated from the Light of Spirit. The earth was beginning to be felt as the home of humanity; and through the agency of man, who found that he could work upon the earth out of the strength of his own will, the glorious rays of the Sun could be made to penetrate the darkness of the earth by means of the plough.

In the Indian period men had lived a nomadic life and nourished themselves on the milk of their flocks and herds and on natural fruits. Only under the leadership of the great Hierophant Zoroaster, in Persia, did they begin to cultivate the soil.[2]

In the third period, a civilisation arose in Egypt and Chaldea, and then appeared the conception of the divine Trinity—Osiris, Isis, and Horus. To the power of Will that had awakened in the souls of men during the Persian epoch, was now added the power of Feeling. Men *felt* the earth which they trod underfoot as a material reflection of the divine measures of the stars. Heaven and earth were divided from one another, but Man could now mediate between the two quite consciously through the science of geometry and the arts. The Creator was the Father; Nature was the Mother; Man was the Child of the past, the present, and the future.

In the following age—the fourth—there began a further maturing of the conception of the Trinity; the Greeks looked up to three generations of Gods, belonging to the three preceding periods. Many Gods dwelt in the Temples and walked with men. Their conception of the Trinity was scattered throughout the vast profusion of Nature's beneficence. Then the power of Thought was added to Will and Feeling.

Those sages of ancient times who understood how mankind makes his way between the " opposites ", regarded the whole process of the evolution of the world as the " dynamic " of the Trinity. It unfolded itself; and must, after a period of maturing, *in*fold itself again. So they pictured this as a succession of seven cosmic ages, a *Manvantara*—to use the Oriental expression—the life of a planetary system. The secrets of these numbers gave the basis for Egyptian architecture.[3]

The idea of the existence of a duality, as the opposition of spiritual and material life for instance, and all other " opposites ", together with the need to discover a third factor which will bring them into harmony, has been present throughout the history of human consciousness; and it is something that is acutely emphasised in the world at the present time. It manifests

itself everywhere. We are overwhelmed by the
questions which arise in the search for a harmonising
principle. Its discovery is the only answer. This
" third " is not sensed by the human soul as a principle
of *compromise;* for there is an inherent health in us
which rejects mere compromise as a false answer to the
real problems of life. But there is, instead, an instinctive conviction that it is man himself who is the
answerer, able to harmonise the opposites; who, by
allowing himself to be even overwhelmed by the
contradictions of life to begin with, will finally emerge
triumphant—a witness in himself, through tribulation,
that the power to become the answerer is given to him
by One who was " crucified between two thieves ".

There are innumerable legends representing the
struggle of the soul to bring these opposites into
harmony: on the one hand the divine wisdom which
for ages had flowed down into the sanctuaries of the
Mysteries in revelation and inspiration, preparing
the way for human reason and intelligence; and on
the other hand the passion—in the true sense of the
word—of human action and experience in the physical
world. Their symbols have been many and various
throughout history, and we have a great heritage of
wealth in every genuine myth and saga all over the
world, to remind us of the threefold harmony of the
world.

In our own time the separation that exists between
the two pillars of life—once so beautifully pictured in
the romance of the Rose and the Lily—shows itself in
the anguish of human souls who cannot reconcile their
sense of inner loss in respect of religion with the sense of
pride and arrogance in respect of a brilliant external
civilisation. And it gives much food for thought when
we pause to look at this external civilisation and see

that in proportion as Science becomes more and more dominant and magical, the wings of Art become feebler, and the great Imaginations that once gave us a common language of Beauty are sinking into the turbid waters of a decadent psychology.

No show of modern Art calls forth the tones of this once universal language, but rather the chattering of opinion and opinion—like the over-tones of a fretful day of English weather. We hunger more than ever for the calm serenity of the Art of the past or of the spacious East, hoping to find there some solace for our unrest.*

One of the greatest of the universal legends is that which tells of the conflict between the wise King Solomon, of the race of Seth, and the artificer Hiram, a son of the race of Cain, in the building of the Temple.†

The Queen of Sheba, whom both desired, is the cause of their difference. She is the human soul. But there are three " evil companions " who see in this disharmony an opportunity for gaining their own ends; their ambitions have been thwarted, and they seek to destroy Hiram's crowning work, the casting of the Brazen Sea.

The Brazen Sea is a compound of the seven planetary metals—lead, tin, iron, gold, copper, quicksilver, and silver; and they represent the culmination of the seven periods of cosmic and human evolution. The making of the Brazen Sea is a supreme mystery of the " Fire " of which the sons of Cain were masters. But the three companions adulterate the mixture with water, and Hiram, in self-immolation, plunges into the fire. This is a spiritual experience. He who can accomplish it understands the secrets of the evolution

---

* Read the Life of Gauguin.
† Hiram and Solomon. Albert Steffen.

of the earth and of human nature. There he sees, in vision, the Master of all earthly sciences and arts, the Master of that wisdom which is not quiet and transparent like the stars, but burning with the passion of enthusiasm and dynamic with the will-impulses of the future—Tubal Cain. From him Hiram receives a hammer and a golden triangle; he returns to his task in the Temple, and the Brazen Sea is made. But the three companions murder him. Before he dies he throws the golden triangle into a spring of living water. There it is found, and is preserved in the Holy of Holies.

This story indicates the preservation, within the Mystery Temples and secret Brotherhoods during thousands of years, of the secret of the Trinity, the " golden triangle ". It is a reminder to mankind that there are three higher members or parts of human nature, corresponding to the transcendental conception of the Trinity, that are to blossom in the future, to make the transfigured, the selfless, the truly living Man; for our thinking, feeling, and willing, are destined to be transformed into higher and ever higher capacities. In expectation of the " golden triangle " and in preparation for it, men looked forward to a time when knowledge of the Spirit would no longer be at variance with the enthusiasm of the " sons of Fire " who build up the physical sciences. The element that must unite them is another kind of Fire: incarnate Love. But in order to comprehend this fully, man must know the secrets of the " seven metals ", that is, of his evolution. It is the crowning work in the building of the Temple.

Therefore certain fundamental truths underlie the researches we must now undertake in Celtic Mythology: namely, that Man passes through his existence

Earth as the harmoniser of opposites; that he has to find the balance between the two extremes, just as he has to live his life always at the ever-moving point of junction between past and future; that the world-evolution follows a majestic sevenfold rhythm, in which is a trinity of phases at either side of a point of balance at the centre: $3+1+3$; and that the " golden Triangle " symbolises the perfecting of the earlier phases in the later. And it is a fact that all the true legends of the world point, in one way and another, to a lost wisdom which man is for ever seeking to re-discover.

So now we can glance at a legend which will be an introduction to our subject of Celtic Mythology; for there perhaps the greatest of all the ancient secrets are concealed.

The very sound of the name of Merlin has magic in it; it sighs like a wandering wind through the forest of Arthurian and Druid legend.

In every mythology there are heroic names that are not the designations of any single individual alone, but are, to use a familiar phrase, a " spiritual calling ". Confusion arises very often from the attempt to fasten such a name to some one particular person; but the spirit " bloweth where it listeth " and is more living than any history. At some point, however, such a name *is* discoverable in association with a particular historical individual, though we may find it in many centuries. But if a person is said to have lived for centuries then history cannot accept him. But history can accept him as the representative of an order, or a teaching, or a power of the human soul building up the folk-soul of a whole people. A study of what has come down to us concerning the acts of a Merlin or an

Arthur or a Tristan may shed its light on many problems, and even lead us to hitherto unknown periods of history.

There was a Merlin—or Merddin—of the sixth century A.D. who was a Bard, called the "Caledonian", and is described by another Bard of the tenth century as "the supreme judge of the North, president of Bardic lore about the waters of the Clyde". He knew the Mysteries that had been taught at Stonehenge. That he was a Master of the secret lore is suggested by the fact that he was called a "swine-herd"—much as we might speak of our clergy to-day as "shepherds of a flock" and the Church as a "sheep-fold". But in the former case the designation is connected with the legend of a mythical Sow which deposited various miraculous creatures upon the Celtic lands. She is the fruitful wisdom of the Mysteries; and one of her deposits was said to be a swarm of bees, the *Melissæ*, or priestess attendants belonging to her cult.

Merlin and his herd of "pigs" are apparently opposed by a certain champion of Christianity; and so he tells his "initiated little pigs" to find hiding-places for themselves in the forests. Merlin himself meets one day with a stranger clothed in dark attire, who is riding upon a black horse, and Merlin, seeing no doubt the winged light about the stranger's head, stops him and asks him if his name is Ys Colan, and the stranger answers in the affirmative. It is Saint Columba. Strange and significant encounter! But sad to relate, any conversation they may have had does not seem to have been recorded; but if the accounts are to be believed, Merlin must have been a formidable adversary, since he is said to have " burnt a church, obstructed the establishment of a school, and drowned a book. . . ." How greatly he dreaded the loss of the old Mystery-wisdom is told in a poem which extols its preciousness not only for himself but for all mankind.

The poem is about a wonderful orchard, called the "Avellenau". This orchard of delicious apple-trees contains the secret of earthly and planetary evolution. It has been revealed to him by Gwenddoleu, his master Hierophant. A translation runs as follows:

"To no one has been exhibited, at one hour of dawn" (the hour of initiation), "what was shown to Merddin before he became aged: namely seven score and seven delicious apple-trees, of equal age, height, length, and size, which sprang from the bosom of Mercy. One bending veil covers them over. . . .

"The delicious apple-tree, with blossom of pure white, and wide spreading branches, produces sweet apples, for those who can digest them. And they have always grown in the wood, which grows apart" (that is, in the sanctuary of the Mysteries).

The key to this passage is the number of the apple-trees—one hundred and forty-seven. It is the square of seven, multiplied by the mystical three, and it refers to the sevenfold system of world-evolution mentioned above. We have seen that this idea is not confined to Celtic mythology. And in our own time it is still taught by representative esoteric schools, that assert the truth of the ancient conception of seven great cosmic periods during which our planetary system is evolving. Each of these seven contains seven lesser periods, and in each of these another seven. Where the planet Earth is concerned, these last occur as successive epochs of civilisation, as indicated in the seven Churches described in the Book of Revelation.

According to this esoteric teaching only three of the greatest periods (with their subdivisions) have so far been completed. The fourth of these, which represents the evolution of our present Earth, has brought the fourth *lesser* period to completion, and four of the seven epochs of civilisation, the fifth being our current one.

In *this* Merddin's time, the fourth epoch of civilisation was in progress, that is, the civilisation built up by Greece and Rome.

So seven times seven, multiplied by three, gives the number one hundred and forty-seven, and refers to the completion of the *three* great cosmic stages with their seven times seven subdivisions and therefore to the whole past history of the evolution of the Earth-planet in the midst of its solar system.

But in this world-conception the various periods are not regarded as a mere succession, but as groups of repetitions or recapitulations of earlier conditions that thus reach an ever higher and higher stage of complexity, both in life, in form, and in consciousness. They are like " wheels within wheels ".* Therefore all initiation into the ancient Mysteries meant *being able to read the present through an understanding of the past,* and *vice versa.* And—the laws of rhythm and repetition being grasped—the future evolution too would be understood as having to follow, so to say, similar laws, but in an ascending arc; that is, that as during the whole of the past there had been a descent of Spirit into Matter, so the future must be an ascent from Matter to Spirit.

Hence the extreme preciousness of the one hundred

* Seen in vision by the prophet Ezekiel.

and forty-seven apple-trees to Merddin and to all the ancient sages. Their " fruits " were the specialised sciences, etc., that could be " eaten " by the initiated, but could not be digested by the profane.

As seven was felt to be related to Time, in the changing positions of the Sun and the seven planets, so twelve, the number of the constellations of the Zodiac, was representative of the Space they dominated. The Platonic Day of 2160 years, during which the Sun rises at the vernal equinox in a particular constellation and then passes to the next, marked the change from one epoch of civilisation to another. This can be proved by history, when allowance is made for the overlapping of the effects of one epoch upon the next. The gradual shifting of the position of the Earth's axis points to the *greater* rhythms, and the corresponding geological changes.

Some knowledge of these things was essential in initiation in olden times. But what has just been described in such bare and dry words was formerly experienced quite unintellectually, and in mighty visions.

Merddin, as well as others who were partakers in the Mysteries, were said to wear the " golden yoke " or " golden collar ", for they felt that they were " yoked " like the planets, to the Sun, the " splendid Mover ". They identified themselves, in knowledge, with the Earth, and knew its cosmic path.

All the Bardic writings that have come down to us are clothed in the greatest obscurity of language and of imagery, probably for the reason that in this obscurity lay the only hope of preserving their wisdom from being desecrated by the unenlightened.

In the poem, Merddin goes on to lament his loneliness as an upholder of the secret knowledge, and expresses his sorrow at its gradual disappearance from the world:

"I am neglected by my former friends, and wander amongst spectres who know me not. . . . Thou sweet and beneficent tree! not scanty is the fruit with which thou art loaded; but upon thy account I am terrified and anxious lest the woodmen should come, those profaners of the wood, to dig up thy root and corrupt thy seed, that not an apple may ever grow upon thee more. . . . Upon me Gwenddoleu freely bestowed these precious gifts; but he is, this day, as if he had never been."

Gwenddoleu's wonderful orchard was guarded by two "dusky birds", and each one wore a "yoke of gold". These birds were said to have consumed two persons—presumably one each—at noon, and two persons for supper, every day. Antiquarian research has made up its mind, shuddering, that this refers to human sacrifice. (How anxious, and almost pleased, people are to comment on the blood-thirstiness of the Druids!) The two dusky birds were eventually destroyed by one who was called *Gall Power*, the "imbiber of learning".

The two dusky birds are similar to the ravens of Odin; they represent divinatory powers, the "organ" of clairvoyant sight, a universal faculty in ancient times, which depended upon a peculiar vibratory relation between two parts of the brain whose functions, to-day, have become more or less atrophied as far as clairvoyance is concerned. The effect, when this peculiar relation was established, was, to the clairvoyant *observer* of the process, like a revolving form of light seen above the forehead, resembling two wings or " petals ". In representations, for example, of the Egyptian God Ammon, they were shown as a knotted or twisted structure ending in two horns. For this reason Moses was also depicted with horns. The old powers of clairvoyance were like " messengers ", or scouts, sent out into the world to discover (and guard) its occult secrets.

The initiated teachers of the Mystery schools employed their pupils, whose souls were still in the unenlightened or " dusky " stage—and so called Ravens—to be the embodied assistants of their clairvoyant powers, as watchers or guardians or messengers of the Mysteries in the outer world. They consumed, not other persons, but *themselves*. For, to accomplish the work to which they were appointed faithfully, they must be selfless—both by day and by night.

The advent of Gall Power who destroyed the birds, hints at the coming of vital changes in civilisation which ushered in *intellectual* knowledge as distinct from the old instinctive knowledge, and so obliterated the old clairvoyance.

What is told in this poem is not " superstition " but exact knowledge, concealed in imagery.

There could be no " orchard of sweet apple-trees " if the " dusky birds " had not been there. Among the relations of Gwenddoleu there were four who bore the following names: *Pabo*, the " producer of life "; *Nudd*, who is " mist "; *Eleuver*, the " luminary "; and *Cov*, " memory ".

But who are these four relations of Gwenddoleu's, Pabo, Nudd, Eleuver, and Cov? Their names tell us that they represent four links in the great sevenfold chain of the stages of planetary evolution. Gwenddoleu, as a master Hierophant, stands as a kind of representative of the whole system of Druid wisdom (even if he *is* also a real person), and so he is bound together by a spiritual relationship with the known sequences of cosmic and terrestrial evolution.

His nearest relative is Pabo. He is the *Earth* in its present form, the producer and bearer of living creatures. The next stage, going backwards, is Nudd, or " mist ". This stage was called in esoteric science the " Moon "; that is, it is a condition when the watery element prevailed throughout the Earth that was covered with a misty veil. Then comes Eleuver, the " Luminary ", corresponding, according to the Mystery teachings, to a kind of Sun-stage of the Earth's existence, a condition of gaseous air. The next is Cov, " Memory ". And this is not quite so easy to grasp. It refers to the primeval state of Fire, or heat without light, and the ancient wisdom called it " Saturn ". What was engendered then, among other things, was that which has now become—for us—the power of memory and the sense of time. One could describe this in all detail, and scientifically, but this is not the place in which to do so.

It is indeed a wonderful hint that is contained in the naming of Gwenddoleu's relations! And it is natural enough that the three elder ones should reveal, in the fruits of the one hundred and forty-seven apple-trees, what these have ripened through eternities for the Earth, and for human knowledge.

The same three steps to the Earth—taught in all the esoteric schools of ancient times—are indicated also in the opening verses of the Gospel of St. John, where the Creative Logos becomes Life, then Light,[4] then Flesh.

In the philosophy of the later Bards, all truth was expressed through the operations of Triads. In the

Three, which they traced in every conceivable sphere of experience, they discovered the key to the understanding of the creation of the material Earth.

This threefold principle abounds everywhere; in Nature, we see it in the kingdom of the plants, in the blossom and the root, sustained in equilibrium by the stem and leaves; in man, in the three powers of the human soul, thinking and willing, harmonised in feeling; in the constitution of the body in nervous system and digestive system balanced by the system of circulation and breathing; in past, and future continually united by the present.

Is it not a matter of common experience that in life, every human being, immortal in spirit, stands always between the outer world of Nature and the inner world of his own soul? Between Science—knowledge—and Art or Imagination? Even as Einigen the Giant discovered all Sciences and all Arts in the Three Rays of Light—and Hermes wrote them on two pillars, where man, as the *third*, could read them?

CHAPTER II

FIRE AND WATER

" Then Being, beholding, said: Let me become great; let me
give birth. Then it put forth Radiance. Then Radiance, beholding said: Let me become great; let me give birth. Then it put
forth the Waters . . . Then the Waters, beholding, said: Let us
become great; let us give birth. They put forth the world-food.
So from the Waters the world-food—*Earth*—is born."

(From the *Upanishads*.)

IN seeking to trace the origins of Celtic mythology
and Christianity, and particularly of the mythology
of Wales, it will be necessary to make excursions
into what may be regarded by many people as a realm
of pure speculation. The writer approaches this part of
her task with great diffidence. So much has been
written, so many eminent antiquarian scholars have
devoted a whole life-time to these things, that the views
that will be expressed here may be considered—to
begin with—as suggestive and empirical.

The writings and researches of the last century on
these matters present a view-point which is too often
limited by the idea that mankind has progressed from
purely savage and ignorant origins, and the discovered
relics of great civilisations and works of art have been a
surprising contradiction, in some respects, to this
idea. But even so it is hardly conceivable to people
to-day that man could have lived outwardly a more
or less primitive existence while possessing at the same
time a great spiritual wisdom. To-day one is apt to

35

think of the " spiritual " only as representing " goodness ", and to associate it with an ethical and moral life
in accordance with present-day standards. But a more
sympathetic and imaginative study of even very
ancient times and peoples will gradually reveal that
men lived very much " between " heaven and earth:
the earthly existence was not nearly so closely absorbed
by their consciousness as it is with us; the body—
death—suffering—these were in a sense apart from the
life of soul which found its own morality in an imaginative and often inspired experience of immortality, and
of the glorious rulership of Gods and Heroes; they felt
that these imparted their wisdom and gave vision to
men, enabling them gradually to accustom themselves
to the physical world. Death was no agonising
problem, but the assured gateway to another existence.
The experiences of clairvoyance and of dream were
more real than those of material life.

The last remnants of a universal clairvoyance were
already fading out some centuries before the beginning
of our era. We have to use this word " clairvoyance ",
although it has fallen somewhat into disrepute at the
present time. It may be that the word " insight "—in
its true sense—might be more acceptable in describing
what was once a universal gift, the power to look *through*
the material phenomena of the world to the spiritual
phenomena behind them. In different ages and
countries the myths by means of which the spiritual
phenomena were interpreted by the initiates to the
people, naturally varied according to the general level
of evolution that the people had attained, and
according to the geographical, racial, and other
prevailing influences. But the fact remains that a
certain kind of rather dreamlike clairvoyance obtained everywhere, and this was enormously enhanced

in the case of those who had undergone initiation in the Temples of the Mysteries.

If one reads, for example, such a book as Wood-Martin's *Elder Faiths of Ireland and pre-Christian Tradition*, or (written in 1856 under the very shadow of nineteenth-century materialism) Nashs' *Taliesin*—one will feel keenly how difficult it is to put forward an explanation, as will be attempted in these pages, which is based on a totally different outlook, namely, on the recognition of the fact of the old powers of clairvoyance. The *facts* described in such books are usually the acme of correctness, but the explanations of the facts, based on a materialistic interpretation, are, according to this view, often quite incorrect. When we read that the discovered remains, let us say, of the old Irish " civilisation " prove conditions of degradation, of cannibalism, human sacrifice, superstitious idolatries, etc., and little else, the question is naturally asked, how could such people have had a real " spiritual " knowledge? This is the question we shall endeavour to answer in these pages.

Anyone who studies the Celtic legends and traditions which are linked with the early centuries of the Christian era, will be impressed by the atmosphere of beauty that pervades them. Mingled with the fragments of an ancient Druid culture and wisdom there is the childlike purity and ecstasy of a Christianity quite unlike that which is to be found later. It is enclosed like a delicate seed within the old and dying splendour of the Great Mystery Centres of Ireland; it is a Christianity that, in its pristine purity is no longer to be found on the surface of civilisation. It is still hidden in the hearts of a few, and in solitary places. More than any other writer Fiona Macleod was its apostle; and he longed for its true history to be made known through the story of Iona:

" What a book it will be! It will reveal to us the secret of what Oisin sang, what Merlin knew, what Columba dreamed, what Adamnan hoped: what this little ' lamp of Christ ' was to pagan Europe; what incense of testimony it flung upon the winds; what saints and heroes went out of it; how the dust of kings and princes were brought there to mingle with its sands; how the noble and the ignoble came to it across long seas and .perilous countries. . . .And how, slowly, a long sleep fell upon the island, and only the grasses shaken in the wind, and the wind itself, and the broken shadows of dreams in the minds of the old, held the secret of Iona."

The foundations of Celtic Christianity had a peculiar and deeply esoteric quality which, giving rise to the great stream of Christian impulse that flowed from Ireland over Europe, was later overwhelmed by a differently experienced form of Christianity advancing from Rome, and yet secretly permeated the world as the great hidden source with which all future revelation concerning Christ must assuredly be united.

There is indeed a feeling in certain circles to-day that in some way the Soul of the Celtic people will again arise, the bearer of some mission to the world; that " Arthur " is not really dead, but living. What this mission is, is no new thing, but is the discovery of ancient truth in the Celtic Mysteries—the very rock of Christian revelation. Consciously or unconsciously, we are all crying out for a " return of Arthur " and for the Wisdom of the Holy Grail! It is not the romance of the adventures of the knights and heroes, it is not the poetry, nor the fascination of research that draws people—as though by a supernatural force—decade after decade to this realm of story. It is the flight of the single human souls to the World-Soul that is hidden there.

The Celts, we must remember, were not inhabitants only of the Northern and Western parts of Europe where we still look for them to-day. They spread far over Europe, over a vast region, called Celtica by Ptolemy; and the British Isles were at first not included in this Celtic world. So that even from this side our Celtic mythology has a widespread foundation related especially to Scandinavian and North-Germanic wisdom, and of which it has been said that " there is no mythology on earth which, in its remarkable constructions and unique development, gives a more significant or a clearer picture of the evolution of the world."[5]

Let us imagine then, the folk-lore of Northern and Western Britain (we shall tell presently of the coming of the Celts) borne upon this foundation, but at the same time having a deeper and older under-structure which is connected with the supernatural wisdom of the submerged continent of Atlantis—now generally acknowledged as having been no fabulous land, but a reality; and developing out of this double foundation the seed of a pure esoteric Christianity.

Let us imagine too, the whole nature of our Northern and Western British country—a region of wild moors and rocky hills and coasts, of seas and lakes, of mists and rainbows and Atlantic storms, and with a vegetation that is curiously stubborn and intensely vital. But we must feel too the significant difference between, for example, the characteristics of the Scotch and Welsh landscapes. In Scotland we seem to breathe an air that blows like cool fire over the primeval granite. In Wales we breathe a kind of twilight air that is laden with the secrets of the grey masses of Silurian shale. For in Scotland, in spite of its frequently wild and rugged quality, there is something like an eternal freshness of youth showing itself as though reborn continually out of the ancient earth. There the skies seem far away, illimitable in light, and the wet mists that fall have no menace in them, but are a reverie. While in Wales, one is led down into the darkness of a terrestrial old age, brooding over deep waters, telling us of the antediluvian world. There the skies are heavier; they bend low over the mountains as though always wishing to converse with them of eternal things. And as we go further South, to Cornwall, the weight of mystery is lifted, and we cannot but think that the golden hair of Isolde or of Gwenevere is still gleaming in the light, and the sun is flashing on knightly armour in the chequered shadows of the woods.

Yes, it is a land full of secrets, and it is bound by strong spiritual bonds with Ireland, the ancient " Paradise "; where, as we shall presently see, Irish priest-initiates of the pagan Temples experienced, ages before our era, a vision of the Christ.

The background of the Northern European mythology is woven out of the whole fabric of Nature. It is as though these people might have said: " Out of the Earth, out of Herda, I can discover the mystery of my own being. Nature has begotten me in her union with the divine-spiritual Fire, the Father; and Nature will lead me again to that Source of my being, to the Waters of the womb of the world, which well up in me continually like a memory of ancient holiness."

The Celtic tradition is full of this twofold origin of man—appearing in many forms—the Fire and Water, the solar and lunar powers—of primeval world-conditions. In Welsh mythology especially there are constant suggestions of a world born out of Water; and these suggestions have provided scholars with the theory that the Druidal religion was " Arkite "—a worship of the Ark as the womb out of which the new humanity, the descendants of Noah, spread over the world.

Everywhere there are allusions to " drowned islands ", or mysterious lands to the far West of Britain, notably the real or mythical island of Hy Brasil, and the " magnetic island " that was the goal of the seven year voyage of St. Brendan. The Cymry (the Welsh) are said to have come from " the summer country, over the hazy sea." Allusions to the " summer country " and the " land of the summer stars " are not, I think, to be interpreted only geographically, but also astronomically, and we may be able to touch on this later in connection with Bardic initiation. But, in another sense too, such allusions are probably astronomical in hinting at periods of *time*, marked by the precession of the equinoxes, and hence to earlier and even antediluvian ages.

Different zodiacal constellations are visible at night above and below the horizon in summer and winter; roughly speaking, ancient tradition could point to seven such constellations and to five, as either " above " or " below". This division of twelve into seven and five has to be taken into consideration in many legends, not only as historical indications, but also as referring to the idea of the twelvefold structure of man and the universe, and this idea played an important part in the ancient myths.[6]

A lovely legend is told by Fiona Macleod in *Beyond the Blue Septentrions*. The boy Arthur, dreaming on the hills at twilight, watching the stars, " climb out of shadowy abysses ", saw in vision the splendid figure of his father Pendragon (the Dragon's Head) who pointed to the constellation of the Great Bear as the place to which he must soon return. Arthur, closing his eyes, felt himself " ascend the invisible stairways of the sky " until he stood on the verge of Arth-Uthyr the Great Bear. There he saw the " Light of the North " as a company of majestic figures seated round a circular abyss of darkness. Each of the seven lordly Kings wore a star upon his forehead. Among them he recognised himself as the King of the Seven Kings. And then a voice that " rose and fell through the eternal silences " like a mighty ocean, proclaimed: " Comrades in God, the time has come when that which is great shall become small."

This is a beautiful illustration of the truth that every earthly event is first " written in the stars ". There it is great; upon the earth it is small. The Round Table is the " circular abyss " of the Earth, and the original foundation of the traditional Round Table—ages before the King Arthur of history—was an ancient wisdom which was based at first, not on a knowledge of the " Twelve ", but of the " Seven ". In other words, on the secrets of *Time*, as calculated by the movements of the seven recognised planets of our system, and the seven periods of world-evolution; and not yet upon the secrets of *Space*. The Twelve constellations of the Zodiac were regarded as a star-picture of all that " dwells side by side in Space "; and in its harmony and majesty encircling the world as the archetype of the universal brotherhood of man.

Hence, in very ancient times, and most especially in those parts of the world that long ago gave a first refuge to the wanderers from the submerged Atlantis, we find to begin with records of the existence of so-called *Mysteries of Saturn*, whom the Greeks call *Cronos*, the Father of Time. Through this wisdom there could flow a perpetuation of the memory of the " Golden Age " of clairvoyance relating to the evolution of the Earth through rhythmic sequences of Time. But let us go back to the Atlantean catastrophe. Edward Davies, in his *Rites and Mysteries of the Druids*, seeks for the whole origin of Druidal tradition in the Biblical deluge. In the margins of our Bibles we see the suggested date of this event as about 2340 years before Christ. But we must look into a much more remote past, more like ten or twelve thousand years before Christ, and think of the " flood " not as a swift and sudden catastrophe but as a prolonged series of such happenings causing, and caused by, enormous geological changes, and commencing thousands of years before.

Nor can we neglect the innumerable references occurring in the legends and traditions of many countries to the secret land of the West, called by various names, and known also to be connected with a healing art, where the mysteries of death and immortality could be solved. There is evidence of this even in so comparatively recent a time as seven or eight hundred years B.C. in the Epic of Gilgamesh, inscribed on tablets in the Library of Nebo at Nineveh, and now in the British Museum.*

Gilgamesh, a ruler in Babylon, was overcome with horror and grief at the death of his friend Eabani (or Enkidu), and the whole problem of death—until then

* The Epic of Gilgamesh. British Museum. Pub.

no " problem " to an ancient humanity that had still so real a sense of the spiritual world—became for him an overwhelming one. Gilgamesh knew that his ancestor Uta-Napishtim had become immortal and so he determined to set out to find him and obtain from him the secret of immortality. The goal of his journey was the Mountain of the Sunset in the West, on the shore of a vast sea. There his immortal ancestor's boatman came to meet him and carried him in his boat over the " waters of death ". Gilgamesh is told: " Shamash the Sun-God hath indeed crossed the Sea, but who besides Him could do so? The passage is hard and the way difficult. And the Waters of Death which block the other end of it are deep." But Gilgamesh arrives in the land of his ancestor, and the latter then tells him the story of the deluge, etc.

The " mountain of the sunset " is an old expression for entering into a different state of consciousness, that of clairvoyance during sleep. Sleep was an " entering into the mountain ", or into the " crystal " of the world. To reach it, the sea or ocean of dream—what the Greeks called " chaos "—had to be crossed. The voyage over this ocean (and it could be undertaken in the waking state as well as in sleep) was a voyage of the spirit through the planetary spheres. Such an experience was connected with all initiations. And Gilgamesh journeyed, to obtain this experience, to a centre of the Irish-Atlantean Mysteries in Middle Europe, near the borders of the present Austria and Hungary. And that was, for him, towards the West; not only geographically, but because the Mystery centre there was an offshoot from the Western Mysteries.

Certain old initiations were often described as a search for the *ancestors;* and between the seeker and his ancestors were the waters of the womb out of which he had been born. Initiation awakened the " ancestral memory " (latent in all people) by teaching the neophyte to extend his ordinary memory beyond the moment of his own birth; and there came to him dim pictures of earthly history—even the visions of the great geological catastrophes, or the deluge. But in this spiritual consciousness all this was experienced not merely as " history " but as the search for the *birth of the soul out of the Divine;* and so led to a realisation of immortality. Such experiences have been recorded in legendary form and in many ancient mythologies.

So the Mountain in the West, separated by deep waters from the seeker is the " place " where the beginnings of post-diluvian (and earlier) history could be found—by crossing the " planetary ocean "; and that is, by an extension of the memory, through initiation, to the time before birth when the soul was on its way through celestial spheres to incarnation. All men live in an *ocean of forgetfulness* of a past which could be known if we could penetrate to the spiritual world where souls live after death and before birth. Merezhkovsky quotes from the Book of Enoch about this:[7]

. . ." ' And he showed me in the West a great mountain. . . . And in this mountain there were four precipices, which were very deep, wide, and slippery; three of them were dark, and one was bright.'

" Here is the kingdom of the dead, the *scheol* of Israel; the *erallu* of Babylon, the Egyptian *amenti*— the eternal West, the ' Setting of all Suns.' This means: the secret of the End, the Apocalypse, is the secret of the West.

" Above the bright precipice was the ' fountain of living water '—very likely the same about which the Egyptians pray for their dead, departed to the eternal West, Amenti: ' Grant thee, Osiris, of cool water! '

" ' And I went to another place, toward the West, at the end of the Earth .. . .' Everything goes to the West; it cannot pause; it is as if it were seeking, and knows, that only there, in the West, it shall find the end of the East—time—in eternity."

This is why Atlantis is both history, myth, and *Mystery*. The secrets of the End can be found in the Beginning; Death is revealed in Birth, and Birth in Death.

Gilgamesh was looking for the " Herb of Life ", as did all who sought initiation in the Great Mysteries of the West.

" The herb of life—the secret of the West—' the rose and the thorn '—the Rose of Love, the Thorn of suffering: *tlao*, I suffer—the root of the name ' Atlas '—is the root to all Atlantis. . . . Gilgamesh does not find the Herb of Life; it is left to Enoch to find it in the image of Him Who Shall be in Himself the Thorn of suffering, the Rose of Love."

No external event was ever regarded by contemporary observers in ancient times from its outer aspect alone; it was always mingled with the visions of clairvoyance. Or, events which were solely the inner experiences of vision in the life of some human being, are clothed in the pictures and images of the material world, and so appear to a later age as actual historical narrative.

The legend of St. Brendan is also one of the last links
with this search for immortality and healing in the far
West. St. Brendan (484-577 A.D.), one of St. Columba's fellow-pupils at the monastery of Clonard, was
known as the " sailor monk ". Tradition tells of a
seven years' voyage that he took in search of a " para-
disal land ". The stories of his travels took so firm a
hold on the popular mind that the islands he is
supposed to have discovered in the Atlantic became—
so says Wood-Martin—" subjects of treaty ". It was
probably St. Brendan's voyages that gave rise to the
account of the existence of an island, far West of
Ireland, called Hy Brasil, and another called Brandion.
As late as 1634 they were clearly marked on a chart
made by the French Geographer Royal. They are not
there now.

In 1674 a certain Captain Nesbitt actually landed
on, and partly explored, Hy Brasil, and—*disenchanted* it.
The pamphlet in which this is described says that
" since then several godly ministers and others are gone
to discover them " (the islands) but no news of their
return had—so far—been received. Neither has there
been any further news of the existence of Hy Brasil.

In connection with this there is a legend of St.
Brendan in *Der Wartburg Krieg* (thirteenth century;
and therefore before the supposed discovery of America
by Columbus). St. Brendan, who is said to have
" found the holy secret on the tongue of a bull ",
sailed to a land which is described as the " magnetic
mountain ". The Saint " knew the mystery of the
Quaternary ", which for this adventure, had to be
known, " together with the secret of the four elements
and the four winds ". He came near the " magnetic
mountain ", but its power drove him away, while
attracting out of his ship all the iron nails that held it

together, and the four bulls which he had on board, drawing them to itself by their iron chains. As to the " holy secret on the tongue of a bull "—this will belong to another chapter.

In this legend we have a combination of a spiritual experience with—probably—an actual voyage to America.

The latter statement needs perhaps some explanation, since the discovery of America has been generally accepted as having taken place at the end of the fifteenth century. This view is now superseded. The existence of America was certainly known in Europe in the early centuries of our era and long before. Occult schools and brotherhoods have always known this. But, for reasons which will be fully explained later, Papal decrees, after about the seventh or eighth centuries, forbade intercourse with the American continent until the fifteenth century. The knowledge of magnetism and electricity—in certain forms—which could be obtained in the far West was considered dangerous.

Adam of Bremen (eleventh century) wrote about Greenland, saying that there were " bishops " there. Other writers, as early as the eighth century A.D., have mentioned the existence of the Western continent. There have been excavations made in Labrador where Irish bells of a very early date were discovered. There are passages in Plutarch which point to the existence of a land in the far West where the Mysteries of Cronos (Saturn) were celebrated. These had their greatest festivals every thirty years, the period during which Saturn completes its orbit. Edward Davies (*Rites and Mysteries of the Druids*) finds, in the Welsh Triads, this Saturn Deity under the name of *Seithenin*, son of *Saidi;* this " prince " was intoxicated, and " let in the sea over the country so as to overwhelm a large and populous district ". Seithenin is the same as the Roman *Septimianus*—suggesting again a link with the *seven*—Saturn being regarded as the Father of the seven periods of planetary evolution.* In Welsh mythology this same " son of Saidi " appears as one of three sovereigns in the court of King Arthur, where he is the *door-keeper*—Guardian of the seat of wisdom. As the outermost planet of the seven, Saturn guards the threshold of the fixed stars.

These brief allusions will help us later, when we shall see how the " Waters of Death ", belonging to regions of the West, are a gateway to knowledge of immortality guarded by the God of Death and Time and Memory, and to knowledge of the secrets of the depths of the Earth—*magnetism and electricity.*

Albertus Magnus (thirteenth century) mentions in his *Geographica* that the reason why the *Westland* is not well known (America) is not only because of the enormous space of ocean that has to be crossed, but also because in that country the magnetic forces of the earth " work on the body in the same way as the magnet works on iron."

The special knowledge of healing possessed by the Druids and some of the earliest Christian missionaries in Britain—and in fact a great part of the fundamental principles of medicine in olden times—was knowledge obtained from America.

Through the agency of water, land-contours are formed. The *shape* of the land, its meteorological phenomena, the clouds, the sighing winds, the mists and rains and the sunshine, and all the general character that we associate with the landscape and

* Chapter I.

climate of different countries—especially coastal landscapes—were experienced by the North-Germanic
peoples as the " qualities ", or as the " Voice ", of the
great Mother Nature, and the forms of the land spoke
a spiritual language to them. They learnt from her the
secrets of Birth and Life.* This is what we feel in the
Celtic souls even of to-day. Only, there is mingled with
this love of the " Waters of Birth ", a brooding, often a
stern and iron melancholy. For the " Mother " of
the Celtic mythology of Britain is born of the " Waters
of Death " that have flowed from West to East over the
old volcanic fires of Atlantis.

It is more than probable that the oldest (Saturn)
form of Mystery wisdom (upon which the " Hibernian " schools were founded in Ireland) were to begin
with of an exclusively Dionysian character—in the
sense that they taught about the depths of the Earth,
and hence had to do with magnetism and healing and
the facts of human illness and death; but also, in
so far as the prophetic element of their seership was
concerned, the future would not be perceived save as a
kind of metamorphosis of an infinite, and perceived,
past; a " looking backward so as to look forward ".
Something of this primeval characteristic still persists
in the Irish soul. The Saturnian element is an extremely important one in the subsequent development
of the Hibernian Mysteries, as we shall see. It was only
much later, when the real Druid culture was brought
to Ireland that a " sunlike " quality was added to it.
Greek colonisation contributed to this also.

There is a legend (mentioned by Plutarch) which
says that Cronos (Saturn) was put to sleep in a rocky
cave somewhere in the West and bound by chains of
gold. Gold is the metal regarded as belonging to the

* The Cult of Herta in Scandinavia.

Sun. The Sun-wisdom eventually overpowered the Saturn-wisdom. Something of this is reflected in the fact that the Romans made *Saturnus*, originally a God of the harvest—the " reaper ", whose emblem was a sickle—into a God of the *seed-time*.

So we see that three " elements ", if we may call them so for the moment, have been mentioned in relation to the foundations of Celtic mythology: Saturn, Sun, and Moon (Water). These three were recognised as the three stages (indicated in the Merddin legend in Chapter I) through which the evolution of the planetary system had passed before the Earth became " dense " physical matter. Veneration for these stages of the world's history through processes of gradual densification was reflected in the religions of different epochs of civilisation, as has already been outlined (Chapter I). But they were never regarded by the ancients as merely *physical* natural processes. Many traditions suggest that they were " seen " in clairvoyant imagination as the mighty deeds of divine Beings. It is for this reason that we find the religious conceptions of Unity, Duality, and Trinity in the old Indian, Persian, and Egyptian ages; and fourthly in the Greek age, there is a mythology which includes *three generations* of Gods representing the earlier stages of the life of the Earth; and below them—Man.[8]

From this it becomes evident that the general trend of the Druidic sciences towards a knowledge of Nature connected with the Sun and the Moon must at some time have grown up upon earlier foundations which already existed in Ireland and the Western coasts of Britain—a " Saturnian " wisdom, of which the number seven is in various ways a representative number.

But we shall never understand Druidism (or indeed any of the religious conceptions underlying the old mythologies) unless we grasp the fact that it was recognised that all knowledge must be sought in two directions: one, by searching the outer world—*Science;* and two, by searching the depths of the human soul and the secrets of the human body—*Art.* For Art is the product of the human soul itself; it is generated by all Imagination, all world-conceptions, all idealism, all capacity to imbue the " science " of the outer world with the forces that bear it onward into the future. This is the great polarity that rules our human life— the Outer and the Inner, the Above and the Below, the Macrocosm and the Microcosm; and between— the individual immortal Spirit of Man.

Religion—that is, man's spiritual link with the Divine—is the necessary and only fruit of a true conception of Science and Art.

We will now try to explore the avenues which led to the meeting of the Celts with the " Fathers " of the post-diluvian world.

CHAPTER III

HIBERNIA

" For enquire, I pray thee, of the former age; and prepare
thyself for the search of their fathers. . . . Shall they not teach
thee and tell thee, and utter words out of their heart? "

(Job viii.)

THE shining land of Death is the world of the
Gods. . . ." On earth man is subject to death—
he belongs to the " shining land ", and is but a visitor
on the dark earth.

The knowledge that men had—it was not " faith "
but clear vision—of this shining land was their guide
ten thousand years before Christ when, owing to the
changing inclination of the earth's axis, the old centres
of civilisation were overwhelmed and a new world-age
began.

An old tradition says that once the " Gods of the
shining land of Death " ruled in Ireland; and that
then men came from the " land of Death " and
conquered them. Half of the Gods went to the West,
and the other half remained in Ireland and hid in
caves.

This tradition is true; but we have to explain it.

There are two ways of regarding the mystery of
death. One way, is to see it as the gateway into the
spiritual world; the other way is to see it as the end of
earthly life. The first is the reality; the second is the
shadow.

In the tradition, the *Gods* of Death are overcome by
the *men* of Death. The old visionary powers by means

53

of which men knew clearly of their spiritual origin, began to vanish away when the post-diluvian age brought the first beginnings of a real material culture. The wandering refugees from the gradually disappearing Atlantis, who had known the " shining land ", turned their footsteps in two directions. Some went to the far West where the American continent lies, and some to the East. Some remained behind ending their journey in Ireland and on the western coasts of Britain. Those who went East were divided into two main streams, the one travelling towards Asia and India by a northern route, the other by a southern route.

An immense amount of scattered evidence has been steadily accumulated with regard to the existence of Atlantis.* In fact a difficulty seems to lie in the very quantity of the evidence, which has been gathered from the far East as well as from the far West, not to mention the Greek, Roman, and other European sources. Yet for some reason it has always seemed very hard for people to accept the idea of a submerged continent. " Suffice it to say," says Scott-Elliott,† " that in India, Chaldea, Babylon, Media, Greece, Scandinavia, China, amongst the Jews, and amongst the Celtic tribes of Britain, the legend is absolutely identical in all essentials. Now turn to the West, and what do we find? The same story in its detail preserved amongst the Mexicans (each tribe having its own version) the people of Guatemala, Honduras, Peru, and almost every tribe of the North-American Indians."

A modern scientific writer, Theodor Arldt, in his book *Die Entwickelung der Kontinente und ihre Lebewelt*, presents a large series of maps showing the stages of the

* The Evolution of Mankind. G. Wachsmuth.
† *The Story of Atlantis.*

evolution of the present continents and the gradual disappearance of Atlantis. The later maps of the series show very clearly what was the last connecting link (in the Tertiary period) between Atlantis and Britain in the North and between southern Atlantis and Africa in the South. We see how the peoples could have dispersed, when all the central part of the continent had gone, by a southern *and* a northern path towards the East (Asia) or towards the *West*, as the various traditions all suggest.

To-day such journeys could be accomplished by millions of people in a few weeks. Then, the very slowness of movement, covering hundreds, even thousands, of years, would tend to make such a catastrophe—gradual though it was—a world-memory in the widest sense. It would cause a process of long-lasting creation and upbuilding and change in humanity, a process that would always bear within it the aftermath of its original impulse, engendered by terrific upheavals and successions of catastrophes. And would, indeed, meet with a kind of renewal in memory through the slow returning of masses of the descendants of the original eastward wanderers, back to their " base " in Britain.

The Biblical story of the deluge describes all this as a brief event and indicates the repopulation of the world by the sons of Noah. It is condensed into this form, and the sons of Noah appear as single individuals—which they surely were. But this pressing together of the history of an immense period into a short space of time should remind us that the old form of ancestral memory—which is somewhat similar to that which may still be gained even in modern times in initiation —did not look back and see the past as extended over the stream of time, but saw it, so to say, " standing upright " with event beside event in a vast panorama much as a person who is at the point of death sees all the events of his life in a single swift impression.

This peculiar form of memory was allied to a certain kind of thinking. Rudolf Steiner, in one of his works, says that the thinking or reasoning of early times was not so much connected with the brain as with the *heart*. The " thoughts of the heart " resembled a direct knowing without the necessity of ratiocination. It was more akin to what we call " feeling ". Job, in the verse quoted at the head of this chapter, is referring to this direct form of self-experience.

It is interesting that many historians, not omitting Cæsar, describe the Celtic population of Europe as the children of *Japhet*. But Japhet, or Japhetos—who is also called *Dispater*—was regarded as a God of Death; not one who inherited a " shining land ", but one whose portion was the *land of Dis*, a plutonic realm of darkness. This means that the people who were regarded as the descendants of Japhet were becoming " earthly ", learning the arts of material culture. Their religion was Dionysian in character.

A part of the " family " of Japhet, the children of *Gomer*, have been regarded as being the Cimmerii or Cymry who, eventually travelling back from western Asia, came to inhabit Britain, and especially Wales. This returning movement from East to West of peoples who had originally wandered from Atlantis to the East, is a fact.

The successive periods of culture after the last deluge, *beginning* with that of the oldest Indian nomadic civilisation inaugurated by the " Seven Rishis " of pre-Vedic times, arose as the result of a kind of urge to discover the possibilities offered by the earth, and so by a process of returning movement, very slowly, from East to West; in a sense " pushing " the developing population before them.

This moving pressure—not a voluntary movement—brought about the eventual approach of the Celtic people of the more northern parts of Europe towards our own land; and roughly speaking, during the so-called third post-Atlantean epoch, probably about 2000 or 3000 B.C. This was the time of the Egypto-Chaldean civilisation.

What would be the result of these millennia of alternating movement and rest upon the soul of a people? How would it contrast with the soul of a people who had remained stationary, where the very ocean washing their shores was still flowing over the old buried secrets, and which they heard whispered in the winds that blew from the infinite and mysterious West, whither the other " half of the Gods " had gone?

Experience of the world such as would have been gained by the returning peoples whom we call Celts would have the effect of advancing their evolution. It is strange that a dimming of the old spiritual knowledge must be regarded, at this point, as a state of progress. But so it was. The greater the intelligence with regard to the material life, the less the need for knowledge to be " inspired " in sleep or in the heightened consciousness of initiation. The Celts of Europe had their Mysteries as we know; but the wisdom taught in them had a character that showed an advance beyond the more Chthonian wisdom of the stationary " Fathers " of the West. They venerated and studied all that is brought to *life* in man and in the universe by the forces of *light* alternating with the forces of *darkness*. They adored the Sun. They learnt their natural science from the shadows that the sunlight creates. They felt that they had come forth out of darkness—out of the " city of Dis " of their ancestry, because the earth had become *intelligible*, and the heavens, provided the starry script by which it could be understood. The Sun and the Moon, day and night, were the portals through which clairvoyant vision could still look to understand the connection between the creative wisdom of the Gods and the world of matter. The leaders of these people were the Druids.

They came to Britain; and they found in the West the " secret of immortality " which Gilgamesh later set out to find, as has been told. In Ireland, and probably especially in all the Western regions which are the last peaks of a primeval volcanic area, they found the descendants of the " Gods of the shining land of Death "—the men who knew the secrets of the interior of the earth and had retained, in the highest possible degree, the old powers of spiritual clairvoyance.

Through the mingling of these people there gradually ripened a school of the Mysteries which influenced Europe right on into the early centuries of our era. Whatever in the course of time has been discovered about the Celtic Mysteries of Britain, has for the most part been described only as Druidism. That is correct. But what has not been clearly understood is that the Druidism we think we know could not have existed without this twofold foundation—the " progressed ", and the " Fathers ".

It is interesting to find that this idea of a patriarchal wisdom (not using the word in its limited Biblical sense) meets us also in ancient Indian tradition. It is not possible, without accepting the theory of the original eastward wanderings from Atlantis, to account for the fact that in India, and in the mythology of the other culture epochs mentioned, mankind had looked

for, and received, a divine teaching directly from the
" Gods ". The Oriental word for these Instructors is
Pitris—Fathers. (Originally: *Ptr.*)

In the eighteenth century a Mr. Wilford, writing in
the *Asiatic Records*, V, 3, says that much intercourse
once prevailed between the territories of India and
certain countries in the West; that the " old Indians
were acquainted with our British Islands which their
books describe as the 'sacred Islands of the West',
calling one of them *Bretashtan* . . . and that one of these
islands was regarded as the *abode of the Pitris*, who were
fathers of the human race."

Edward Davies,* commenting on this makes the
following suggestive remarks:

" The Pitris of the *West*, and the honours done to
them, could not have sprung originally from India.
From the earliest periods, their abode had been in
the sacred Islands of the West, in which Islands we
find the Cymry (Welsh), who emphatically call
themselves the *first*, or the oldest race. These
Islands could not have been consecrated by the
Indians. Had the mysteries of the Pitris *originated*
with the Hindus, their sacred abode would unques-
tionably have been fixed in a recess of *thir own
country*. . . . This veneration then, for the Pitris,
and the usage of consulting them, were necessarily
derived, by the Hindus, from the religion of that
race in whose land those consecrated Personages
were acknowledged—uniformly—to have resided.
And this was the country of the same people to whom
the ancient poets of Greece and Rome conducted
their Heroes, when they were to consult the *manes
of the dead*."†

* *Celtic Researches.*   † Homer's *Odyssey*.

This country is Ireland. And before Ireland—Atlantis.

Davies is right in placing the original knowledge of the Pitris in the West. But who were they originally?

If we were to say simply that these " Fathers " were the " Gods of the shining land of Death " who had remained in Ireland we should be guilty of superstition; but we should not be guilty of superstition if we said that they were *the divine Instructors who appeared to the earthly Initiates in their clairvoyant visions in the Mysteries.* In that sense they " lived in Ireland ". We are familiar enough with the title of " Divine Father " bestowed on the initiated Priests of the Egyptian Temples. They, too, had the vision of those whose designation they bore.

Occult Science—which is our modern term for the wisdom of the " Mysteries " as taught by Initiates to-day—asserts that in Atlantean times humanity was hardly yet " awake " in the physical world; so that spiritual Beings (our Angels and Archangels) were visible to them in the earthly environment. We know that this was still the case in Biblical times. And that as much longer ago, men were still able to look back by means of that peculiar form of " panoramic " memory which has been described, into the earlier stage of the earth's evolution, and particularly so under the conditions attached to the training for initiation, they could, by inspiration, receive instruction from the spiritual Beings whose creative powers had permeated that primeval " lunar " earth.

The capacity for holding this mystical intercourse must have been still present among the leaders and descendants of those Atlanteans who remained behind in Ireland as well as among those who wandered to

Asia and India. They learnt about the Earth from the Lunar Pitris.

The moon in the sky, whose phases we know so well, was regarded as the " doorway " into this ancient wisdom. The sphere enclosed by the moon's orbit is— if regarded as a region only accessible to human knowledge through initiation—that part of the spiritual world that the soul first becomes acquainted with after death.[9] If so, then it would be admissible to say that the " Moon " can instruct us about " Saturn "; that is, that the lunar Fathers could teach men about Death—not as a sorrowful problem, but as the gateway to life; and, too, about the *shadow-land* of Death, which is the deepest level of earthly matter, the inner fires of the earth's core.

Therefore it is not so difficult to accept the tradition that " the Gods (Pitris) of the shining land of Death " once lived in Ireland in the visions of the sages.

And now we can see in what way the coming of the more intellectually advanced Celtic *Druids* changed a little what was still left of the wisdom of the Fathers. They brought the *Sun* to the Saturn-Moon. And with the Sun-worship—the possibility of the culture of Music.

All Celtic researches divide the Druid " schools " which arose on these old foundations into three classes: the Priests—who were also orderers of the social system—the Bards and the students. The Priests, as we can understand, were the masters of the Wisdom itself, regarded as *a means for creating the outer culture of the time*. We can think of them as " officiating "— as mediators—between the secret knowledge of the Mysteries and the outer world.

But who were the *Bards*? They were not, in the earliest times, inferior to the Druids—that is, to the

Priests—as is now generally supposed, but superior.
The Bards were the descendants of the *Fathers*, the
" Vates " or " Pitris ". Their name shows this.
That is to say that the Bards, during the best and
noblest period of Druidism many centuries before
the Christian era and only for a much shorter period
after it, were *par excellence* the Seers, the Prophets.
They had not, as had the Druid Priests, advanced
so far in the more earthly form of intelligence, but
their spiritual knowledge was greater. One might
perhaps say that they were secondary to the Priests
only because they " stood behind them ". They had
a different degree of initiation.[10]

Of all the Bards of whom tradition tells we have one
whose name in familiar to all, *Merlin*—or *Merddin*.
But this is not *one* Bard. It is a designation—the
" signature " of Bardism as a whole; and there were
several Merddins of greater or lesser fame.

Mer-din means " dweller of the sea ". But this name
has also been bestowed on Britain itself " before it
was inhabited ", so say our British Triads. It is the
land dwelling in the sea of the West like a star. The
twin-sister of Merddin is *Venus*, the morning star,
called in Welsh *Gweddydd*. Merddin, the twin-
brother of the morning star—changing places with
her in morning and evening as we know—is *Mercury*.
And Mercury is Hermes, the teacher of the secret
wisdom and the Messenger of the Gods; in British
Mythology, Merddin.

So the general designation of the ancient Bards,
" Merddin " (as Mercury with his twin Venus)
suggests the alternations of morning and evening, the
moment of waking and the moment of falling asleep,
and these are the times, above all, when souls, living
on the earth, are crossing and re-crossing the threshold

of the spiritual world in sleeping and waking up and are best able to receive impressions of the " shining land ".

> " Knowest thou what thou art
> In the hour of sleep—
> A mere body—a mere soul—
> Or a secret retreat of the light ? " *

The sea, when the evening star glows above the horizon, is like the spiritual " ocean " where the soul finds its inspiration and meets the " Fathers ".

Strange that Britain, the gateway between East and West, should once have borne the name of the evening or morning star!

America, the land which received the " other half of the Gods " who went there after the destruction of Atlantis, still reveals the remains of a worship of the " Great Spirit ". What this originally meant was that the world was conceived by those ancients as the creation of a Supreme Spirit—the Father-God— who, in His omnipotence, *included* in Himself not only the whole spiritual world but also every manifestation of the material world. The depths of the Earth were as much a part of Him as the heavenly heights. A knowledge of the nature of the Earth was therefore a knowledge of the " Great Spirit ", the Father. But the Earth brings about death;[11] so Death is the Father. *Through* the Father—that is, through Death —the Father is found as the source of Life. This is the same fundamental principle as that which underlies the Hibernian Mystery-wisdom.

But how should one know the way through death while still living, and so during life, find the secret of Immortality? That was the great question which

* From a Bardic poem of the sixth century.

the neophytes in the Hibernian Mysteries longed to
solve. . . . Man may accumulate all knowledge, all
science, so it seemed to them, but the very core
seething within the accumulation of such a mass of
knowledge, and its inevitable accompaniment, is:
the effect it has on the human soul.   Does knowledge
—in itself and for itself—make for happiness, either of
ourselves or of others?   Is it not a fact, even of
modern experience, that the accumulation of *mere*
knowledge—without the " dream " of the soul that
it must have a purpose—turns to ashes and bitterness?

Then, suppose a man were to turn altogether away
from the search for knowledge of the outer world and
contemplate only, with ever deeper and deeper
intensity, the nature of his own soul, he would find
there endless contradictions; he would find in himself
a world of imagination, and the inward search for
thoughts, ideals, fantasies, dreams, passions, and a
tremendous force urging itself towards the creation
of something in the outer world, which, *without
knowledge of the outer world*—as little knowledge as
if he were blind and deaf and dumb—would be a
nightmare of illusion and loneliness and despair.

He would question: can I find happiness and
fulfilmeht through the possession of the whole external
universe in knowledge?   No.   For there I see only
an endless succession of how the world has *become* what
it is.   I see æons and æons of the Past which is frozen
into form.   I see *Death*.   I die into a vast and endless
Winter in the illusion that knowledge can be fulfilment
of the Being that I feel I *am*.

And he would question again: Then can I find
happiness and strength in the possession of my own
soul alone?   No.   For there I burn in a consuming
fever.   In myself is a fantasy of perpetual creation,

which falls every moment into ashes and dust through
the power of a divine Imagination which is without
my will, but which wills itself in me with the urge of
an everlasting Future—a perpetual fertilisation whose
fruit rots away in unfulfilment, while the æons that
are to come approach me and reproach me.

De profundis ! " *Out of the depths* have I cried unto
thee, O Lord! "

My soul waiteth for the Lord *more than they that
watch for the morning !* "*

These two, the cry out of the Past, the cry out of the
Future, represent the Way of Initiation for those who
were the pupils in the ancient Mysteries of Hibernia.
They were Mysteries of *Time*—of Cronos—the Father
of Evolution Who enclosed within Himself all opposites: the Macrocosm and the Microcosm, Past and
Future, the Outer and the Inner, the Below and the
Above. The fulfilment of the initiation of the
candidate lay in his finding the solution to these
two overwhelming problems. And it could be found.

I have tried to couch these experiences in words that
might help to bring them in some slight degree before
the modern mind. The actual cult and the mantramic
sayings of these Mysteries have been described only
by Rudolf Steiner in the approximate form and
words in which they were experienced even three
thousand years ago.†

It is most important to try and gain some idea of this
Mystery cult, for it was the product—although having
but a faint reflection of its original majestic solemnity—
of the wisdom of the " Fathers ", those great Teachers
who must have ruled over the oracles in Atlantis and in
ancient Ireland, who had been able to hold mystical

* Psalm cxxx.
† *Mystery Centres.* Lectures by Rudolf Steiner.

intercourse with the Lunar Divinities. The original Hibernian Mysteries, as such, were at their height, we must assume, before the coming of the Celtic Druids. What the latter were able to add to them, thus changing their character, will be described later. But at this point it may be said that what the Hibernian wisdom contained was inseparable from a plunge, if one so describe it, into the Depths. And it was *this* element which survived, in the later Druidism, as the doctrine of *Annwn*, the Underworld, which had first to be passed through (in inner experience) as countless legends tell us, before the higher spiritual worlds could be known.

A necessary function of all the old Mystery cults was to present to the pupils or candidates for initiation an *external visual representation* of what, when initiation was once fully attained, would be an indescrible and unrepresentable supreme mystical experience.

So there were, for instance, the dramas of the Eleusis Mysteries in Greece; the representation (probably by highly skilful mechanical contrivances) of the Sun, planets, etc., in Egypt; or the being led into darkness, into caves, the worshipping of the new-born child—as in the Mysteries of the Serapæum in Alexandria and so on. These things are well known. All this was necessary not so much because it stimulated the imagination, but because, before our era, human beings did not possess the same faculty that we possess of being able to bring purely inner mystical experiences *so far* as to a conscious entrance into the spiritual world—unless they had help. So their will was made subject to the will of the initiating Priest. The candidates' preparatory trials of the soul enabled the Initiator finally to induce in them a state of deathlike trance, during which their " spiritual senses " were opened. And afterwards they remembered all that they had experienced; and so much so, that by this " loosening " of their whole spiritual nature from the physical body they could, for the rest of their lives, continue to extend these experiences, and give them, as divinely inspired knowledge of the arts and sciences and religion, to the world. There was no other way of learning. " In those days," says Steiner, " the pupils of the Mysteries could actually see how the spiritual Powers let Themselves descend into the multitudinous forms of life. There was no other Science save that which men also *perceived* " (clairvoyantly); " no other Piety save that which dawned in the soul when the Mysteries were seen; neither any other Beauty save that which men knew when the Gods came down to them."

In Hibernia the external representations of the two-fold problem which has been described, were two statues, one male, one female. The whole surroundings, the darkness of the rock-hewn temples, sounds, lights, together with the mantramic utterances of the Priests, and many other things, following upon months and even years of preparatory scientific and religious learning, eventually brought the problem —which I attempted to describe in present-day language—to so great an intensity, that the pupil became " as one dead ".

What he had experienced was the tremendous enigma of *Humanity*. The problem of his own being flowed together, in an indescribable mingling of contraction and expansion, with the problem of the Being of the Universe, its Past and its Future. He saw that what men call knowledge has no value for the spiritual world—it could tell him nothing of it. And that what appears to have value in the life of the soul, such as happiness and joy, has, for the spiritual world, no truth. The value of everything that belongs to the life of man on Earth must be changed into another value when the threshold of the spiritual world had to be crossed. The two statues appeared as though, over their heads, flaming signs suggested the words *Knowledge* (or Science) and *Art*.[12]

As in ancient Egypt the new initiate was led out of the chamber of death to behold the rising Sun, so the initiate of Hibernia was spiritually led out at last by his Initiators to behold the vision of Christ. In that moment he knew that the warmth and strength of Love could flow into his heart, and that from this strength came the recognition of the harmonious unity of the " Science " and the " Art " of Life. He knew what the statues concealed; he knew the answer to all his questions.

The Hibernian Mysteries were *a way to the remembrance of Atlantis*—to the visions of the Beginnings of man, even long before Atlantis, and in the Beginnings the vision of the great enigma of the Future, the Apocalypse. Why should Atlantis be remembered? Why should *we* remember it?

Past and Future—these were spread out before the spiritual gaze of the Hibernian initiate. But the lesson of the fall of the Atlanteans was learnt there— and the Son of Peace held out His promise to men. And this is why we must remember Hibernia, and behind it—Atlantis. The War in Atlantis was the war of white against black magic—between those who saw in Nature the great Divine Mother of men and used her gifts for human welfare, and those who saw in Nature the satanic Temptress, offering dark dominion and cruel power.

How was it possible that the Hibernian initiate, a thousand years or more before the Incarnation, could have had a vision of Christ?

To answer this question as it should be answered would require a volume to itself. But let us try to understand it from one aspect which has already been touched upon. In the preceding chapters it was said that, according to universal mythology and also according to the teaching handed down for centuries in the esoteric schools (even to our own day), the evolution of our planetary system as a whole has to pass through seven stages; that these are echoed in shorter periods within the Earth itself. The *third* of these shorter periods is said to have reproduced at a quicker tempo the original creation, or separation from the general cosmic substance, of the Sun and the Moon; and that this is the period described in the Book of Genesis, where seven "days" are spoken of. The seven "days" are of course immense periods; but the word *day* (in Hebrew *Yom*) represents not only an age of time but also a sevenfold group of spiritual Creator Beings, the *Elohim*. One of these "Groups" (the word is very inadequate) whose titular Head was Jehovah, had a Moon-like nature; and this Group was especially associated with the power of reflectung, upon the Earth, those influences which were poured forth by the other Groups who represented the spiritual force of the Sun. Therefore, being in a sense " nearer " to the Earth they could impart to humanity wisdom concerning the spiritual Sun.

These Beings were variously described in all ancient mythology and religion as "Moon-Beings". They have already been mentioned as the *Pitris*. They were, for the West, the "Gods of the shining land of

Death ", who inspired the initiates in the Mysteries. But, as " reflectors " from the Moon of the glory of the Elohim of the Sun, their supreme mission was to prepare humanity, in all the different Mystery-sanctuaries of the world, for the Advent of the Sun-Logos, Christ.

This Being held the central place in all the old Mysteries. He was spoken of in ancient India as *Vishvakarman*, who was the " Light of the World "; in Persia as *Ormuzd*; in the *Zend-Avesta* it is said of Him: " He will descend to Earth; He will overcome age, death, decay; He will create free decision; then, when the time is ripe for the resurrection of the dead, He will have the victory of life. He will be the victorious Saviour, surrounded by Apostles." In Egypt, He was known as Osiris; in Greece as Apollo; by Moses, as the I AM.

The influence of the lunar Beings, as Teachers about the descent of the Sun-Logos to Earth, is also to be found in the wisdom known as the *Gnosis*, which, in Christian times appearing as a sect of Christianity, came to be regarded as heretical. Why? Because this wisdom (as so wonderfully written down in the well-known *Pistis Sophia*) could fully understand the cosmic nature of Christ but could not explain—for the satisfaction of the Church—His *humanity*.

The mission of all this old wisdom was primarily to remind human beings that they were " born out of God ". As, from the physical point of view, all men had their ancestors behind them, so from the spiritual point of view they were " sons of God " Who was the Father of all. The content of all the Mystery schools consisted in educating such people as were especially fitted for it, to eliminate the physical consciousness (for the time being) and attain a clear

spiritual consciousness in which they could perceive
something of the manner of their descent from God.
And in all the Mysteries it was taught that there was
one Son of God Who was supreme, and of Whom
it was foretold that He would one day descend to
the Earth, in a *Man.*

If we look carefully at the four Gospels we shall see
that these two points of view are shown. The God
descended is especially to be found in Matthew, and in
John. (The Word of the Beginning made Flesh.)
And the heights from which He descended are alluded
to in Luke's genealogy: " from Adam, which is the
Son of God "; and also in Mark, where we are
immediately made aware of the Divinity in Jesus
in the way in which the Gospel opens and specially
in the recognition of the God in Him by the demons:
" We know Thee Who Thou art, the Holy One of
God." (Mark i, 24.)

These are the most sublime things that it is possible
for us to imagine. But we can surmise that in any
revelation given to mankind concerning the descent
of the Spirit into Matter, these two poles of existence,
the divine and the human, both in doctrine and in
ritual, would necessarily be represented in some form
in every school of the Mysteries which was concerned
with the *central* idea of Earth-evolution, namely, its
Creative Logos. There were also other schools of
wisdom connected more particularly with other
aspects.

If we see this whole question of mythology in this
light, then the somewhat ironical disdain cast by some
scholars upon the " solar myth " idea will be relegated
to its proper place. Sun, Moon and stars were, to
the leaders and teachers of the ancient peoples, not
merely *physical,* but " pictures " of the hidden and

the divine. Misunderstanding of the myths would cease once it were universally recognised that, outside the Mystery-Temples, only the language and imagery of ordinary life could be used to describe the realities of spiritual experience obtained in the " holy of holies ".

To-day our modern intellectual arrogance is shocked at the descriptions of divine Beings given in mythology that make them seem like men and women—occasionally graced with wings, and arranged in family relationships. We call the ancient people " anthropomorphic ". But in reality it is *we* who are guilty of anthropomorphism for we have for so long denied the possibility of spiritual vision that we are unable (or unwilling) to accept the " imaginative translations " of indescribable experiences which issued from the Temples of old, and think them " superstitious idolatry ". Even Sabianism—the worship of stars—was not an idolatry of physical stars, but arose *to begin with* from a clairvoyant knowledge of the spiritual Beings whose habitations were " expressed " through those radiant worlds. But it goes without saying that everything of this kind passed through decadence and final obliteration, as the old forms of " clear-seeing " disappeared, and intellectual theory began to take its place.

Few indeed could find words or pictures in which to clothe their visions of the ineffable vortices of light and flame and colour that drew near to them in sleep. Some of the great poet-prophets—such as Ezekiel, Isaiah, or Enoch, or the compiler of the noble Bhagavadgita, can still overwhelm us with their descriptions: "... and the likeness of the firmament upon the heads of the living Creatures was as the colour of the terrible crystal, stretched

forth over their heads above . . . and when they went,
I heard the noise of their wings like the noise of great
waters . . . . As the appearance of the bow that is
in the cloud in the day of rain, so was the appearance
of the likeness of the glory of the Lord.   And when I
saw it, I fell upon my face . . ."*

Or Enoch, telling of the inscrutable and terrible
Beings of Darkness: ". . . *their faces were like extinguished
lamps. . . .*"

Or Arjuna's vision in the Bhagavadgita:

" Shining, a mass of splendour everywhere,
  With discus, mace, tiara, I behold:
  Blazing as fire, as sun dazzling the gaze,
  From all sides in the sky, immeasurable.

Lofty beyond all thought, unperishing,
Thou treasure-house supreme, all-immanent;
Eternal Dharma's changeless Guardian thou,
As immemorial Man I think of thee.

Nor source, not midst, nor end; infinite force,
Unnumbered arms, the sun and moon thine eyes,
I see thy face, as sacrificial fire
Blazing, its splendour burneth up the worlds . . .

Radiant, thou touchest Heaven, rainbow-hued,
With open mouths and shining vast-orbed eyes.
My inmost self is quaking, having seen,
My strength is withered, Vishnu, and my peace . . . "

The vision of the Christ in the Mysteries of Hibernia
—how may we imagine it—we who are living two
thousand years after the event that they only foretold?
Before He came to Earth how did He appear?   As a
God-Man surely.   For the Priests pointed to Him as
to a living Being, but spoke of Him as One Who
could give a gift that only the Spirit can bestow—
strength in the heart.

* Ezekiel.

This vision could take another, and another, form. He was seen, much later, in these same Temples as the God who had at last completed the sacrifice of His descent and was hanging on the Cross. The events that took place in Palestine were seen, *at the moment of their happening*, in the Hibernian Mystery Temples. There were no earthly means of immediate communication between Palestine and Ireland. But the Crucifixion was instantaneously reflected in the Æther— *there*; in the " sacred island " where had dwelt the Gods of " the shining land of Death ". And nowhere else in the world.

But among those whose clairvoyant sight was directed towards the great world of Nature in Hibernia, the vision of the Crucifixion was amplified and extended from the Earth into the infinities of Space. The Being whose Incarnation had been foreseen for thousands of years was a God; for a God to die upon the Earth, as any man, must be a cosmic event of stupendous significance; the sacrifice of His Body must surely transform the visible as well as the invisible worlds; and all who could see with " opened eyes " must have been astounded at what they saw.

And this is described in a legend.

The version of the legend that I give here is taken from a note by W. B. Yeats to his poem *The Secret Rose*.[13]

There was a King in Ireland called Conchubar, who had once been struck by a ball made out of the dried brains of an enemy and hurled out of a sling, and this ball had been left in his head, and his head had been mended with a thread of gold because his hair was like gold. Keeling, a writer of the time of Elizabeth, gives the rest of the legend in this form:

" In that state did he remain seven years, until the Friday on which Christ was crucified, according to some historians; and when he saw the unusual changes of the creation and the eclipse of the sun, and the moon at its full, he asked of Bucrach, the Leinster Druid, who was along with him, what it was that brought that unusual change upon the planets of Heaven and Earth. 'Jesus Christ, the Son of God,' said the Druid, 'who is *now being crucified* (my italics) by the Jews.' 'That is a pity,' said Conchubar; 'were I in His presence I would kill those who were putting Him to death.' And with that he brought out his sword, and rushed at a woody grove which was convenient to him, and began to cut and fell it; and what he said was that if he were among the Jews, that was the usage he would give them; and from the very excessiveness of his fury which seized him, the ball started out of his head, and some of the brain came after it, and in that way he died."

No one " inventing " such a legend in later times would have been able to stress—as the most important part of it—the fact of the " unusual changes of the creation ". It is the very simplicity and directness of such a statement which reveals its truth. A seer of that time would have perceived just that; and even the reversal of the " direction " of the elementary powers revealing themselves in the rainbow-hued aura of the Earth. The Earth had received a force of Ascension which would enable it, in the far distant future, to lose its planetary character and become a *Sun*, for Christ had entered into its substance. It was the vision of the " Secret Rose " whose

" . . . . great leaves enfold
　The ancient beards, the helms of ruby and gold
　Of the crowned Magi ;　and the King whose eyes
　Saw the pierced Hands, and Rood of elder, rise
　In Druid vapour and make the torches dim . . . "

Conchubar's strange wound and its stranger healing
—the " dried brain of his enemy " bound to his head
with a golden band—are a clear reference to his
gift of second-sight.　The enemy who causes this
wound is the light itself: Goethe says " the eye was
made by the light for the light "—it is a veritable
wound in the body of man;　but if you take your
" enemy "—the *physical power of seeing*—into yourself
and bind it to you with the spiritual power of the
Sun, and do so for the mystical " seven years ", physical
sight becomes the clear-seeing of the Spirit.

Death, as we know it, the greatest of earthly
sorrows, is a false image;　and by dying we overcome
this false image and find the reality: for Death
overcomes Death—whether it be a physical dying or
the mystic death of initiation.　In the legend there
is a kind of " imagination " of this in the account of
Conchubar's onslaught upon the trees;　he kills their
life, and this is the false form of Death;　and in his
own death, he embraces its true form, Life everlasting.

There is sometimes greater wisdom in a single
legend than in many volumes of history.

CHAPTER IV

HEAVEN AND EARTH

I

" Whence didst thou proceed? and what is thy beginning? "
" I came from the Great World, having my beginning in Annwyn."

(From the *Barddas*.)

THE fact that in the enclosed Temples of the oldest Hibernian Mysteries (they may have been partly natural rock-temples, or underground)* there were two statues representing the two poles of human experience which had to be balanced by the vision of a " Third ", provides a clue to the understanding of the Druid trilithons, two great stones roofed over by another, which we know so well. These stood in the open air, generally situated in wide spaces, freely accessible to the sunlight.† As to their purpose, this will be described later; but they show that the Mysteries of the Depths were slowly giving place to the Mysteries of the Heights. Nevertheless, the peculiarity of Druidism was that it combined both.

The Hibernian Mysteries in their oldest " Saturnian " form based their wisdom fundamentally on Time. Their initiates, as has been described, had to pass through experiences which gave them an extended vision of the Past and the Future. The Druids looked out into Space; but in Space they

---

* Like New Grange, Ireland.   † Stonehenge.

discovered the " Time-Kings ". They were astronomers, but directed their knowledge towards the
regulation of social and agricultural life in accordance
with the changing seasons. But in directing the social
life, they studied the *human being*, and they were able to
discover very much about the constitution of the body,
as well as the " light " and " darkness " which are
woven together in the soul, in moral and immoral
impulses.

The centre and heart of the Druid cult was the Sun,
and not, as some scholars have thought, the Ark of
the Deluge and its creator Noah. But the Sun is
also reflected by the Moon. Lunar and solar influences, observed in relation to the twelvefold order
of the zodiacal constellations, were the basis of the
Druid wisdom. Only we must remember that these
alone would have little value; they must be related
to the Earth. And the Earth is not merely a surface,
it is a globe, and its crust is undoubtedly penetrable
by these influences; they descend into the depths,
where, in fact, they already are, having been deposited
in the Earth during the processes of its formation.
These cosmic influences, radiating through the Earth
from " below " as well as from " above ", affect, and
have always affected, not only the Earth as a globe
but the beings that live on it—men, animals, and
plants, and even minerals.[14] Cosmic forces stream
into us through the centre of the Earth from the
other side. This fact is not unconnected with our
moral impulses. Man is really placed between
powers that work centrifugally—away from the Earth
—and powers that work centripetally—towards the
Earth's centre. The interaction of these powers
causes—speaking in a general way—motion; expansion and contraction. Rhythm too plays its part in

this " world-breathing ". The whole world of Nature is permeated by it; and this knowledge formed part of the secret wisdom of the Druids. They knew that the " Great World " reflects itself in man; its living-ness and mobility are imitated in man's breathing and circulation. The rhythms of our solar system—even to exactitude of number—are repeated in miniature in the processes of the body.

This principle of expansion and contraction was associated with the whole idea of death and birth, and of sleeping and waking. The teaching of all the ancient Mysteries attempted to disclose how the Spirit of man belongs to the entire universe (conceived in a spiritual way), and how at birth his spiritual nature becomes contracted and compressed into the body (which is made of earthly material), while at death the Spirit is set free and again expands into the light-realms of the heavenly spaces. The same principle was recognised as underlying the alternations of sleeping and waking. While awake, the human being is contracted into himself, and while asleep his soul and Spirit—all that makes his conscious waking life, that is, are " spread out " in another state of existence, that of the spiritual world.

The law of the change over from expansion to contraction rules in every kind of physical birth, and even in the changing seasons from summer to winter. If we imagine this, in the case of a human being, as a *spiritual* process accompanying the formation of the body, a good idea will be obtained of the importance, in olden times, of seeking to gain knowledge, by clairvoyance, of the contracting and expanding laws working in all natural metamorphoses.

The same thing applies to the Earth in spring, when expansion takes place through the " greening " of the vegetable kingdom—the rising of the sap and the shooting out of innumerable branchings, carrying this life outwards into the sunlit air. Then the Earth  dreams and sleeps. And then in the Autumn, the seeds fall and are ripened in the Earth, which becomes like a pregnant mother —all the forces are drawn inwards, and the Earth is wide awake and full of fiery germinative energy. Many animals feel and live in this process instinctively. The dormouse, for instance, curls itself up into an embryo-like form, and sleeps, in order to be " shone upon " by the cosmic warmth of the Earth-Mother.

The Druids knew that the contracting and hardening forces are at work in the *roots* of plants, and the forces of expansion in the *blossoms*; and in between, in the stem and leaves, the intermediary " mercurial " forces. From this whole conception there has arisen the universal symbol of the " rod of Hermes ", the symbol of healing; and it is, too, the symbol for the waking and sleeping life, the central line representing the Spirit, or Ego, of the human being that progresses permanently through these alternating states. The idea being that when one is *awake*, one is " asleep " in regard to the mysterious processes of life that are flowing through the body; and when one is asleep, this life expands and is met and nourished by the universal Life. The true being is then awake, while the body sleeps.

There are many traditions and writings that point to the fact that before the time of Christ, and more and more so the further we look back into the past, the state of sleep was not a wholly unconscious one, though what consciousness there was, was not of the *physical* world, for it was the soul, not the body, that could be aware of the " shining land " and the spiritual beings of many kinds who inhabited it. " He giveth [to] His beloved in sleep " means that supernatural vision was the gift of God to the sleeping man. The more such knowledge was intensified and elaborated by passing through the trials of initiation in olden times, the clearer would become the understanding of the relation between the Macrocosm and the Microcosm— the Great World and the Little World. Long ago, people did not live so apart from the rhythm of sunset and sunrise as is the case to-day. Their sleeping and waking, like that of the animals, and even the plants, corresponded with the natural rhythm of day and night. Since the greatest experiences could be had concerning the secrets of existence during sleep, when the physical Sun was absent, it can be understood that at the time when the sacred Mysteries were at their height it was not the physical Sun that received the greatest adoration, but the " Midnight Sun "; that is, the *spiritual* powers of the physical Sun that streamed through the Earth from the antipodes.

To " see the Sun at midnight " is a well-known expression for the visions of the soul in sleep. The " Sun " denoted the spiritual world.

In Egypt, the transition from the adoration of the Spiritual Sun to a beginning of the adoration of the Sun as the giver of Life to the physical Earth, occurred at the time of the Pharaoh Akhenaten, Amenhotep IV, who forsook the worship of Amen—the representative

Sun-God of the old clairvoyance—for the worship of
Aten, " Giver of Life ". He was a preparer, and did it
quite consciously, for the time when the atavistic form
of clairvoyance should have died out. It is an interesting fact that in the West, in the British Mysteries, this
transitional point in the evolution of human consciousness occurred more than one thousand years
later; so that the Druidic wisdom retained much of its
mystical knowledge right on into early Christian times.
And this is one reason why the seed of Christianity
found such fertile soil in Ireland and the Western Isles.

The Hibernian Mysteries, with their ritual of the two
statues, represent the very essence of the problem of
human life. The pupils' experiences, left alone as they
were in darkness in the presence of these statues, alter-
nated between the feeling of being lifted out of themselves, with their consciousness extended over vast
periods of Time and regions of Space, and the feeling
of being pressed and contracted into themselves. In
both directions such a pupil would feel a kind of
annihilation of his ordinary self-hood; because, *in*
himself, he knew that he had been " born out of the
womb of worlds, out of the great Universe ", as an
individual Spirit, and this was contracted into his
earthly personality. This has already been described,
but I have repeated it, because it will presently be
seen that it is connected with something else.

The British Druids, who were the representative
teachers of the various Celtic peoples that had moved
gradually westwards—the descendants of the original
eastward-wandering Atlanteans—had lost a little of the
old visionary powers of sleep, with the natural result
that the waking life, the ordinary day-time consciousness, was more—if one can use the expression—" under
the Sun ". It was more intellectually observant. One

must try to imagine (for it is very important to grasp
this in attempting to study our Celtic mythology from
this new angle) how it feels when one is passing from a
deep twilight into a full daylight. All objects become
clearer and more defined; we can *know* more about
them. In the twilight, our imagination is stimulated;
in the sunlight, our intelligence. And in the brightness
we are less able to be *wise*, to use the deep instinctive
powers of the soul, and more able to be *clever*; and
we should have to make a certain effort to recall, in the
light, the deeper thoughts and feelings that the
twilight had engendered. So we can see from this
how important for the Druids would be the influences
of the morning and evening stars—Venus or Mercury
—and how these " twilights " were mystically and
mythologically combined in such a figure as Merddin
or Merlin, who could bring *divine wisdom* into *human
intelligence.*

It was this quality (still far, far removed from what
we should call " intellectual knowledge " to-day) that
the Druids grafted upon the original wisdom of
Hibernia some three thousand years ago.

But before we consider the nature of their teachings
we must see what other influences were at work.

The British Druids were connected, through the
distribution of the Celtic peoples, with the Trotten
Mysteries of northern Europe. The northern Mysteries
shared with those of other parts of the world, especially
Egypt, a certain characteristic, which was based on a
universal principle. It is this: all ancient wisdom
regarded the twelve encircling constellations of the
Zodiac as spiritual Powers, groups of creator Beings,
who worked formatively upon the whole structure of
man's body,* and upon the capacities (senses) to

* See frontispiece

which this structure belongs. The ancients recognised twelve parts of the body, and—not all of them clearly —twelve senses. The Zodiac was, to them, a principle of perfection. This twelvefold order is once more beginning to be recognised in our own time, not only in connection with the senses, but also with the classification of the plant and animal kingdoms.[15] It is the principle of the archetypes of all things. And it is the principle upon which the foundations of the " New Jerusalem " are built.

Therefore, should one member of this twelvefold order be missing it is no longer perfect. So in the Mysteries, in order to accomplish something as perfectly as possible, one human being alone did not suffice; he must be surrounded by twelve others each of whom was allotted a special task. Wherever in history we find mention of twelve human beings surrounding a thirteenth, it is an echo of what was practised when anything that was inspired through the Mysteries had to be carried out, either in connection with initiation, or in affairs in the outer world. And within the Mystery schools themselves as part of the necessary procedure in the attainment of initiation, twelve " helpers " were present. These twelve worked in such a way that, by their capacity to direct their thoughts to higher spheres, they supported the one who was being initiated, by strengthening him when his feeling of self-hood seemed to be annihilated by the overwhelming majesty of the Macrocosmic powers: or, when in the experience of his own inner life of soul, he was in danger of cramping isolation through his own newly discovered superabundant self-ness.

The *physical image* of the Thirteenth in the midst of the Twelve is the Sun in the midst of the twelve zodiacal constellations. The *reality* was the knowledge that behind the physical image were all the hosts of heaven and their creative activity surrounding the *human being*.

Not only was this principle applied as among thirteen separate people, but in the Mystery Temples the one who was to be initiated had to feel himself as the Sun, and rule—in himself—over the twelve members of his body and his twelve senses; so that he could at last truthfully say: " I rule in the mid-space as the Sun; I am Master of the Stars."

Needless to say, so high a degree of development was only possible for those who are known in our modern terminology as " Culture Heroes ". They were " Sun-Heroes "—full Initiates. . . . We will return to this subject later.

There is a poem attributed to the Bard *Taliesin* (sixth century A.D.) called *Canu y byd mawr*, the *Song of the Great World*, in which the soul is said to be seated in the head of man, who is composed of *seven* elements, Fire, Earth, Water, Air, Vapour, Blossom, and the Wind of Purposes. He is endowed with *seven senses*, which include " appetite " and " aversion ", or, as one might say, " attraction " and " repulsion ". Above him are *seven skies*, or spheres; and *seven planets*, Sun, Moon, Mars, Mercury, Venus, Jupiter (called Severus), and Saturn. The Earth is said to have *five* zones; counting from the centre, one is hot, and uninhabited, two are cold, the fourth contains the " inhabitants of Paradise ", and the fifth is the dwelling-place of mortals.[16]

This classification presents an approximate picture of the twelve spheres of existence (seven above, five below), which correspond to the twelvefold forces that sustain the life of the Earth. The Bard relates the seven superior forces to the senses of man; and where the seven elements are mentioned, as part of man's "head", it is not unlikely that he means to indicate the seven elementary processes of Life, such as, for instance, breathing, nutrition, and so on.

If this whole question is studied esoterically, we find that the twelve senses may be divided into seven "ordinary" ones, and five that are less known, and which may be said to be more "spiritual", for they are more deeply concealed in our nature. Modern research already recognises (one somewhat doubtfully) *nine* senses. The remaining three that are not yet fully recognised, are those that are most deeply concealed: the sense of "I am", or of the Ego; the sense of Thought; and the sense of Speech.*

The fact that the Bard only mentions *seven* senses is really quite an important clue to the general nature of the ordinary consciousness of life possessed in early times. It suggests (what other research confirms) that the sense of being an *Ego* was not fully awakened, except in the case of highly developed people. The general feeling was, as is well known, that the whole tribe or family represented the "*Ego*", and each person was only a part of this group-soul. Moreover, if one does not feel one's own individuality strongly it is not possible to feel that *other* people are separate individuals and the full significance of "I" and "thou" is not appreciated. And so the *thought*, and the *inner meaning of the speech* of others (both higher "senses") is not so well understood.

That the "sense of Ego" is placed in the diagram under the sign of Gemini, the Twins, is very suggestive. The "sense of Life" is the general feeling of inner vitality which is really contributed to by all the other

* See *The Riddle of Man*. By Rudolf Steiner.

more external senses; and is also connected with all those life-processes to which the Bard gives such delightful names. It is nice to think one may be blown through by the " Wind of Purposes! "

The purification necessary for any initiation consisted (and still consists) in first of all mastering all elements of selfishness and desire in ordinary life. The higher stages consist in doing the same with the more "spiritual" senses. But here again, what is selfishness and desire to the common man had a different character in ancient times. *Courage* was the greatest virtue; and this covers a very wide field. The " power of overcoming ", applied to life as it then was, is indicative of mastering all the obstacles in the way of knowledge, whether such knowledge was concerned with man himself or with Nature. To overcome is comparable to the conflict between Light and Darkness; darkness must be known before light can be revealed.

To the ancients, *darkness* was the physical world of matter, the kingdom of Pluto; and in Welsh mythology it is called *Annwn*. So that the question and answer quoted at the head of this chapter are really two questions and two answers, and include the two-fold origin of man: his spirit comes from the Great World, and his body from Annwn. This has not been recognised in comments that I have seen on these words, where the two questions have been regarded as one.

All this will be more fully dealt with in connection with the Bardic initiation.

The zodiacal constellations belonging to the "seven" are those that the dwellers in the northern parts of the world are most familiar with for they are visible in the long nights of the more wintry months. In the summer, others appear, which in the winter nights had been below the horizon; and these are those that are connected with the more spiritual human senses. The greatest heroes of Celtic mythology were said to come from " the land of the summer stars ", or from the " summer country ", because they had, as initiated people, found their way, with the " Midnight Sun ", to these deepest—or highest—levels of the soul, and become " Sun-Heroes "—Masters of all the twelve constellations. All this however points more to the mystical experience of the individual initiate, rather than to that other oath of knowledge which could bring illumination and a skilled and imaginative science concerning the kingdoms of Nature and the cosmic powers working within them.

But everything that has been said here about the twelve senses and the seven and the five, and the experiences of sleeping and waking in ancient times is only approximate, for there are great differences in the quality of our senses to-day as compared with three or four thousand years ago. And not one of the human senses is confined to its particular sense-organ alone—as smell to the nose, taste to the tongue and so on, but each is related to all the living processes of the other bodily organs. In the same way, not one of the constellations of the Zodiac was felt to be an isolated citadel, but each responded, in the influences it rayed out, to the passage through its " house " of the seven planets.

In Egyptian mythology (the same period) there was a Celestial river Nile, inhabited by *five* crocodiles. When the Osiris Sun dies, or sets, the crocodiles plunge into the watery abyss of the celestial Nile, and when the Sun rises, they reappear. They vanish into the spiritual and reappear in the physical—a heavenly picture of man's sleeping and waking.

Among the Gnostics,* *five words* were said to be written on the shining garment of Jesus at His glorification: *Zama, Zama, Ozza Rachama Ozai:* " The Robe, the glorious Robe of My Strength." The initial letters Z, O, R, O suggest the name Zoro-aster, the " blazing Star ", the sign of the complete fulfilment of initiation.

All this points to the mystery of the " higher man " who is revealed in the " lower man " when he has passed through the mystic death or trance and become acquainted with the Twelve.

These things will help us to solve some of the problems of Celtic legend, and especially the poem of *The Spoils of Annwn.*

The various numbers so frequently alluded to in Celtic mythology almost always refer in one way and another to the correspondences that exist between the Macrocosm and the Microcosm. *Twelve:*—the principle of spatial perfection, pointing to the heavens and to the anatomical structure of the human body, and to the senses. *Seven:*—the principle of motion and Time, as revealed through the planetary movements; also to the seven senses that are most apparent, and the seven life-processes of the seven principal organs of the human body, in their relation to the planetary influences and to the senses. *Five:*—that which is most concealed in man and the universe, all that lies nearest to the sacred mystery of the " I am "—and therefore " dark ", because the secret is Dionysian, internal, reflected in the core of the Earth. *Three:*—in the universe; Sun, Moon, and Earth. In the human being and in Nature: the secret of the " dynamic " of the Trinity and its evolution in Past, Present, and

* *The Secret Doctrine,* Vol. II, page 613. H. P. Blavatsky.

Future,—really including the principle of metamorphosis. *One:*—the " thirteenth in the midst of the
twelve ".   The intervening numbers need not be
mentioned here.

The number Three is continually met with in
Druidism and especially in the whole theology of the
Bards. A reason for this is that the Celtic mythology of
the West reached its zenith during what has been
mentioned as the third epoch of culture (corresponding
to the time of the Egypto-Chaldean civilisation),
when the trinitarian conception of the divine rulership
of the world prevailed.   The word " Druid " also
comes from " three "; it is associated with the third
epoch and also signifies an initiate of the third degree.

During that epoch the Sun, at the vernal equinox,
rose in the constellation of Taurus, the Bull. The Sun,
in its 25,960 years' passage through the twelve signs of
the Zodiac, rises in the month of the spring equinox in
some one particular sign during a period of 2160 years.
Then it enters a new sign.   This fact colours, in one
way and another, everything that takes place during
such a period of 2160 years.   The constellation of
Taurus, as all the constellations do, sends down its own
particular characteristic forces to the Earth. Those of
Taurus are said to have to do most especially with the
reproductive powers in man and Nature, with inner
secretions, with the juices and saps of plants, and with
what is, in man, the sublime counterpart of these
processes, the powers of speech. There is a connection
between the reproductive organs and the larynx.

This explains how it is that in our Celtic mythology
related to the Taurus epoch we have innumerable
legends about bulls and cows. The great central
myth of this whole Celtic pantheon is that of Hu, the
Sun-Hero, whose sacred Bulls draw the mysterious

" Avanc " out of the waters of a lake. This legend will be described later. In the Western Islands and High-lands of Scotland there are still remnants of an ancient midwinter festival connected with Bull-Mysteries (Hogmanay). The Mithraic Mysteries, with the Hero Mithras as their founder, who conquered the Bull, belong also to this period. The mystical conquest of the Bull signified not only a knowledge of processes in Nature connected with the healing art, but also a deep insight into the characteristics and functions of the human organs, and of the " sense " of speech, its meaning and its spiritual power.

This makes the Bull symbology of special importance when we are studying the functions and doctrines of Bardism. For the Bards are those who, above all, " declared their dark speech upon the harp ". *Music* and *speech*—these are faculties that come from the highest spheres. Let us say that they come through the spiritual influences of the Sun, and the constellations of Taurus, Gemini, and Aries.

No doubt it will seem to many people to-day that to attribute our human faculties to the benevolence of the heavenly bodies is a superstition. But to the men of old it was as natural to regulate their lives by, and feel their connection with the holy Twelve, as it is for us to regulate our lives by our watches and clocks. Never-theless, the day will surely come when science, climbing its spiral staircase, will find itself once more at the same, but higher, point of observation as that occupied by the men of the third epoch.

2

The oldest Greek writers (and Strabo refers to his-torians " still more ancient ") ascribed the name of *Hyperborea* to some land in the north-west of Europe.

They believed that their Sun-God Apollo travelled thither every winter-time and returned to the Grecian Mystery-sanctuaries in the summer. Apollo was not, in ancient Greece, worshipped as the *physical* sun, for they called the physical sun *Helios*; but Apollo was the Spirit of the Sun, who worked upon the Earth and all its kingdoms by sending his powers through the four (or five) elements, which were, in a very real sense, regarded as his messengers and servants. Through them Apollo brought inspiration to the priests of the sanctuaries, and withdrew his inspiration in the winter months to the land of Hyperborea, where other Mystery centres were established to receive them.

So there was a living link between Greece and the lands of the North, and these were the lands of the Celts; and the link was ratified, so it was said, by the sending of a wheat-straw in the hands of travellers between Greece and Hyperborea. Moreover, there was another link with the Greeks, and that was their knowledge that in that same northern land secrets of the Depths, of Death, of the origin of the Earth, could be learnt. Aeneas (Virgil's *Aeneid*) may have taken his journey to Hyperborea, the land of Dis, in search of the Golden Bough (mistletoe) which would admit him to regions of the spiritual world where he could converse with the dead. This, too, is a reference to the Celtic-Hibernian Mysteries. Hyperborea is described by Hesiod as at the " ends of the Earth, in the island of the blessed, and by the deep ocean ".

Another writer, Diodorus Siculus, says:

" Opposite to the coast of Gallia Celtica, there is an island in the ocean—not smaller than Sicily— lying to the north, which is inhabited by the Hyperboreans, who are so named because they dwell beyond the north wind[17]. . . . In this island there is a magnificent grove (or precinct) sacred to Apollo, and a remarkable temple, of round form, adorned with many consecrated gifts. There is also a city sacred to the same God, most of the inhabitants of which are harpers, who continually play upon their harps in the temple, and sing hymns to God, extolling His actions. . . . The supreme authority in that city and sacred precinct is vested in those who are called *Boreadae*, being the descendants of Boreas (or Bore) and their governments have been uninterruptedly transmitted in this line."

Edward Davies commenting on this passage remarks:

" We discover no considerable Druidical monument, where the language of Britain is preserved, without finding also, *Tre'r Beirdd*, the *town of the Bards*, or a name of similar import, in its vicinity."

Diodorus says further that this island, Hyperborea, had " remained unmixed by foreign power, for neither Bacchus, nor Hercules, nor any other hero or potentate had made war upon it." This is true of Ireland, whose people had lived for so long " unmixed " from the time of the Fathers until peaceful colonisation took place from other nations, and from Greece itself. Commentators on the ancient Greek and other authors conclude that Hyperborea is Celtic Britain, and that the great temple referred to is Stonehenge.

I am more inclined to think that the pilgrimages that were made from south-eastern Europe to the Hyperborean land, had, as their *ultimate* goal at any rate, Ireland; although Celtic Druidism, with its Sun-Moon wisdom, was probably more intensely cultivated in Wales than anywhere else, Ireland was still the holder of the most ancient form of the Mysteries of the Depths. And there was a part of Ireland, says an old tradition, that has never " descended to the Earth "; that is, the hardening, materialising forces of the Earth do not " enter into human souls and bodies ", and the shadowy form of Death can be held at bay. Moreover it was in Ireland and Wales particularly that the art of Song and the music of the harp—gifts of Apollo during his " northern visits "—had their true home.

Turning now from the ancient writers to a modern author, Rudolf Steiner, we find some interesting statements about Ireland.*   He tells us that at a particular period of the third post-Atlantean epoch (the time already referred to in this chapter) Greek colonists from Melos came to Ireland. That is already known. But what is *not* generally known is that this colonisation was undertaken for a special reason, which shall be dealt with more fully later, but which can be briefly indicated here. Such colonisations were, in those times, thought out for quite different reasons than the reasons we have for colonising in modern times. They were *spiritual* reasons; and the colonisations were arranged by the initiated leaders of the people who could foresee what the future development of humanity would require.

Ireland, the first halting-place of a part of the original eastward-wandering Atlantean population, had, in its geographical and geological character, a certain effect upon its inhabitants: it held back the development of intellectual observation and the growth of Ego-consciousness; which must be thought of in the

* In a privately printed lecture-course.

sense that strong personality, strong ability to make decisions, did not develop there. Instead, the old clairvoyance could continue for a long time after it had faded out elsewhere. So those people who had an "Apollonian" nature (the Celtic Druids), mingling with those whose nature belonged to the deeper sources of earthly genesis, the "Dionysian" men, were really like "light shining in darkness", but in a darkness that held the key to many mysteries. The Greeks therefore were people who physically and actually came from the "summer country" of Apollo. But this does not contradict the mystical and symbolical "land of the summer stars", which was the heavenly "picture" of the Sun-initiation—the selfless attainment of the twelvefold wisdom of the Zodiac.

The Greek initiates foresaw that out of this mingling of peoples, descendants would come who would have special qualifications, in the whole constitution of their psychic-spiritual life, for *understanding* the Mystery of the Incarnation, Death, and Resurrection of Christ. They would be, so to say, "Ego-less" men. It is from this mixture of peoples that the Irish monks at last appeared, and were able to go forth, utterly selflessly, as the greatest Christian missionaries. The spiritual heritage of the great Hibernian Mysteries permeated their souls through the magical breath of Nature; that "water-fall land", as St. Columba called it, brought the Sun-song to birth in their hearts, and the fiery depths gave strength to their consecrated will.

So far, we have attempted to gather together a few of the threads out of which Celtic mythology is woven; and in the next chapter we shall have something to say about the Bards—whose writings are so obscure, and who have been so little understood.

CHAPTER V

THE BARDS

" In all that I speak there shall be sight."
(Œdipus.)

I

I SHOULD like to refer the reader once more to the
first page or two of Chapter I and the story of
Einigen the Giant.

There it was said that the name Einigen is related to
Enoch, in the sense that this name denotes an initiate,
a seer, or prophet. Books or writings that are called
*Apocrypha** or *Enoïchion*, are secret books or documents
which belonged in olden times to the archives of the
Temple Mysteries, and were not accessible to the
"profane". The tradition that the ancient wisdom was
preserved in *two* parts is to be found in many countries.
Josephus tells us that Enoch hid his precious books
under the two pillars of Mercury, or Seth. The same
thing was said of the great Hermes of Egypt, Thoth.
But he hid his "books" first under a single pillar, and
afterwards found their content written on *two* stone
pillars. Moses also had to write the Commandments
on two tables of stone. And we have already described
the two statues of the Hibernian Mysteries.

The mysterious accounts that exist everywhere of the
"translation" or disappearance of the great initiates of
the world, the statements that they did not die and will

* From the Greek *crypto*, to hide.

96

come again, all point to a continuance of the secret
wisdom, either in the Mystery Temples, or, when these
came to an end, in the various secret brotherhoods
even up to our own time. But, let it be understood,
only in the real and genuine occult schools, not in
those that have from time to time presented some kind
of pseudo-occultism to the world.

Whatever we may think of such a statement, the fact
remains that when we examine the records of the past
we find a certain uniformity of idea—a wisdom of the
spiritual world (religion), and of the sciences and the
arts, which appears under the guise of a unity—a
single " pillar ", then of a duality, then of a trinity.
Further that there were in different parts of the world,
generic names—Enoch, Thoth—(or Mercury),
Orpheus, Hu or Hesus (Jesus), Jonah—the same as
Iona;—and the names of the so-called " culture
Heroes " such as Arthur, Merlin, and many others,
which denoted not single personalities *only*, but a title
of initiation.

Certain attributes are found to be connected with
such names: the seven-stringed phorminx or lyre of
Orpheus, the twelve knights of the Round Table,
etc., etc.

In the presentation of all wisdom a twofold source is
implied. Orpheus called the two principles of the
universe Æther and Chaos; Pythagoras and Plato,
the Bound and Infinity. In the latter we sense the laws
of contraction and expansion, as already described.
And it is natural somehow to experience this as a
circle, and to feel in the circle, a point; and in relating
circle and point to feel the necessity of expansion and
contraction as the very life of the concept. This is the
rather chilly intellectual picture that we can make of
what was once a grand and sublime world-conception,

not vague and empty, but filled with very precise knowledge of the relation between the Macrocosm—Infinity—and the Microcosm—the Bound.

The diagram on p. 110 shows, in the form of *stones*, the metamorphosis—from the earliest known world-conception up to Druidical times—of the Mystery cults connected with Celtic mythology. But first there is something else to be said so that the connection with the Taurus Age may be apparent.

In the two vertical stones of the Druid trilithons, united by the horizontal covering stone, we have something like a picture of the horns of the celestial bull—which represented two great cosmic forces—separated, but united by the universal power of the Sun, or of the

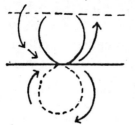 spiritual world. The two cosmic forces were the same as those represented by the two principal Gods of the altars of the Mysteries of the Kabiri in Greece, *Mars* and *Mercury*. The sign for Taurus ♉ may be thought of rather as a lemniscate, open above, and not as a closed circle with two horns or a crescent above it (see fig.).

On one side the forces are descending, on the other ascending. The warlike powers of Mars were to be led through the Earth and transformed into the love-bearing light of Mercury, by the might of the Sun.

The ancients thought—and rightly—that the horns of an animal were cosmic radiations bearing the *instinctive* sentient life of the animal, that had become " frozen " in matter. So the stones of the Druid cromlechs could represent powers of the World-Soul, creating the world; but the horizontal stone " captured ", so to say, these radiations and cast a physical shadow when the Sun was shining.

If one could visualise, in imagination, such a two-pillared doorway, and add, in the imagination, a blazing and dazzling light in the space between the two pillars—a light so intense that it could give one the impression of an emptiness, a vacuum—one could say to oneself: " *There is God;* but we cannot look at Him, He is too bright. But if we make a shadow, we can see in this shadow *how God works in His creation.*" This, as we shall see in a later chapter, is what the Druids did. Their God, the representative of the whole spiritual world, the British Druids called *Hu the Mighty One,* whose Bulls were yoked to the Sun.

Here we can sketch the metamorphosis from the " Atlantean " Mysteries to the Druids as shown on p. 110.

The constellations of the Zodiac, while they certainly are spiritually connected with the senses and also with the structure of the body, were experienced in the higher states of consciousness induced in the Mysteries, as the source of man's capacity to utter *consonants*; the planetary divinities gave him the capacity to utter *vowels.* Therefore the power of the Word was felt as altogether divine, and the utterance of the sounds of speech were recognised as an imitation, by man, of the spiritual tones of the Creative Word. But the vowel sounds—and one can feel their inherent music when one makes them—could be experienced as containing within them the spiritual counterparts of the primal consonants. Thus, for example, the word *Jehovah* as we speak it on Earth, could be perceived as consisting only of vowels, " spiritually impregnated " by consonants. So we get I, O, A, and similar combinations of vowels for the divine Name.

The fixed stars were felt as the formative power in creation; but the planets as movement—that is, as the *deeds* of Beings who carried out the *thoughts* of the fixed stars.

The utterance of vowels and consonants is connected with breathing, and among the ancients there was a very profound knowledge of this; it was possible, through speech, to produce really magical effects. Such speech contains elements of healing. The very last fragment of this old knowledge of the formative and healing powers of speech survives to-day in the West in our ideas of modern hygiene, in the " deep

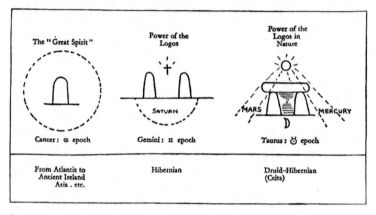

The " Great Spirit "	Power of the Logos	Power of the Logos in Nature
Cancer : ♋ epoch	Gemini : ♊ epoch	Taurus : ♉ epoch
From Atlantis to Ancient Ireland Asia . etc.	Hibernian	Druid-Hibernian (Celts)

breathing " practised in physical culture. *How* the inbreathing really restores the life of our organs is no longer understood except as a purely materialistic idea of " renovation ".

To-day when we look at the stars we look at them from the standpoint of the Earth and of our earthly consciousness; after death, or in the case of one who is initiated, the " other side " of the stars is seen. But what is the " other side " ? It means that the veil of physical perception—sight and hearing—has fallen away, and the consciousness, expanded and spiritualised, sees no " stars " but is aware of spiritual Beings instead.

In an article on *Speech and Song*, Rudolf Steiner gives a beautiful imaginative picture of the heavenly sounds of cosmic speech, in the following words:

" Imagine yourself out there in the Cosmos; now the planetary world is farther from you, and the twelve constellations of the Zodiac nearer. From all the heavenly bodies there is singing—speaking as they sing to you, singing as they speak; and all your perception is a listening to the speaking song, the singing speech of the World. . . . The planetary sphere is singing to you in vowels—singing forth into the cosmic spaces; and the fixed stars permeate the song of the planetary sphere with soul from the consonants. Picture it to yourselves as vividly as you can: the sphere of the fixed stars at rest, and behind it the wandering planets. Whenever a planet in its course passes a constellation of fixed stars, there bursts forth, not a single note, but a whole world of sound. Then as a planet passes on, let us say, from Aries to Taurus, a different world of sound rings out. But behind it there follows another planet—Mars. Mars passing through the constellation of Taurus causes a different world of sounds to ring forth once more. So in the Zodiac you have a wondrous cosmic instrument of music, while from behind, the planetary Gods are playing upon this instrument."

Only by conceding that experiences like this were possible is one able to imagine that the utterance of speech in the Mysteries must have been held most sacred. The true Names of the " Fathers in the Heavens " could not be spoken outside the sanctuaries. The clairvoyance obtainable in the Mysteries showed how different sounds, when seen spiritually, possessed the *forms* that are repeated in the structure of the human body and its organs.

Speech could be used in a certain way as a means of healing; or as a means of producing visions, for or in others, of the anatomy and life-processes of the body. In Egyptian times this very profound insight into the connections between the Macrocosm and the Microcosm had already lost much of its purity and fell at last altogether into decadence. In the later periods of Druidism this was also the case. Human sacrifice was probably a result of the attempt to recapture the lost wisdom of the " Word " by means of a degenerated magic. . . . But we are trying here to reconstruct the earlier experiences.

When we think of the Bards we think of Music, rather than of Wisdom. But music, like everything else, has been born into physical existence out of a spiritual realm. The world of colour, too, has entered into visibility out of an existence that, to our modern blindness, is invisible. We see a dark cloud in a rainy sky, and suddenly, as though out of nothing, the rainbow appears. . . . For one brief moment the hidden and ever-present ethereal world of colour has stepped over the threshold from the spiritual into the material world. So we feel: colour is *there*—it exists— it has revealed itself to us!

In the same way we can think of music. It is there, in eternal and inaudible beauty, and we still speak of this —to us—inaudible music, as the " harmony of the spheres ". Sometimes, in the moment of waking out of sleep, we can feel ourselves streaming earthwards in a river of light and of great organ-tones—a magnificent and indescribable harmony comes with us, " trailing clouds of glory ". Then suddenly we are awake, and it is silent.

Who first "fetched" music from the heavens? Tradition tells us that it was Orpheus, the son of Apollo. But now we know that "Orpheus" is the name of an initiate, and of a school of initiates founded by him. But everything has its beginning, and so it is no phantasy to say that at some time or other there was a real single Orpheus-personality, who was the original Bard.

And we have to ask too, Why does music exist? . . . It is much easier to imagine why sculpture or painting or architecture should exist, because in a sense the very life and forms of the Earth present them to us in idea. These arts belong to our more direct experiences of life—the necessity to build, to form, and so on. But music expresses something deeper, something nearer to our inner life of thought and emotion. It is like light, and carries warmth, and expresses love.

In the third epoch, mentioned previously, love was still confined to the sphere of blood relationships, and inhered in the Group-soul of the tribe or family, and was, in that sense, instinctive. It was not natural to love all, or any, people outside this narrow limit. The great "lovers" of the world were only to be found among the initiates, who had broken through the bonds of blood by the very fact that in their initiation they experienced the true Ego, which is eternal, and which "shines like a star" above the mere physical personality. If the true Ego, or Higher Self, is found it is a natural consequence that other human beings are perceived as one's spiritual brethren; all are equal in God.

So without wisdom (which was then not cold intellectual knowledge) this all-embracing love could not be

found. This implies that the " path of overcoming "
which, through Courage, led to the attainment of
initiation, included, at any rate for those who were to
be initiated *Bards*, the overcoming of all lower forms
of love and of self-love. But no one can overcome
what they have not experienced. The lower forms of
love could be symbolised by the Bull. So also could
the higher. For then the Bull could wear the " golden
yoke " and be the servant of the Sun. Or, if we take
the Orpheus legend, we see how it is described that *all*
Nature, all plants and animals, bowed down to the
music of Orpheus' lyre; they were overcome, and
embraced in the light of the sphere harmonies.

There was then, an initiate whose " generic " name
we may say was Orpheus, and who knew, by his
peculiar initiation wisdom, that mankind needed
music. Occult science shows that the transition from
an instinctive form of clairvoyant knowledge and of
feeling, to a more clear-cut and defined *thinking*,
conjured forth—so to say—the birth of music; or,
more precisely, the birth of music in the form in which
it could be expressed on a stringed instrument (instead
of a wind instrument) and be accompanied by the
measures and tones of song.

The effect of music was *to build and strengthen the
organ of thought*. Thought is akin to light. When we
understand something we still say: I see. So thought
and music, music and light, are akin. And light is
wisdom—the pure virgin wisdom of the celestial spheres.
The Bards could understand how music comes from
the " eternal feminine "—from the Virgin Sophia
(wisdom), the Virgin of the Light—where knowledge is
unsullied and pure; and where, in the radiance of the
stars of Gemini, there is understanding of the brotherhood of man, of " I ", and " thou ". And that is Love.

But the teachers of music could not yet aspire to inculcate eternal love, through music, in others; though they had to discover it themselves. The effect of their music, to begin with, was to clarify the " Gemini " powers in other people as *separation and association of ideas*—light in thinking—logical thought. So we find, among the later Bards, a great deal of logical thinking, of theological and philosophical doctrines, mainly in the form of poetry. Logical thinking (we can all be aware of it) tends to tear one away from dreaminess or instinctive action and impulse; it works separatively, separating us from our surroundings so that we can observe them. And this, strangely enough, is the *path of love* for all of us! It creates the possibility of selfless devotion to something other than ourselves.

These connections are difficult to grasp at first. And no one will easily admit that clear thinking could be engendered by music in primitive times, unless he is able to concede the fact that the development of human consciousness was the result of *spiritual and not* (at first) of physical changes in man; and that man was still in those times under the protective and creative powers of the spiritual Hierarchies. Only those could be music-initiates who had the greatest insight into the Mysteries—who knew the " Fathers ". But it was not the function of the Bards to deal with science, with the outer world, for that was more the task of the Druid priests; but it was their function to be " psychologists "—if one can use the word. They had to suffer and endure and overcome all that belongs to the tragedy of the impurity of the human soul in face of the Divine Soul, the eternal Feminine— the Goddess Ceridwen. Every poet knows this suffering. Theirs was a Dionysian, a Kabirian, cult. But, inseparable as had been the two statues of Hibernia, so this Dionysian-Orphic way was inseparable from the Apollonian Sun-wisdom of the Druid priests. They were distinct, but together and interwoven.

As music and song prepared the way for the burning, dissolving, and combining in the realm of thought, so the Druids prepared the way for the burning, dissolving and binding in the realm of alchemy. The Bards represented the inner, the Druids the outer, path.

We begin to see another aspect of the significance of the intercourse between Greece and the West of Britain, in the fructification of the Dionysian wisdom of the original Fathers by the *Orpheus* Mysteries. Legends tell us that Orpheus appeared unexpectedly in the turbulent bacchanalian orgies of the sanctuaries of Thrace, like a ray of peace and healing. But his message was still immature. So he went to Egypt and was initiated in the Egyptian Mysteries, returning to Greece to found his own Mysteries there. He is represented in many ancient carvings and drawings as a Fisherman. But why? The Fish is the emblem of Divine Life—the Light of the Sun—hidden in the dark depths of the waters of the soul.

Orpheus with his music sought to draw sun-like beauty out of the turbid secrets of the darker side of the old Dionysian cult—to give it the clarity of Thought, Music, the heart of Love, that fervently longs for the pure and eternal Feminine, the Virgin of the Light, and not for the raving lusts of the Bacchantes.
. . . But in Greece they tore him to pieces. There, he could not complete the mission that was destined to be carried, like the Sun itself, from the East to the West, to wander over Europe and sink down into the hearts of the Bards of Britain.

We can perhaps try to make all this a little clearer, though it must remain to some extent symbolical and mystical because what we are attempting to depict from the facts that have come down to us belongs to another age of consciousness than our own. Moreover we are trying to go back behind the generally accepted historical records, as these dealt with the time when pure Druidism and Bardism had become a mere shadow of its former greatness.

There is some connection between the Egyptian cult of the Goddess Hat-hor and the initiation experiences of the Bards. The cult of Hat-hor had to do primarily with the development of the sexual organs at puberty. It was known that the natural powers of clairvoyance could be prepared at that time of life so as to be developed more intensely later. The Hat-hor Mysteries seem to have been a kind of preliminary stage on the way of initiation for those who were going to devote themselves to the attainment of higher degrees. Hat-hor was the " Queen of Heaven ", and her name means the " house of Horus ". She was represented as a cow with the Solar Disk between her horns. Such an image was symbolical of birth. Man is born, so it was said, not only of a human mother, but of the lunar envelope or surrounding moist sphere of the Earth— thought of as an albuminous but immaterial fluidity, a spiritual-astral world through which the Spirit of man descended into the womb of the physical mother. This sphere was the " womb " of Hat-hor. In the Germanic Mysteries—Herta.

The fluidity and plasticity of the supersensible " matter " of this realm was life-giving; it was the " milk " of the World, the " Soma " of Oriental mysticism. When the human being was born and the physical body was formed, it was known to contain this life-giving element in all the fluids of the body. Every process of nutrition and metabolism was concerned with this inner life-giving " milk of worlds ". Its most secret functioning is in the cerebro-spinal fluid; and this is connected (among other things) on the one hand with the sexual nature, and on the other hand with the " single eye " of seership. If a man could set his consciousness free from the attraction of the body, by initiation, he could " enter again into his mother's womb "—that is, into the *womb of Hat-hor,** and be born, not in the earthly realm, but into the spiritual world, whose Beings and laws would then be revealed to him.

This experience of the " element of water ", and the other elements, is found in the Celtic mythology in everything that has to do with the mystical *Cauldron of Ceridwen†*—which " would not boil the food of a coward ". Three drops of its precious fluid gave inspiration to him who could partake of it.

The initiation-steps of the *ancient* Bards represented the quest for this second birth, but in cosmological and astronomical experiences. But revelations of higher things always bring knowledge of the corresponding lower things. Imagine, that you are ascending a staircase which is reflected in a mirror on the floor; with every step you take in ascending the staircase you appear to take a step, in the mirror, into an abyss. With every stage of mystical communion with the elementary, planetary, and stellar powers, there was a corresponding step in knowledge of the depths of the soul and of the body.

Then imagine, that the search for the Virgin of the Light undertaken in Bardic initiation is a mystical and

* In Celtic mythology, of *Ceridwen.*
† To which a chapter will be devoted.

clairvoyant wandering through those things, first of all, that are the elemental constituents of the physical world—the operations of Nature; and you get thereby to know something of the natural structure and life of the physical body. Then you reach to the sphere of the Moon, and then to the other planets; and you begin to learn about the organs of the body and the life of desire and passion and emotion, and the meaning of the fluids and " humours " of the body, and the temperaments. And as the inner experiences reveal the evil that is in you, and what has to be overcome, so the cosmological imaginations reveal the " images " of the Gods, sometimes in terrible, and sometimes in beautiful forms.

And then begins the crossing of the boundless ocean —the voyage from constellation to constellation of the Zodiac, thus expanding again the miracle of the upright human man, who is formed in the form of a Cross, into the miracle of the infinite (circular) individual spiritual man eternal in his resplendent " revolving " *Caer*. Then all the twelve senses are filled with life; and the great Time-Kings, the twenty-four Elders, are there, seated at the heavenly Round Table. And everything is sounding with " singing speech ".

2

We can now glance at that most obscure and seemingly incomprehensible of Bardic poems, and see whether all this can help us to understand it a little.

The poem, written down probably in the sixth century A.D., but far more ancient as to its content, is known as the " *Spoils of Annwn* " (the Deep), and is attributed to the Bard *Taliesin*, whose name means " the radiant brow ". One commentator says of this poem: " All connected train of thought seems to have

been studiously avoided." Another writer says that it
is the " mythology of the Deluge and the Mysteries
celebrated in connection with it ". The poem is about
a series of seven *Caers* visited by a number of people
who went with Arthur " in his splendid labours ",
accompanying him in his ship *Prydwen*.

I give here some fragments of Edward Davies' prose
translation of the *Spoils of Annwn*, and will then
comment on it.

> " I will adore the sovereign, the supreme ruler of
> the land. If (though?) he extended his dominion
> over the shores of the world, yet in good order was
> the prison of Gwair in the enclosure of Sidi.
> Through the mission of Pwyll and Pryderi, no one
> before him entered into it.
>
> " The heavy blue chain didst thou, O just man,
> endure: and for the spoils of the deep, woful is thy
> song; and till the doom shall it remain in the Bardic
> prayer—*Thrice the number that would have filled
> Prydwen* (the ship) *we entered into the deep; excepting
> seven, none have returned from Caer Sidi.*"

2nd stanza:

> " Am I not contending for the praise of that lore,
> if it were regarded, which was four times reviewed in
> the quadrangle enclosure! As the first sentence was
> it uttered from the Cauldron, which began to be
> warmed by the breath of nine damsels. Is not this
> the Cauldron of the ruler of the deep! What is its
> quality? With the ridge of pearls round its border,
> it will not boil the food of a coward, who is not
> bound by his sacred oath. Against him will be lifted
> the bright gleaming sword: and in the hand of the
> sword-bearer shall he be left: and before the

entrance of the gate of hell, shall the horns of light be burning.—*And when we went with Arthur in his splendid labours, excepting seven, none returned from Caer Vediwid.*"

3rd stanza:

" Am I not contending for the honour of a lore that deserves attention! In the quadrangle enclosure, in the island with the strong door, the twilight and the pitchy darkness were blended together, whilst bright wine was the beverage, placed before the narrow circle.

" *Thrice the number that would have filled Prydwen, we embarked upon the sea; excepting seven, none returned from Caer Rigor.*"

5th stanza: (part)

. . . " They know not the brindled ox with the thick head-band, having seven-score knobs in his collar. *And when we went with Arthur of mournful memory; excepting seven, none returned from Caer Vandwy.*" . . . etc. etc.

Davies translates the names of the Caers as follows: Caer *Vediwyd*: the enclosure of the inhabitants of the world. Caer *Rigor*; the enclosure of the royal assembly. Caer *Golur*, the gloomy enclosure. Caer *Vandwy*: the enclosure resting on the height. Caer *Ochren*: the enclosure whose side produced life. There is also the enclosure of glass—Caer *Wydr*.

Nash sees nothing in this poem but a muddle of allusions to various romances. Davies sees only allusions to the ark and the deluge. My own interpretation may be at fault. But one thing is certain, and that is that in nearly all these poems actual happenings, or perhaps romances, are used as a veil behind which mystical or *alchemical* experiences are concealed. The colours and movements of the Knights of Arthur's Court are often used as images of the work of higher alchemy. The legends of the Cauldron of Ceridwen are throughout mystical experiences. Actual references to the ritual of the Mysteries are also mingled with the visions of the soul.

What is a Caer? Davies thinks it is the Ark of Noah. Translated, it appears to mean a fenced " enclosure ", a circle, a sanctuary, or, according to Davies, also an island. The greatest of these Caers (they are mentioned in many legends and poems) is *Caer Sidi*. Taliesin, as a great leader of Bardism, was described as occupying the " Chair " or Presidency of Caer Sidi. At all events, Caer Sidi appears to have been the most important, the most wonderful of temples—whether earthly or heavenly—and its " language " was what was pronounced from that Chair. To reach it, it was necessary to cross the " Great Deep ".

The ship of Arthur, in which the adventures are undertaken in the poem, is filled with three times its appointed number of persons, and Arthur himself. In all probability this number is *four*; and it is multiplied by three, and so the total is twelve, the basic number of the Round Table. There is a good foundation for this statement. In the Mysteries of Northern countries the four seasons of the year were studied with great intensity, as were also the four elements; and anyone who was about to be initiated into the secrets of Nature had twelve helpers, who were divided (says Rudolf Steiner)[18] into four groups of three, each group taking upon itself the arduous " adventures " necessitated by their particular task. Each group of three persons had to be entirely devoted to all the wisdom the Mysteries could bestow concerning each of the four seasons.

The Arthurian-Druid Mysteries consisted in the search for illumination concerning the influences of the stars in the four elements of Fire, Air, Water, and Earth; and in tracing their effects in a "natural science", there was included, as in all initiation, a profound knowledge of man, and the attainment of purity in the soul: and in the Arthurian Mysteries, the practice of chivalry. It was felt that the "order" of the stars must be imitated on the Earth. The chivalry of the Knights was a great step forward in the general impulse of civilisation, and was the very first beginning of the institution of civil rights. So the Arthurian Druidism was, in a sense, a "secular" form of the Mysteries because its exponents had to be "men of the world"—or, to use the Gnostic expression: "he shall be a man of the world but a King of the Light".

The boatful of twelve people with their thirteenth, is an image of the Zodiac with the Sun in its midst. It is a sort of clue to the Arthurian Mysteries when we find in legends that what is a heavenly reality is mirrored on the Earth: "when that which is great shall become small".

So what is contained in this poem is a picture of the seven planetary spheres "visited" by the twelve constellations, i.e. influenced by them; and the constant mobility and constant presence of the planets give us a picture, always, of the permanence and stability of the Universe; only the "seven" return again and again to our consciousness, while the "twelve" are, in their totality, a vast celestial "Caer", majestically revolving . . . something that is too sublime to return into the consciousness of man after his brief ecstatic vision of them.

And not only are there seven planets, but these must have had their representations on Earth in the seven holy " fortresses " of the seven " white " Kings of Atlantis. In *The Secret of the West*, Merezhkovsky says:

" Atlantis perished, but its gods were saved. There are seven of them: the Cretan Adonis-Adonai, the Egyptian Osiris, the Babylonian Tammuz, the Hittite Attis, the Iranian Mithra, the Hellenic Dionysus, and the ancient-Mexican Quetzalcoatl. They all show one face, like brother-twins. The swastika is on their brow: it is possible to say these are the ' baptised ' gods.

" There are seven of them like the seven colours of the post-Deluge rainbow: ' I do set my bow in the cloud, and it shall be a token of a covenant between me and the Earth.'

" They are more than twins, they are each others' doubles, so that if you know one you know all; they mix in one another, like the colours of the rainbow, behind which is one sun."

So, if the poem the *Spoils of Annwn* refers *also* to post-diluvian history (as an experience of initiation) it is still correct to say that " only seven " return; because, in Atlantis, only the seven god-accepted sanctuaries and their Mystery-wisdom survived, and those under the " Lords of the Dark Face ", the black-magical Kings, perished. The offspring of these seven Mystery-schools, devoted to planetary wisdom, are to be found —historically—scattered all over the world of the " second humanity ".

On the other hand, the inward mystical reflection, in the human being himself, of the seven Caers is the seven recognised stages of clairvoyance, the seven centres of higher consciousness. At each stage the seer experiences what his inner vision reveals.

Therefore, if we interpret the poem from the aspect of inner mystical experience, the " prison of Gwair " in the enclosure of Sidi expresses in reality the incarceration of the human being within his skin—that is, in his body—whose outermost limit, whose *form*, is created by the twelve constellations. All this must be " in good order " before the journey is begun. The just man " endures the heavy blue chain "; that is, he is, however ennobled, subject to the heaviness, or the fall into sin, of humanity, which expresses itself through the nature of the veinous blood that is burdened with the inevitable impurities of the bodily life: the " heavy blue chain ". (Stanza 1.)

Then the poet speaks of Caer *Vediwid*, which is the first clairvoyant experience, the " first sentence uttered from the Cauldron ". Vediwid is the *world*—all people —all that lives: it is the experience of first going out of oneself to " know the world " in North and South and East and West (" four times reviewed "), and so to unite oneself with the world, feeling its spiritual reality, not the illusion of its physical nature. Otherwise, the " bright flaming sword " will be lifted against the candidate, and he will not cross the Threshold into the spiritual consciousness. If he *does* cross it on the journey into the depths of his soul, then even the entrance to hell will be illumined by the *horns of light*— i.e. by that organ of clairvoyance or centre of consciousness in the forehead which, in olden times, was imagined and actually perceived as " horns of light ".

And so one might find one's way in every detail through the whole poem after this fashion;[19] but that would be tedious for the reader. In the end, the " seven " remain; not the twelve. For the latter must always, every time, be summoned—the " twelve legions of Angels "—when the adventure is to be undertaken.

Western (and Eastern) occultism speaks of six centres of consciousness, but their summing up constitutes and culminates in, a seventh. In the poem, it appears to be this seventh whose character is alluded to both as " the animal with the silver head ", and, in the previous verse, as having " seven-score knobs in his collar ". That is, the *totality* of experience, which includes the sevenfold nature of man and the sevenfold evolution of the seven cosmic ages. " Seven score " is 140, the number—as well as 147—already mentioned in this connection. The " silver head " is the complete Saturn-Sun Wisdom, reflected from the *Moon*; imparted, that is, by the spiritual " lunar " Instructors in the Mysteries.

Both the constellation Taurus, and the planet Mars, were imaged as Bulls. In fact it seems as though this taurine character is reflected *throughout the stellar spheres*; and we can well understand that this would be so in the third epoch—the epoch when the Sun rose, at the vernal equinox, in the constellation of Taurus. The God *Hu* (of whom more later), who represented the whole spiritual world, was attended by his oxen who " roared in thunder and blazed in lightning "—a thrilling allusion to the music of the spheres! Even the officiating Druid Priests identified themselves with this taurine power, in the saying: " I am the cell—I am the opening charm—I am the Bull of Flame."

Mars too—(in the Orphic hymns which have an undoubted connection with Bardism)—is called " the Deity with two horns, having the head of a Bull, even Mars-Dionysos, reverenced in a double form and

adored in conjunction with a beautiful star ". And the
Bacchantes invoke Dionysos by calling him:

> " Come, heifer-footed Deity to thy sacrifice! . . . Hear
> us, O Bull, worthy of our veneration; hear us, O
> illustrious Bull! "

All the starry worlds are Bulls. The thunders and
lightnings of the Ruler of the Age permeate the whole
firmament. And all are *Caers*, because each one is a
citadel of spiritual Mysteries.

The whole poem must be regarded as an account of
the experiences of an initiation, but presented, purposely, in the most obscure language. And the
difficulty of interpreting it is probably all the greater
owing to the fact that it is written down long after
the greatest period of the Celtic Mysteries, and it is
never possible to be sure to what extent later trans-
cribers or translators may not have thought that they
knew better than the earlier ones!

The more one studies Druidism, and especially that
side of it connected with the Bards, the grandeur of the
Dionysian Depths—the *reflection* in Man of the sounding thunders and organ-tones of what the old Indians
called the " Formative Voice " of the Heavens—moves
us profoundly. Human speech, human song, human
music, comes from the regions of the Light! . . . In
that extraordinary document, the *Pistis Sophia*, we
read that Jesus says to His disciples:

> " Do ye seek after these Mysteries? No Mystery is
> more excellent than they; which shall bring your
> souls into the Light of Lights, unto the place of
> Truth and Goodness, unto the place where there is
> neither male nor female, neither form in that place
> but Light, everlasting. Nothing therefore is more

excellent than the Mysteries which ye seek after, *saving only the Mystery of the seven Vowels and their forty and nine Powers.*"

The capacity to " think into " the qualities and meanings of speech is a higher gift than that of mere speaking, and is highest of all when it is combined with love.   Then it is musical, because it is a spiritual power working directly from soul to soul, and has no tyranny in it—nothing of the thrusting violence of the *untamed* Bull; and musical speech is formed in complete harmony with the laws of the spiritual structure of the body.   The harp of the Bards is a symbol of the love-impregnated soul which is able to transmit the heavenly wisdom (no matter how concealed in earthly images) from age to age.

It is noticeable that the Bards were lovers of peace, and not combatants.   Yet they sang always of the prowess of others.   And if we read the poems of Ossian the two poles of masculine war-like tendencies and the feminine musical and artistic tendencies are often set in contrast to one another.   The warriors are always in some way represented as under the protection of the oak-tree, which is the tree of Mars;   and after their battles they come to the birch-trees—which are dedicated to Venus—under whose shelter the harps are played.   Music is always related to the feminine element.

The Bards' way to the " Virgin of the Light " may be said to be in three stages: the passage through the elemental world, through the planets, and at last to the fixed stars.   A true Bard could say, as Taliesin did, that he had been born three times:

" Thrice have I been born.   I know how to meditate.   It is woeful that men will not come to seek all the sciences of the world, which are treasured in my bosom; for I know all that has been, and all that will be hereafter."

If music be not only the " food of love ", but the builder and nourisher of the powers of clear thinking, it could be no other than the preparer of the age when, the great visions of the past being lost, man had to find his way to a precise and objective intellectuality in regard to his knowledge of the world and of himself. It was the Swan-song of the old Gods; and we hear it still in the Fire-music of Brunnhilde's sleep. . . . There is in Wagner a true echo of the magic of Merlin.

The extract quoted a little way back about the music of the spheres may be taken as an illustration of the mystical experience of an initiated Bard; but let us imagine further that the Bard felt that he *himself*—as a copy in miniature of the whole living starry system— was the one who, looking back from the heights upon the great " cosmic instrument " in its twelve and sevenfold order, played upon it and extracted its melodies and harmonies. It was not his own lower personality that could command this heavenly music, but his Higher Self; and the name for this Higher Self, identified with Divinity, was IAU, called the " Younger ". In oriental mysticism, presented in a certain poetical form in the *Stanzas of Dzyan*,* we read:

" Behold, O Lanoo, the Radiant Child of the Two, the unparalleled refulgent Glory, Bright Space, Son of Dark Space, who emerges from the Depths of the Great Dark Waters! It is OEAOHOO the Younger. He shines forth as the Sun. He is the blazing divine Dragon of Wisdom."

* H. P. Blavatsky: *The Secret Doctrine.*

In the name OEAOHOO we have the same, or nearly the same, vowel tones as in IAU, OIU, IOA, etc., which again and again are found as expressive of the Divinity, but without the exoteric addition of the inwardly perceived consonants. The meaning of these sounds can be summarised in the following way:

A, (as AH!): We receive all the powers of those regions of the Cosmos whence our Being comes to us. We express Wonder.

O,: the world experiences something through man himself. There is an intelligent relationship between ourselves and that which calls forth our wonder. I, and thou.

I,: the forces stream from our own centre outwards. *I am.*[20]

The idea that this Being IAU is the " Younger " will remind readers of the Dionysos myth. IAU is the re-born Dionysos—the God who was " dismembered " in the Plutonic (physical) world, and re-created in the Light: i.e. *the initiated human being himself.*[21]

This conception of the Higher Self, the " Younger ", born out of the human personality, in initiation, is probably the key to the understanding of the collection of poems known as *Hanes Taliesin*, the History of Taliesin, which shall be considered in the second part of this chapter.

But first, a word or two about a certain confusion that exists in the minds of some students with regard to Caer Sidi and the " revolving Castle " mentioned in the Welsh Sant Graal. Lewis Spence, in his *Mysteries of Britain*, says that Caer Sidi " sometimes means the Zodiac and sometimes Annwn ". And in his *History of Atlantis* he quotes from the Welsh Sant Graal as follows:

"And they rode through the wild forests, and from one to another, until they arrived on a clear ground outside the forest. And then they beheld a castle on level ground in the middle of a meadow; and round the castle flowed a great river, and inside were spacious halls with windows large and fair. They drew near the castle, and they perceived the castle turning with greater speed than the fastest wind had ever known. And above on the castle they saw archers shooting so vigorously that no armour would protect against one of the discharges they made. Besides this were men blowing horns so vigorously that one might think one felt the ground tremble. At the gates were lions in iron chains, howling so violently that one might fancy the forest and castle uprooted by them."

Then he says: "This revolving castle is unhesitatingly the Castle of the Grail; we find this mysterious stronghold mentioned also in one of the poems of Taliesin:

'Perfect is my chair in Caer Sidi;
Plague and age hurt him not who is in it;
They know, Manawydan and Pryderi,
Three organs round a fire sing before it,
And about its points are ocean's streams,
And the abundant well above it,
Sweeter than white wine the drink in it.'"

But these two are not the same. What is described as the "revolving castle" is an allegory of the experience of the elemental or imaginative world where it imposes a test on the soul's steadfastness; and a similar experience is described in Wolfram von Eschenbach's *Parsifal*, where Gawain makes his entrance into *Chatel Merveil*, the Castle of Wonders, and

lies upon the " couch marvellous " with its ruby
wheels, and is whirled about the hall whose floor is
like slippery glass; is deafened with sounds, dazzled
with colours, shot at by arrows, and attacked by a
lion. It represents the bewildering visions of the first
stage of clairvoyance. The test is whether the soul
can find poise and self-possession in the midst of
visions.

But the verse, beginning " Perfect " (or tuneful) " is
my chair in Caer Sidi ", is the opposite pole to the
former experience. It represents *attainment*; and is,
actually, a cosmological *and* physiological allegory.
The " abundant well " is the source of inspiration, and
the seeker finds it in his *own head*, when he has gained a
certain control over the movements of the cerebro-
spinal fluid and the circulation of the blood. From the
other standpoint the seeker has risen in his consciousness " behind the stars ", and hears their music.
Pryderi is the same as Parsifal, whose name is also
Perce-val—the light that pierces the valley of the
shadow of death.

3

The life and works of Taliesin, the great Bard, are
shrouded in mystery, and any study of them which
seeks to penetrate behind the strictly historical and
critical researches of the last century is fraught with
difficulty. A later Bard, Cyndellw, of the twelfth
century, says of him: " From the mouth of Taliesin is
the Bardic Mystery, concealed from the Bards." This
may mean either that Taliesin gave out the greater
Mysteries, that were unknown to later Bards; or that
he gave them out in a secret and concealed form.
It is interesting to contrast two opinions of Taliesin's
works, that which is given by Edward Davies (1809) in

his *Mythology and Rites of the Druids*, and that which is given by D. W. Nash in his *Taliesin*. They represent two opposite views.

Davies approaches his subject with imagination and sympathy, searching for the true background for his work in an ancient Mystery wisdom. Nash writes in a mood of cold intellectual analysis, and often holds Davies' views up to scathing scorn, together with those of other writers who show a similar tendency. He gives translations of an immense number of poems attributed to Taliesin or his imitators and successors from the sixth century up to the thirteenth, and interlards his commentary with emphatic denials that there could be anything of wisdom behind the fantastic imagery of the poems.

The nineteenth century (Nash wrote about the middle of it) was a century of militant materialism, and its supporters scrutinised everything " ancient " from the standpoint that the " scientific outlook " had once for all lifted human knowledge to a safe and lofty pinnacle built of proven facts. Nothing else had any importance save as material for enquiry, all of which must reveal the superiority of modern intelligence. Few troubled to seek for the foundation upon which the poetic imagery of the distant past had been based. Nash concludes his learned book with the words: " The Welsh poems, such as we find them in the Myvyrian Collection, we have shown to be replete with references to the extant tales, and to others of a similar nature not now known to exist; but of any other mysteries than such as can be explained by reference to the current religious philosophy of the age, or to these romantic tales, not a particle of evidence can be discovered."

I have alluded to this method of criticism which ruled in the middle of the nineteenth century, because everything that is stated in these present pages is the direct opposite. The reader is free to choose between them.

And now we can make some slight acquaintance with a small portion of the " mystery " that surrounds Taliesin by considering a series of poems known as *Hanes Taliesin* the History of Taliesin. Nash gives them in full; and a good summary of them is given in Lady Charlotte Guest's edition of the *Mabinogion*. In the light of historical criticism it is not certain that all these poems are actually composed by this Bard of the sixth century A.D. But the whole traditional story of Taliesin and the sequence of the poems is highly remarkable, and I have ventured to suggest that it presents a kind of clue to a very great deal that may some day come fully to light concerning the meaning of the imagery employed when a more *spiritual* study of Celtic tradition shall be undertaken.

The story of Taliesin's extraordinary birth is probably well known to all who have turned their attention to Welsh traditions. He says of himself that he comes from the " country of the summer stars ", and the legends of him tell that while still an infant he sang and spoke as a Bard.

The Taliesin of history is a son of Saint Henwyg the Bard, and has royal blood in his veins. But mythically, he bears to begin with the name of Gwyon Bach, and he is appointed by the Goddess Ceridwen to stir her magical Cauldron. She is brewing the Cauldron in order that her ugly son Avagdhu may drink the prescribed three drops of its precious fluid and so become inspired. But by chance the three drops fall upon Gwyon's hand, and he sucks them off for their

heat scalds him; then he immediately foresaw everything that was to come, and knew that he must flee
from Ceridwen, for she would be angry, and work
against him with her cunning.

And so he fled to his " own country ". But Ceridwen
pursued him. However, Gwyon had now received
magical powers, and so he changed himself into a hare;
but Ceridwen transformed herself into a hound and
ran after him. Then he fled into a river and became a
fish. But Ceridwen changed herself into an otter and
chased him under the water. So then Gwyon became
a bird of the air, and Ceridwen a hawk, and she gave
him no rest in the sky. And flying down, and nearly
exhausted, he saw a heap of grain in a barn and
changed himself into one of the grains. Then Ceridwen became a hen and swallowed him. She bore
him within her for nine months and then gave birth to
him. He was so beautiful that she had not the heart to
kill him, so she put him in a leather bag and cast him
into the sea. . . .

The rest of the legend, too long to give fully here,
tells how he was found by Elphin the son of Gwyddno
" in the leathern bag upon the pole of the weir "
where Elphin had gone to look for fish. Elphin took
care of him, but later was thrown into prison by his
powerful and wealthy uncle Maelgwyn, and Taliesin,
by his genius of song, obtained Elphin's deliverance
and prophesied the downfall of Maelgwyn.

The whole legend, from beginning to end, is an
allegorical description of an initiation, and the
ascending stages of the power of vision.

The first stage, described in the song that the infant
Taliesin sings to Elphin when he finds him in the water,
is that Taliesin has the vision of his prenatal existence
in the " elemental " world, where he shares in the

divine activities of the World-Soul Ceridwen, the
" dark giantess " who is the Goddess of Nature. She
impels him to flee into his " own country " the Earth.

Then, as it were, she tells him in pictures how he has
passed through all the four elements during the
creation of his body *before he was born*. But he sees them
in reverse order: as the hare, he was connected with
the earth element; as the fish, with the element of
water; as the bird, with the air; and as the grain of
wheat, with the fire. So he is " swallowed up " in the
whole of Nature. Then he is in the womb; and his
whole embryonic life is clothed with the elements.

To have the vision of one's pre-natal life and birth
was regarded as one of the necessities of Bardism, and
was called having the " memory of Annwn ".

Elphin, who first receives Taliesin (or " Gwyon " as
he then was) from the ocean—the physical maternal
womb—and brings him to Earth, *is Taliesin's own
earthly personality*; that Elphin is human is indicated in
the fact that he is the son of Gwyddno whose *horses*
(intelligence) are poisoned by the earthly residues of
the Cauldron. That stamps his descent as human.
Elphin is a son of humanity. But *in* him, in Elphin,
lives *Taliesin* the immortal spirit, who has imbibed the
three drops of the " Trinity's words "; and in this way
he describes the mystery of his pre-natal existence:

" I was first modelled in the form " (spiritual
archetype) " of a pure man in the hall of Ceridwen.
. . . Though small within my chest and modest in my
deportment, I was great." (Consciousness in the
spiritual world is expanded to the whole circum-
ference of the universe.) " A sanctuary carried me
above the surface of the Earth. Whilst I was
enclosed within its ribs the sweet Awen " (the

Cauldron of Ceridwen) " rendered me complete, and my law " (destiny) " was imparted to me without audible language by the old Giantness darkly smiling in her wrath."

Elphin is not able to continue being the protector of Taliesin, for he is entangled in his worldly destiny. He is imprisoned by the royal state of earthly existence, and for a time is separated from his Higher Self, Taliesin. This " separation " occurs in various forms in many legends, as, for instance, in the finding of some miraculous object or animal, which is then lost for a time.

The legend tells how Maelwgyn throws Elphin into prison, but Taliesin, his initiated Self, comes to deliver him. Maelgwyn does not believe that any Bard could rival those of his court, but Taliesin sings to Elphin's wife (his soul) and tells her how he means to put the other Bards to shame and so obtain Elphin's release. When he comes into the hall all the other *twenty-four* Bards are silenced by the might of his genius. And then Taliesin's inspiration is fully awakened and he sings of his own spiritual origin. This is a further stage of the initiation. The poem is too long to quote in full; the following are some of the verses according to Nash's translation:

> . . . " My accustomed country
> Is the land of the Cherubim.

> Johannes the Diviner
> I was called by Merddin,
> At length every King
> Will call me Taliesin.

.   .   .   .   .

I was with my Lord
In the highest sphere
When Lucifer fell
Into the depths of Hell.

I carried the banner
Before Alexander;
I know the names of the stars
From the North to the South.

     .   .   .   .

I was in Canaan
When Absalom was slain;
I was in the Hall of Don
Before Gwydion was born.*

I was on the horse's crupper
Of Eli and Enoch;
I was on the high Cross
Of the merciful Son of God.

I was the chief overseer
At the building of the tower of Nimrod;
I have been three times resident
In the castle of Arianrhod.†

I was in the Ark
With Noah and Alpha;
I saw the destruction
Of Sodom and Gomorra.

     .   .   .   .

I was with my King
In the manger of the ass;
I supported Moses
Through the waters of Jordan.

I was in the firmament
With Mary Magdalene;
I obtained my inspiration
From the Cauldron of Ceridwen.

     .   .   .   .

* Gwydion is Mercury or Hermes.
† Or *Iris*. The rainbow-hued aura of the Earth.

I have been instructed
In the whole system of the universe;
I shall be till the day of judgment
On the face of the Earth.

I have been in an uneasy chair
Above Caer Sidin,
And the whirling round without motion
Between three elements."

One of the greatest sources of misunderstanding has been in connection with the idea of the " transmigration of the soul " from one form into another.   In another poem, not included in this particular series, the *Battle of the Trees*, we read:

" I have been a drop in the air.
I have been a shining star.
I have been a word in a book.
I have been a book originally.
I have been a light in a lantern . . .
A year and a half . . .

I have been a sword in the hand.
I have been a shield in the fight.
I have been the string of a harp,
Enchanted for a year
In the foam of water.
I have been a poker in the fire.
I have been a tree in a covert.
There is nothing in which I have not been."

One will find this " universalness " of the soul's experience described in two ways: either the individual describes himself as being a definite *thing*—many different things—or else he states how he has shared in, or been present at, the experiences of countless other human—or divine—beings, throughout history. The former is an experience which may be described roughly as the " expansion of the consciousness " into every phenomenon of Nature, every object

of man's creation.   The human soul feels itself as
though broken and scattered and everywhere existent.
This was one of the vivid experiences in the Hibernian
(and many other) Mysteries.   We can compare the
speech of Johannes in the modern Rosicrucian drama
The Portal of Initiation, by Rudolf Steiner:

>   ... " I change
> Each hour of day, and am transformed by night.
> The Earth I follow on its cosmic course:
> I seem to rumble in the thunder's peal,
> And flash along the lightning's fierce-looking tongue—
> I AM!—Alas, already do I feel
> Mine own existence snatched away from me." ...
>
>   (*Translation*)

The other experience (described above in the long
poem) is a higher form of intuition; it is the capacity to
enter into the " universal memory " of the Earth
where the effects of all operations of the human Will
are inscribed.   The Eastern term for this universal
memory is the *Akasha*, in which the Seer is said to be
able to " read ".   Interwoven in this " reading " are
also memories of the individual's own earlier incarnations.   Both of these two kinds of experience, variously
attributed in a loose way to the so-called " doctrine of
metempsychosis ", have left their traces all over the
literature of antiquity.   In studying the history of
mythology and legends generally, it is extremely
important to remember that in ancient times there was
a great " elasticity " in the consciousness of man, and
he could transpose himself with ease into the " consciousness "—if the word can be used—of everything
around him; and with extraordinary intensity during
the stages of initiation.   It needs much study to be able
to distinguish, even a little, between these ecstatic
conditions and the real *doctrine* of reincarnation.

But to go on with the story.

Maelgwyn continues to question Taliesin when he has finished the poem quoted above, and he replies first of all with songs that refer to Elphin who is " secured with thirteen locks and a golden fetter ", from which Taliesin will deliver him;[22] and he speaks of *retrieving the loss* he has suffered in losing Elphin. This makes it clear that Elphin is his *earthly* self; for this self must first be lost, and then redeemed, on the path of initiation. Moreover, Taliesin regards Elphin with veneration, even calls him his " lord " and his " sovereign "; and it is remarkable that while Taliesin means " the radiant brow " or " radiant front ", another title of Elphin (*Rhuvawn Bevyr*) means " he who radiantly shines forth ". So they have the same name.

The whole sequence of the events of the story represent the true order of initiation experiences: first there has been the passage through the elemental world and the memory of pre-natal existence; then the loss of the earthly personality (or lower self) who is in prison and, in a sense, suffers because of his humanity; and then, when face to face with the loss (which is a loss on both sides) the whole reality of the *spiritual* nature of the human being is recognised and the path of evolution is seen " from the beginning ". And then something of the *law of destiny* reveals itself. For there follows next a poem which is formed somewhat on the lines of the old poetic riddles, where something is described without being actually named. In this case the poem seems to be describing the power of the wind. But this wind is to come in a manner unknown and terrible—" thou canst not tell whence it cometh nor whither it goeth "—and it is to overwhelm

Maelgwyn.   Throughout the poem Taliesin is pro-
nouncing the judgment of fate upon Maelgwyn, the
inexorable onward rush of his destiny.

> " Discover thou what is
> The strong creature from before the flood,
> Without flesh, without bone,
> Without vein, without blood,
> Without head, without feet,
> It will neither be older nor younger
> Than at the beginning . . .
>
> It is in the field, it is in the wood,
> Without hand, and without foot,
> Without signs of old age,
> Though it be co-eval
> With the five ages or periods
> And older still,
> Though they be numberless years.
> It is also so wide
> As the surface of the Earth;
> And it was not born,
> Nor was it seen.
> It will cause consternation
> Wherever God willeth. . . .
> One Being has prepared it
> Out of all creatures,
> By a tremendous blast
> To wreak vengeance
> On Maelgwyn Gwynedd."

Vividly Taliesin pictures the paradoxes that work
themselves out in destiny even as they live in the
invisible winds of Heaven.   And the strong blast is to
sweep upon Maelgwyn. . . .

Who then *is* Maelgwyn? He is yet another " self "
of Elphin's, for he is all that represents his *lowest*,
sensuous, nature; and Taliesin, dwelling in Elphin as
his Higher Self, knows that the lowest part of his
nature, Maelgwyn, must suffer and be overcome if
Elphin (the human personality) is to be free to be the

worthy vessel for himself, for Taliesin, who has the
" radiant brow ". *Then Elphin will become the one who
" radiantly shines forth " in the full possession of his higher
Self.*

So in these poems it is shown how knowledge of
destiny, and of the evolution of the world, is born out
of self-knowledge, and freedom is attained. The
Trinity—that rock of Bardism—rules in the whole
picture: Taliesin, Elphin, and Maelgwyn, as *three
aspects of the same being.*

Elphin is the human being in his absolute humanity
—he is like *all* human beings. In discovering his own
higher Self he really discovers his own " radiant
brow ". But this is only the beginning of his path of
knowledge. He finds he is early led captive by the
powers of the physical world. What can deliver him?
Nothing save the power of his higher Self, Taliesin,
who has been in Caer Sidi. So he is set free. And all that
belongs to his lower nature, Maelgwyn, is destroyed.

In the case of an individual so developed as Elphin-
Taliesin it often happens that what is on the one hand
taking place in the life of the soul, is also present in
historical external events. It is as though the force of
such development must run side by side with—or, if
one can say so—be taken hold of, by the outer events.
This is the secret of many legends. It explains why
facts known to history are sometimes included in the
most fabulous tales which are really allegories of the
spiritual life. Maelgwyn, the *historical* personage, died
later of the plague which, sweeping like a hurricane
over the country, caused dreadful destruction between
the years 552 to 557.

After the song of the wind, Taliesin invokes the
Supreme Being, and that is when Elphin's fetters fall
from him. Then follow poems which are a challenge

to the other now silent Bards. The legend continues by relating how a horse-race is run—Elphin riding against the *twenty-four* horses of Maelgwyn, and by Taliesin's magic assistance, he wins the race. On the spot where he drops his cap, a cauldron full of gold is found.

According to the summary of the legend and its poems as given in the *Mabinogion*, Taliesin then sings the poem which has been called " One of the four pillars of Song ". It is a history of the creation. The most noteworthy verses are the two where he mentions Christ:

> " The wheat rich in grain
> And red flowing wine
> Christ's pure Body make,
> Son of Alpha.
>
> The wafer is flesh,
> The wine is spilt blood,
> The Trinity's words
> Sanctify them."

Earlier verses had described the original cultivation of the earth. And in these two verses there is a beautiful recognition that the substances of the earth make the Body of Christ.

Whether we accept, or not, all these poems as having been written by the historical Bard Taliesin himself, is not important.   What *is* important is the whole artistic structure of the legend, and we should notice how it combines the old forms of inspired clairvoyance with the recognition of Christ in the Earth—the Earth transformed by Christ, the final culmination of what had been foreseen in the Mysteries.

Taliesin—whether we regard him as an individual or as the noble representative of a great School of the

Mysteries that was fading into oblivion—climbs to his height as one of the last of those to show how the Christ-vision might be attained *through the old clair-voyance*. That Sun had to decrease. That way of knowledge had to disappear. It sank into darkness.

That Elphin seems to represent more than the mere earthly personality whose initiation-name is Taliesin, and that he is all humanity, waiting for liberation, is beautifully suggested in these lines from the " Royal Cadeir " (Myvyrian Collection):

> " At the end of our toil
> Languages shall pass away.
> The ardent soul
> Shall be voyaging through the clouds
> With the children of the Seraphim,
> Gliding on shall be thy people
> To the liberation of Elphin."

CHAPTER VI

THE CAULDRON OF CERIDWEN

" Come with me into the City, thou shalt have mead which I
have prepared—O thou with pure gold upon thy clasp."

CERIDWEN, the great Goddess of Celtic mythology, has already been mentioned in the story
of the miraculous birth of Taliesin, that took place
after the draught of three " precious drops " from the
seething Cauldron.

" It will not boil the food of a coward
  Who is not bound by his sacred oath.
  Against him will be lifted the bright gleaming sword
  And in the hand of the sword-bearer he shall be left;
  And before the portals of Hell the horns of light will be
    burning."

That such words were spoken of the quest of the
mysterious Cauldron shows very clearly that it was not
mere fairy-tale, but had to do with the trials of the soul
that were undergone by those seeking the first stages of
initiation.

Steiner describes this initiation as follows:

" All that lies hidden behind the material world as
the sun behind the clouds, the hidden Spirit, was
known in these Mysteries by the name of *Hu*.
Ceridwen was the seeking soul. And all the rites of
initiation were a means of revealing to the pupil that
death is only one of the many processes in life.
Death changes nothing at all in the innermost core

136

of man's being. In the Druidic Mysteries (*Druid* means an initiate of the third degree) the neophyte was put into a condition resembling death, so that his senses could not function as organs of perception. A man whose only instrument of perception is the physical body or the physical brain has *no* consciousness if he is in a condition when his senses cease to function. But in initiation, the senses—feeling, hearing, and so on—cease to function, yet the neophyte is able to experience and observe.

" The principle that observes was called *Ceridwen* —the soul. And that which came to meet the soul (as light and sound come to meet our outer eyes and ears) was called *Hu,* the spiritual world. The initiate experienced the union between Hu and Ceridwen . . . When we are told to-day that the ancients paid homage to a God Hu and a Goddess Ceridwen this is simply another way of describing initiation. And with this the true myths are always concerned."[23]

It comes naturally enough into the mind to suppose that the *Cauldron* of Ceridwen is a kind of " pagan " Holy Grail. But to describe all the correspondences and differences would fill a volume.

The " Wisdom of the Grail " was, in ancient times, the wisdom of the stars conceived as the whole " secret doctrine " of the spiritual world and spiritual man. Later, it was the wisdom concerning a particular Star, singled out among all the hosts of heaven—the Jewel, as a legend has it, that was struck from the crown of Lucifer—and became the Vessel that was to contain the Blood of Christ. This Vessel is a Human Being, the Star that shone over Bethlehem, *Jesus of Nazareth,* into whom the Christ-Spirit descended.

In the age of which we are writing, the wisdom of the " Cauldron " was, also, a Star-Wisdom, as can be seen when we read how the Goddess Ceridwen gathered all the herbs and other ingredients for the Cauldron according to astronomical laws. The whole of Nature, and that includes the whole nature of the human being, is seething in the Cauldron of Ceridwen. And the whole of Nature—the Earth itself—was in the future to become the Holy Grail in another sense; for the Earth received, as though it were itself a Chalice, the Blood of Christ that fell from the Cross on Golgotha. Then the wisdom contained in Nature was transformed into Love that, in Christ, permeated the whole world, and even descended into Hell.

The legend of the Quest for the Holy Grail became known exoterically in the twelfth century A.D., in Europe; but it was known in esoteric schools long before, and indeed emanated from them as a " picture " of the quest of the soul for Christ in the Earth.

In Wolfram von Eschenbach's *Parsifal* we read about a certain man called Kiot, a Master of astronomy, who found in Spain a book written in Arabic characters by *Flegetanis*, " the first who wrote on the Grail ". But Flegetanis was a heathen; he was said to be of the lineage of Solomon, and to have worshipped God in the image of a calf.[24]

The name Flegetanis is Persian, and means " one who knows the stars ". Dr. W. J. Stein points out that the mention of Flegetanis' descent from Solomon (in the *Parsifal* poem) is an expression signifying that he was *one who had visions*, that is, that he did not know astronomy as a science, but knew it through his natural inherited powers of seership. A distinction was made in olden times between those who were of the " lineage of Solomon " and those who were of the "lineage of Jonah". The latter achieved their knowledge by inner spiritual training.[25]

So we find in quite another direction than that of the Celtic mythology an indication that the secrets of the "Grail" were known to a heathen who had worshipped God under the symbol of the "Bull" (Taurus), and who was a seer.

The Cauldron of Celtic mythology was the object of a quest, conducted first through the elemental world, or "Underworld"—that is, what is concealed behind the physically-perceived world of Nature—in order to gain initiation into higher Mysteries. The soul had to know not only creative, but *destructive* processes; and Ceridwen is often called the Goddess of Death.

At the time of which we are speaking the Christ had been revealed to the Initiates in the Hibernian Mysteries, but He had not yet descended into His bodily "vessel", Jesus of Nazareth. He was still, so to say, above the Earth; His presence was felt in the *world of the elements*. In still older times, His presence was perceived in the planetary spheres; and before that, in the Sun. Thus the ancient sages sought to find Him Who is the Logos; and in the Celtic mythology they represented the realm and the Being of the Logos to themselves as the God *Hu*. Hu was also called Hesus, which is the same name as Jesus, and means a "healer".

Most wonderfully is this Quest described for us in the imaginative pictures of the Goddess Ceridwen, the great Demeter of the Celts, who weaves the garment of the Sun-Spirit out of the elements of Nature.

Ceridwen is the soul that is initiated and able to perceive this spiritual life. In order to make the soul capable of perceiving it, trials and tests must be undergone and "adventures" must be undertaken.

In many legends—and not only in Celtic ones—we find that the heroes go on these adventures sometimes in a *glass ship*: " the multitude could not see the hero's progress after he had entered his glass vessel ". Arthur had a boat of glass. Taliesin says that Alexander the Great went on voyages in a boat of glass. Condla the Red of Ireland was spirited away to fairy-land in a glass ship. The boat of Osiris in Amenti was made of glass. Even our own Cinderella found her Prince because she could wear the glass slipper.

The mysterious *Mwys*,* the dish or vessel belonging to Gwyddno which, " though all the world should approach it, thrice nine men at a time, they would find in it the food each liked best "—this too is another " Grail ", which was said to have been spirited away by Merlin when he disappeared into his Glass House in Bardsey.†

Glastonbury is often supposed to be so named because it was the Isle of Glass, *Ynesuuitrin*, the *Insula Vitria*—where there was no thunder or lightning, nor tempest, nor serpent, nor excessive heat or cold. This is the " blessedness " of the state of consciousness that has passed through the tumult of the " Chatel Merveil " and attained the Quest of the Grail.

Glass—or a kind of glass—is supposed to be the material out of which the so-called " serpent's egg ", the well-known talisman of the Druids, was made. Whatever it was, it was said by Pliny to be able to float in water and resist the flowing stream, like a boat that is propelled. St. Columba had such a talisman, a white stone that could " swim ". These objects were

* One of the " thirteen treasures of Britain".
† J. Rhys: *The Arthurian Legend*.

called " the splendid product of the adder, shot forth by serpents ", which could " cast its rays to a distance ".

There were certainly various objects of a glassy nature in existence in Wales called Gleiniau Nadredd, or Glains, which as talismans had the same virtue as the " serpent's egg ". When a stranger sought entrance to the ceremonies of the worship of the Moon (Ceridwen Mysteries), Taliesin tells us he had to exhibit his " boat of glass " as a sort of guarantee of good faith.

All these references have to do with a spiritual-alchemical secret, as can be seen from the following.

In Wolfram's *Parsifal*, Trevrezant tells Parsifal about the Grail—that it is in the Castle on Montsalvatsch, and that all the knights live there by virtue of a certain Stone. Its name is *Lapis exillis*, and it is created in the fire. Basil Valentine* says of this Stone: " When ashes and sand have been timely heated in the fire, the Master makes therefrom a Glass, which henceforth is always able to resist the fiery heat. In colour it resembles a transparent Stone and is no longer recognisable as ashes. For the unknowing this is a great and secret Art; but not so for those who know, for its their craft, attained through knowledge and experience. . . . At the end, the world will be judged by Fire and return again to ashes; out of these ashes the Phœnix can at least gather his young ones (or disciples). For the true Tartarus is concealed in the ashes and must be set free, and after its dissolution the Strong Door of the royal Chamber can be opened."

So we see here too that the glass object, the transparent Stone of the Wise, is needed if spiritual know-

* *Twelve Keys.* In the collected alchemical writings.

ledge is to be fruitful; and the attainment of it means first the purification of the soul in the Fire of self-sacrifice and devotion, even unto death.

Ceridwen was a hard task-mistress. She is sometimes represented as the genius of a sacred ship of death. Arthur himself is said to have " died " in " contending with the Fury (Ceridwen) in the Hall of Glaston-bury ", the " Island of Glass ".

In the poem, *The Spoils of Annwn*, already discussed, there is the passage that alludes to the " island with the strong door where the twilight and pitchy blackness were mingled together "—the same strong door that Basil Valentine tells of. And further on there is the " enclosure of glass " beyond which no one beheld the prowess of Arthur.

The " transparency " of the soul when it is embraced in a higher, non-physical consciousness, and so is " out of the body ", becomes one with the transparency of the world of Life—the etheric world. No *mortal* eye can behold it.

It may be that the familiar proverb which says that " those who live in glass houses cannot throw stones " has an ancient origin and meaning: that in the higher consciousness no *physical* matter can be perceived or handled, neither can the profane disturb its serenity. We might guess this to be the explanation, too, of the fairy-tales' magical cloak of invisibility. The "mantle" of King Arthur, " King in the Light ", was, like the fabulous Myws, one of the thirteen treasures of Britain, and is another mode of higher cognition.

All these are immortal symbols. There is a poem ascribed to Gwyddnaw—though having a more ancient foundation—which tells of a dialogue between a disciple and his Hierophant, and the Hierophant says: " To the brave, to the magnanimous, to the amiable, to the generous, who boldly embarks, the *ascending Stone of the Bards will prove the harbour of Life*! It has asserted the praise of Heilyn the mysterious impeller of the sky; and *till the doom shall its symbol be continued.*"

So the way of the soul is through the fire and the darkness and the strong door, into—or through the power of—the transparent enclosure, the deep mystery of purified wisdom that " casts its rays afar ", yet is concealed from the unawakened. It is called the " egg of the serpent " because the whole wisdom of the third epoch, up to the time of Joshua's leadership of the Israelites was, all over the known world, called the " Serpent Wisdom "—the wisdom of Lucifer, the Light-Bearer. It is the *reflected* Sun-wisdom, a moon-light of knowledge, which could only be revealed in its fullness and its direct and penetrating rays, by Christ, Who did not " destroy the law " but fulfilled it. And He alludes to the devotees of this ancient wisdom as the " generation of vipers " . . . .

The " boat of glass " (the same material as the " egg of the serpent ") was therefore essential if any hero was to discover the Cauldron of Ceridwen and drink its three drops—the three degrees of initiation—and become like Taliesin of the Radiant Brow, " thrice-born ".

The mystical death that was necessary in the old initiations—and it was a condition of deep trance lasting three days—together with the whole intense experience of the destructive powers interwoven with the processes of life both in Nature and in man was never completely spiritually vanquished in the partaking of the *pagan* Grail. But all this was transformed in the Mysteries of the Christian Grail. In the latter, the Grail *Itself*, Jesus of Nazareth the bearer of the

Christ-Spirit, passed through Death and changed it into Life, wholly and fully, for all mankind.

The experience of the Quest in the case of the secret Brotherhoods of the Middle Ages, for instance, was a different one from that of earlier or pagan times. The " transparent Stone " was then a symbol for the *human skeleton*; this is a vessel that contains living blood in the marrow; and the purification of the soul (and thereby of the passionate blood) through selfless devotion, revealed to the aspirant for spiritual knowledge, in a vision, how his *skeleton* which is the densest and stubbornest of matter, became transparent and sparkling—like glass—through the force of the chastity of his Christ-redeemed blood. He saw his skeleton crowned with Roses. This was *foretold* by Job: " Yet in my flesh shall I see God." And it was expressed in the Middle Ages by the verse:

> " Schau den Knochenmann
> Und du schaust den Tod.
> Schau das Innere der Knochen
> Und du schaust den Erwecker."*

Throughout the ages the symbols vary, but the Truth is the same.

Arthur's sword, Excalibur, is the power bestowed by the " white stone " in which, as a legend tells us, the sword was embedded and from which he had to draw it forth. Its name (Excalibur) means that it is made or created out of the *darkness*. And a legend tells how in order to reach it he had to cross a narrow bridge of iron and steel—i.e. to pass over and beyond the blood and nerves of his inner experience to the very citadel of his being.

---

* See the skeleton
And thou seest Death.
See the interior of the skeleton
And thou seest the Awakener.

The " bright-flashing sword " of the *Spoils of Annwn* which bars the way of the aspirant if he is cowardly, is the *same* power as that of Arthur's Excalibur, but it turns *against* the owner if he is unworthy; it is in the hand of the " Guardian of the Threshold "—like the flaming sword of the Cherubim when Adam and Eve were driven from Paradise.

The ceremonies of the Mysteries of Ceridwen very likely included an actual vessel or chalice from which the aspirant had to drink. If so, this must only be regarded as a symbolic act, confirming what had been and were to be the experiences of an enhanced consciousness.

Ceridwen's Cauldron was " warmed by the breath of nine maidens "; which reminds us of the nine Muses of Apollo; and the liquor in it was the medium of inspiration, science, and immortality. What was left over of this liquor was deemed poisonous and accursed. For it is always the case that knowledge is like a two-edged sword; it can be the source either of white or black magic.

That the contents of the Cauldron are said to seethe and boil is an image of how the seer perceives the weaving and seething of the supersensible elements of life of which the whole world of Nature is composed.

It is of course quite possible to conclude that the tradition of a " boiling vessel " (a tradition not by any means confined to our own country) is an image of the purification of the human race through the Deluge, and the destruction of the unrepentant in the poisonous overflow of the World-Cauldron. But if in the whole system of ancient wisdom it is recognised that initiation for leaders of the people was a universal custom, and that it was secret and veiled in imagery from the general mass of the population—if this be taken into account, then interpretation becomes a matter of esoteric understanding, and not mere analysis and comparison.

The neophyte, in his first meeting with Ceridwen, discovers her in the character of a hag or a fury, or as a wrathful giantess. This is an absolutely true image of the experience of anyone who first looks into his own soul, or discovers behind the beauty of Nature her destructive powers. The beginning of initiation must always be a descent into the depths—into Annwn— the kingdom of Hades.

Every day the Goddess Ceridwen was supposed to gather various charm-bearing herbs for her Cauldron, the " sweet Awen ", choosing her time according to the planetary positions. Taliesin gives a long list of these plants and other ingredients, but it is not clear from the poem (*Cadeir Taliesin*) whether all of these were brewed in the " stream of Gwion " as the liquor was sometimes called. There are red berries, cresses, wort, and vervain; and a plant called selago which is supposed to be the hedge hyssop. But in Nash's translation the latter is not mentioned, but only the " tree of pure gold ". The tree of pure gold is the " golden bough " of Virgil's *Æneid*—the mistletoe. Selago is, however, mentioned by Pliny, and the passage is quoted in the *Antiquities of Cornwall*, telling how the selago is a most precious ritual herb which must not be touched by the hand, nor cut with iron, and must be gathered by a Druid whose garment is white and whose feet are washed in pure water.

The gathering of mistletoe was also a sacred ceremony; it must be detached from its tree with a golden hook and on no account be allowed to fall to the ground. Its character as a plant of the *air* (hence sometimes called the " lofty tree " or the " ætherial tree ") was not to be violated by any contact with the earth.

The Druid initiates were perfectly aware of the connections between the various plants and the planets—an ancient lore which has since been lost but is to-day being once more revived. The plants too would each have an affinity with one or other of the " elements ".[26]

The preparation of the Cauldron, as I have already suggested, was no doubt an actual ritual in the Ceridwen Mysteries; but the ritual is never more than a symbol of higher realities; and the aspirant for initiation had to experience the " seething elements " as the world of *life*, the etheric world, and to discover its relation to his own life-forces interwoven with all the fluid processes in their circulating movements within his own body. He perceived in himself life intermingled with death.

This " entering into the water " is similar to what is described in Indian mysticism as the " drinking of the Soma ". Such experiences help to lead the memory back to the time of birth—whether of the individual, or of the Earth itself when it rose from the Waters. And so we have the story of the miraculous birth of Taliesin who, as " little Gwion ", sucked the scalding drops of the brew from his fingers. From that moment of vision of the past begins the ascent to the higher spiritual knowledge and revelation of the future.

Animal symbolism occurs in connection with Ceridwen as well as plant symbolism; and perhaps the most important of the former is the symbol of the horse. This is probably a much later development than the original Ceridwen myth. But it is a subject that covers so wide a field that it is only possible here to refer to it briefly.

The first use of horses as carriers of the soldier-guards, knights, or paladins of a ruler, was in the time of Akhenaten, Pharaoh of Egypt. This fact is really an indication, strange as it may appear, that the *conscious-ness* of the more advanced humanity was changing. The horse was the universal image in the mind of man of cleverness, intelligence, as against the old and fading inspired seership, or inherited clair-voyance. The symbol of the horse appearing in legend and myth denotes the approach of the " Twi-light of the Gods ". In the " Götterdämmerung ", when the last of the Norns breaks the rope of destiny, they cry:

> " Zu Ende ewiges Wissen!
> Der Welt melden Weise nichts mehr! "[27]

Then the heavenly twilight recedes; day—an earthly day—dawns; Siegfried and Brunnhilde appear, the former fully armed, and Brunnhilde leading her horse. Siegfried, as *man*, without the old godlike clarity of wisdom but supported by human *intelligence*, is to plunge into the maelstrom of destiny.

Or, in Plutarch's *Isis and Osiris* we see how this change is suggested in the story of Osiris and Horus. Horus is seeking to avenge the murder of his father Osiris; and Osiris, appearing to him from out of the Underworld, asks him what animal he thinks would help him best in his struggle against Set. And Horus replies: " The lion is useful for him who is in need of help; but the horse is useful for pursuing and scattering the flying foe so that the battle may be ended utterly." Osiris was satisfied, for now he regarded Horus as fully equipped for the task.

And now we can come back to Ceridwen. She was described by Taliesin when he was seeking to escape from her wrath, as appearing as a *hen*, yet she caught him in her fangs. Then she appeared as " large as a proud mare, which she also resembled; then she was swelling out like a ship upon the waters." . . .

The accompanying sketch from an engraving in Borlase's *Antiquities of Cornwall*, is one of various British coins or medals of Ceridwen or Druidic talismans, of about the first century A.D. The figure represents a mare with a bird's head and beak, a body shaped somewhat like a boat, and surrounded by many circles and crescents —possibly " glains " —seeds or stars; and a form under the belly of the mare resembling a cloud.

A COIN OF CERIDWEN

From Borlase's *Antiquities of Cornwall.*
(Enlarged.)

Below is a horizontal line and objects that look like Druid stones.

There is a variety of such horse-coins. Another drawing shows a wheel under the animal's belly, which is supposed to be the sign of the " Goddess of the Silver Wheel "—Iris—(or Arianrod) of whom more later. The horses of more ancient mythology were *heavenly* " astronomical " beings.[28] The later ones are quite earthly; while the symbolic horses of the transitional time seem to have been a mixture of the two. For the Intelligence was descending to the Earth, and the old star-wisdom vanishing away.

The fifth century A.D. saw the first seeds sown in Britain of the Anglo-Saxon race, when Britain was invaded by *a mare and a horse*, the brothers Hengist and Horsa. This was the time when the Druid Mysteries were in decay. It was a physical occurrence that pointed to the final overthrow of all that had been so jealously guarded from the past. This was already threatened at the time of the first Roman invasion. And we see Ceridwen—not as a very earthly horse!— but armoured with the sharp attacking bird's beak, and having her body like an " ark " or womb of the concealed Spirit. The new age is already heralded, but unformed and chaotic, like the drawing.

There are many references in Welsh mythology to Arianrod, *Iris*, the Goddess of the Silver Wheel. She is generally supposed to have been the Goddess of the rainbow; but not the rainbow that we are accustomed to see. In the poem called the Chair (or doctrine) of Ceridwen, this Goddess tells us how there was a great conflict between Gwydion (Hermes) and the Birds of Wrath; and that for the protection of the world, Iris, the Goddess of the Silver Wheel, " speedily throws round the hall the stream of the rainbow, which scares away violence from the Earth, and causes the bane of its former state, round the circle of the world, to subside ". And we are told that Iris is actually created by Hermes out of flowers; she is intended to be the consort of the Sun.

This is a great cosmic secret that Ceridwen announces ! We find the same secret told to the neophytes in the Egyptian Mysteries.

After years of preliminary training they experienced a kind of clairvoyant dream; and the ecstatic state in

which they found themselves when they had this
dream-like vision, was brought about partly by their
training in the Hermetic Mystery-school, and partly
by ritualistic devices. They looked back into the
past evolution of the world and saw the separation
of the Moon from the composite body of the Earth-
planet; and with it the departure of Osiris, who,
though a Sun-divinity, chose to work creatively upon
the Earth from the separated Moon. Then the
divine beneficence of Osiris caused the Earth to
appear as though clothed in a wonderful rainbow-
coloured *aura*, and this was called Iris—the consort
of Os—Iris the Greater Aura.

This teaching—that the aura of the " renovated "
Earth, now freed from the density of the lunar forces—
was the source whence came the vivid imaginations
and visions of the young initiated soul, and that these
visions could save him from the dark " birds " of
the merely physical senses—was an essential element
of instruction in the Ceridwen Mysteries. Iris, or
Arianrod, was always there as a refuge, or (as she is
called), as the " dawn of serenity ", for the neophyte.

One would naturally imagine this rainbow aura as
a circle bent round the Earth, and so, pictured from
the merely *human* standpoint—as from " below "—
it would appear to imaginative vision concave, like
an inverted bowl; but seen with the opened eyes of
initiation, from *outside*—or " above "—it would appear
like a Chalice, supported in the heavens and embraced
by angelic Forms, and containing the rejuvenated
Earth. It would seem like a celestial Grail or
Cauldron of living essences nourishing the Earth with
colour.

And so we can imagine, that when Ceridwen made
herself known in her *true* form, all terror and fury of

darkness overcome, her Cauldron of Nature would be the Iris itself, radiant, glowing, living, creating— the Girdle of Hu the Mighty.

In concluding this very brief account of the Goddess Ceridwen it is necessary to draw attention to her " family ".

She had two sons and one daughter. One of the sons was called Morvan, the Son of Serenity; the daughter was Creivyw, " lovely damsel ", the Persephone of Celtic mythology. And the other son was the hideous Avagddu—*darkness*. His ultimate redemption from ugliness and stupidity was awaited when the Cauldron should have boiled for " a year and a day ".

So the World-Soul Ceridwen appears in *humanity* (her children) in a triple form of soul: there is the true son of serenity who is above temptation and grief; there is the lovely damsel who—as Persephone was also—is the power of " clear-seeing " perception or vision; and there is the son of darkness, that in each one of us waits for redemption.

The esoteric teaching of the Mysteries, as we can still find it to-day though in another form, points to Avagddu as a great secret of human existence, the " Double ". This is a problem of immense significance, not only in its original connection with the Mysteries of the West, but in our own time. And we shall try in a later chapter to lift a corner of the veil in which this " son of darkness " is shrouded.

CHAPTER VII

HU THE MIGHTY

" The smallest, if compared with small,
    Is the Mighty Hu, in the world's judgment,
    And he is the greatest, and Lord over us,
    And our God of Mystery:
    Light is his course and swift:
    A particle of lucid sunshine is his car:
    He is great on land and seas,
    The greatest whom I shall behold—
    Greater than worlds—Let us beware
    Of mean indignity, to him who deals in bounty."
                    (Poem by Rhys Brydydd:
                                15th century A.D.)

THE God Hu was the all-ruling Divinity of
Western Celtic mythology. He represented the
power and glory of the spiritual world, and in that
sense, the spiritual, not the physical Sun. He was
wedded to the Goddess Ceridwen; and Ceridwen was
the Soul of the World, bestowing the power of vision
upon the human soul.

The Mysteries of Ceridwen led the aspiring soul
first through the realms of darkness which are inseparable from the ascent into higher states of consciousness. The soul, in attaining Self-knowledge, must
be aquainted with the Depths into which existence in
the physical world, through the " fall into sin ",
has conducted it.

The Mysteries of Hu revealed the other pole of
human life: the ascent out of the body into the

153

" glorified " state of expansion of the consciousness in the spiritual world.

Ceridwen, the " darkly smiling Giantess ", was the fruitful Mother of the world, bringing all things and all men to *birth*. Hu, wearing the golden yoke of the Sun and the girdle of the Iris of the world, accompanied the human being when he was united with the " power of vision ", out of the Depths, into the light. He pointed the way to the Light where he revealed himself fully.

It is difficult to avoid an element of confusion in studying the meaning of this mythology: Hu appears as a God; but he also appears in legend and tradition as a human being. How can we reconcile these two things?

In ancient times, as has been described, all culture epochs, the lesser and the greater, were created and fostered by initiated leaders of humanity. They were " leaders " in quite a real sense very often—wandering with the people who were under their care, as Moses did, teaching them, bringing to them whatever of *new* knowledge, suited to the age, they received in inspiration in the Mysteries from their angelic " Fathers ", with whom they had intercourse in the Mystery Temples.

If we say that the people merely " deified " their leaders after their death we are guilty of introducing an element of superstition into the consciousness of the people, which, three or four thousand years ago, was not there. To-day, Death hides from us those who pass away from life. Formerly, they were visible to men in certain states of consciousness; and in the case of a great initiate, visible in a truly glorified form; not as " vision " only, but the vision was accompanied by a direct consciousness of co-operation between the living and the dead.

Great leaders became in this way the continuous representatives of the age-long Mystery cults they may have founded; even in some cases their name passed from leader to leader who was able to reach the highest degree of initiation in such a cult. This is one of the reasons why so much confusion enters into any attempt to disentangle history from legend in connection with—for instance—" King Arthur ".[29]

Hu, in his human aspect, is said to have led the Cymry into Wales; to have introduced the use of the plough (connecting him with the first Zoroastrian Mysteries of Persia); to have brought to the people mead and wine, and *music*. In his name *Hu*, the primal vowel sound indicates darkness—the Earth-depths; and in this Dionysian character he is the bringer of the purple vine. But another form of his name is Hesus, or Jesus, and means a " healer ".

The fact that he is connected with the bringing of music is most important in relation to his name and his general attributes in the Celtic myths. It emphasises what has already been mentioned, that music is *Light*; that it comes down into the ancient dream-life of clairvoyance as a healing power, educating humanity towards the future attainment of individual reasoning intelligence. So Light and Darkness are woven into the being of Hu.

And all this strengthens the connection between the Orpheus Mysteries of Greece and the Mysteries of the Bards; and it strengthens too the mystical conception of the " eternal Feminine." . . . The sun-rays of the Virgin Wisdom may be imagined shining in the golden hair of an Isolde, of an Œnone, or a Eurydice, threaded as strings of light and love into the harps of the Bards. Orpheus brought his message of healing to the dark Dionysian Mysteries of Greece; Hu brings the same

message to the Saturnian depths of the Mysteries of
Hibernia. Orpheus is called the " Fisher "; so too is
Raphael the Archangel who shows Tobit how the fish
will heal the blindness of his father; and Hu draws the
Avanc out of the depths of the lake for the healing of
the land . . . .

They are not separated—they are united—Hu and
Orpheus; in the eternal Spirit of the World.

In the *Triads of Theology* as given in *Barddas*[30] there
is a conversation between a Master and his Disciple.
The Disciple asks, "Why is IAU (Hu) given as the
name of God?" . . . Here is it pointed out in a footnote
that Iau means a " yoke "—" the badge of power on
the part of him who imposed it; and indicates preservation, creation, and destruction." Then the Master
tells the pupil that " God is the measuring rod of all
truth, all justice, and all goodness; therefore He is a
yoke (Iau) on all, and all are under it, and woe to
him who shall violate it . . . Hu the Mighty—*Jesus the
Son of God*—the least in respect of his worldly greatness
whilst in the flesh, and the greatest in heaven of all
visible majesties."

Taliesin describes the God Hu as " God of War, the
ethereal one, with rainbow girdle. Hu with the
expanded wings; Father and King of the Bards,
Sovereign of Heaven ". Or he is described as a Bull,
with other Bulls in attendance; or as a mighty Dragon.
He lived in the " stall of the Ox ", and was " subjected
to the sacred Yoke ". In his human aspect he is
described in the *Triads* as " one of the three benefactors
of the race of Cymry "; one of the " three primary
Sages "; one of the " three great Regulators of the
Island of Britain ". Taliesin says that he came from
the land of Gwydion, that is, the land of Mercury,
or Hermes, having therefore the wisdom of Egypt.

It was said at the beginning of this chapter that Hu represented the " spiritual world " in this mythology.

That Hu was called " Jesus the Son of God " in the conversation just quoted, is an identification, by the Christian Bardic teacher, of the spiritual being of Hu with the whole of his initiation-inheritance, in which he is one with the *Jesus* (not the Christ) of the Mysteries: one with the Healer: one with all Initiates who, by virtue of their supreme initiation, are " Sons of God ".

We may compare the God Hu and the Goddess Ceridwen with the two statues of the Hibernian Mysteries, but the content of those Mysteries is now given in the form of the myth of Hu and Ceridwen, and the myth is the image placed before the uninitiated of the inner experiences of souls who could perceive spiritual realities. The philosopher Sallust says: " If truth is given in a mystical veil, it is assured against contempt and serves as a stimulus to philosophic thinking."

" The images forming the contents of a myth", says Steiner,* " are not invented symbols of abstract truths, but actual soul-experiences of the initiate. He experiences the images with his spiritual organs of perception, just as the normal man experiences the images of physical things with his eyes and ears. But as an image is nothing in itself if it is not aroused in perceiving an outer object, so the *mythical* image is nothing unless it is excited by real facts of the spiritual world."

This statement provides the only real clue to the method of interpretation of myths: they are *visions*; but visions are nothing more—to begin with—than intimations of inexpressible things, impressed by the spirit upon the soul, who perceives them in artistic

* *Christianity as Mystical Fact.*

imaginations. Mystical, and that is spiritual, experiences, arouse in us every shade of feeling, and if these are intense enough spontaneous images flow into us that are not symbols or allegories, for these latter are creations of the *mind*. The soul is a spiritual part of us, but it is not the spirit. Nevertheless, being immersed in the bodily nature and in the physical world, it sees the spiritual world, at first, " painted " in forms and colours and movement, which in reality conceal and do not reveal the divine events. Visions are a " secret writing " that can only be read when the source of them is understood.

> " One who lives merely in the images lives in a dream. Only one who has got to the point of feeling the spiritual element in the image as he feels in the sense-world a rose through the image of a rose, really lives in spiritual perception. . . . On account of their illustrative character, the same myths may express several spiritual facts. It is not therefore a contradiction when interpreters of myths sometimes connect a myth with one spiritual fact and sometimes with another."*

The popular worship of Hu and Ceridwen degenerated, like everything else, into mere outer observances and customs—(the Scottish feast of *Hogmanay* is a relic of the Hu Mysteries)—and lived on in fairy-tales and legends whose true meanings were at last altogether lost, except for those few—and they became ever smaller in number—who had the duty of preserving as much as could be preserved of the esoteric wisdom, in secret. Up to the sixteenth century A.D. a kind of worship of " Hu Gadarn " still persisted here and there but was finally suppressed.

* *Christianity as Mystical Fact.* Rudolf Steiner.

The famous legend of Hu and the Avanc has been the subject of a great deal of enquiry and investigation and may be told in a very few words. The substance of various versions is that Hu the Mighty harnessed his splendid Bulls, attached their harness to the Avanc and drew it out of a lake, so that " its waters might burst forth no more ".

Nobody knows what an " Avanc " is. Usually it is said to be a beaver; but if it was it must have been a gigantic one! . . . Some adopt the Arkite theory of Welsh mythology and say that the Avanc was a shrine, or the ark, and that Hu was Noah. It is suggested that the ark is a " beaver " because the beaver builds himself a house of two storeys, one in, and one out of the water, and so can live either on land or not, as the inhabitants of the ark are said to have done when the flood subsided. These interpretations belong rather to the " symbolic " category; they do not take into consideration the *drama* of the events, but are caught up in the interest of the " picture ". The drama is in the appearance of the majestic sun-radiant Hero, the powerful forces that obeyed his will, the mystery of the depths that could be overcome by these forces, and so on. Such dramatic elements belong equally rightly to cosmological *and* human mysteries.

One who was an initiate and leader of men like the earthly Hu could only have attained his degree of enlightenment by first gaining the power of mastering those forces of matter (the Avanc) which deaden the spiritual senses and make the soul blind instead of " seeing ".

The oldest form of spiritual clairvoyance had come over from that period of the Earth's history when its matter was strongly permeated by lunar forces, and these tended to create gigantic physical forms; while human souls, seeking to escape from becoming entangled in their densifying influence, were caught up in a dream-world of visionary wisdom.

On the other hand, their wisdom could be abandoned to these chaotic influences in the practice of evil magic. One can well imagine how the attraction felt for the " monstrous " might present itself in just such an image as that of the Avanc, which could

A RIVER BULL-GOD.
From a Greek Vase. (Louvre.)

only be overcome by a struggle to attain a clearer and more " sunlike " intelligence. And the whole series of geological catastrophes—the deluges, the subsidence of Atlantis, the rebirth of the world out of the depths—all this would lead to a lightening of the lunar burden, and to a clearer consciousness, as though the Sun had drawn nearer with a heavenly beneficence.

And, in a spiritual sense, that was true.

One could say that the legend of Hu and the Avanc illustrates the above, and marks a step in the evolution of Hu as representative deity of the Hibernian-Druid Mysteries.[31]

The worship of Hu shows us something like a combination of the cult of Dionysos (Bacchus) and Orpheus; but of a Dionysos who is primarily the source of Life—spiritual Life—from the Sun; he is, like the Greek Dionysos, divided in his nature in that the other " half " of Life, that of the Depths, has its source in Ceridwen—in the Earth. In Ceridwen is the " milk and honey ".

In the *Bacchæ* of Euripides this double nature of Dionysos is expressed:

>   . . . " If any lips
> Sought whiter draughts, with dripping finger-tips
> They pressed the sod, and gushing from the ground
> Came springs of milk. And reed-wands ivy-crowned
> Ran with sweet honey."

And Hu, as the bringer of music in the Celtic mythology, is associated, not with the flute, but with the harp or lyre, the instrument of Orpheus. It is as though the " intimate and bitter hostility of things akin ", as in the Bacchus and Orphic Mysteries of · Greece, fount their harmony in the Celtic Hu.

> " Orpheus never plays the flute ' that rouses to madness ' . . . he plays always on the quiet lyre, and he is never disturbed or distracted by his own music. He is the very mirror of that ' orderliness and grave earnestness ' which Plutarch took to be the note of Apollo. . . . His music is all of the North."*

This " orderliness " is characteristic of the Celtic Bards who were initiates of Hu; they have a sweetness as well as a gravity; a peaceableness, though they sang

* *Prolegomena to the Study of Greek Religion.* Jane Harrison.

of war; a boundless love, though it seldom seems to have been the subject of their poetry; for the impulse of love lay in the music itself.

In his Orpheus-nature, Hu descends from the Sun to the Depths to conquer the Avanc:

> " And the trees awoke and knew him,
> And the wild things gathered to him
> As he sang among the broken
> Glens his music manifold."

And in his *true* Dionysos-nature he is the one who slakes all thirst and revives the memory of the Beginnings, the " memory of Annwn ". So we may quote for him the Orphic Tablet (*Petelia*):

> " Thou shalt find on the left of the House of Hades a Well-
>   spring,
> And by the side thereof standing a white cypress.
> To this Well-spring approach not near.
> But thou shalt find another by the Lake of Memory,
> Cold water flowing forth, and there are Guardians before it.
> Say: ' I am a child of Earth and of Starry Heaven;
> But my race is of Heaven (alone). This ye know yourselves.
> And lo, I am parched with thirst and I perish. Give me
>   quickly
> The cold water flowing forth from the Lake of Memory.'
> And of themselves they will give thee to drink from the holy
>   Well-spring,
> And thereafter among the other Heroes thou shalt have
>   lordship."

There is another and much later version of the story of the Avanc, this time in connection with the Arthurian legends; and the hero of this story is not Hu but Peredur. Peredur is the same as Parsifal or Percival. The dramatic incidents are set forth in great detail in the narrative of *Peredur the Son of Evrawc*, in the *Mabinogion*.

The Avanc, or Addanc, as it is called in this version, does not live in a lake but in a cave, and certainly is not a " beaver "; but is apparently a monstrosity in human form, and slays all who approach him by throwing a spear at them. In this way he has killed every day three knights, whose bodies are afterwards strapped to their saddles and their horses bear them to the " Court of the Countess of Achievements ". There damsels anoint the corpses so that they come to life again, and return on the following day to the Addanc for their daily death.

But Peredur succeeds in killing the Addanc because a most fair and lovely lady gives him a *stone of invisibility*, so that the Addanc cannot see him. The whole story is very long, and the general trend of its drama is similar to that of other legends, notably that of Owein.[32] The Peredur story is quite obviously an imagination drawn from the early adventures of a soul on the quest for the Holy Grail. (A most skilful and masterly analysis of the Parsifal (Peredur) legend from this point of view is given in Dr. W. J. Stein's book, *World History in the Light of the Holy Grail*, based on Wolfram von Eschenbach's poem.)

The terseness of the Hu legend compared with Peredur's encounter with the Addanc rather suggests that the former is the original substance of a cosmological myth, which, in course of time, becomes one of the experiences of all Grail initiates, namely, when the cosmological secrets have to be rediscovered by clairvoyant *memory*; and then all the visions of the soul on this path of enlightenment are recounted (and embellished) in romantic form as in the story of Peredur.

Peredur—but not Hu—has to make himself invisible for the great encounter, which takes place in the

" land of marvels ", namely, in the stage of imaginative vision; (and this corresponds to the Chatel Merveil of other legends). The reference to invisibility is a manner of suggesting that the greatest and most implacable of the soul's adversaries (the state of *dullness* or ignorance which may be of monstrous proportions) can only be met in a condition of consciousness that is raised above the physical consciousness of ordinary life. In such a consciousness the soul is in concealed and inward activity and so " invisible "; and the power for this can only be given by the " fairest damsel "; this is always the higher soul, the " Ceridwen ", who is the power of vision that rises to inspiration, and so sees beyond the mere Imaginations.

The three brothers who are killed daily are the three capacities of the human soul that work as thinking, feeling, and willing; for these, except in the case of enlightened or initiated persons, are " killed " by every night's sleep, when the dark dream-images represented by the Avanc, finally obliterate all consciousness. Then the damsels—like the aerial spirits in Goethe's *Faust**—call the soul-capacities, the three brothers, to life again at daybreak: when

> " Phœbus' wheels roll forth in thunder
> What a tumult brings the light! "

In *Faust* the healing powers of the night and the dawn are described. But first:

> . . . " Ye round this head in airy wheel that hover,
> In noble elfin-guise yourselves discover.
> Soothe ye the bosom's unrelenting strife.
> Withdraw the bitter darts of self-upbraiding,
> Purge ye his soul from horror of past life.

* *Faust*, Part II, Act I.

Four watches night hath—ere her fading
Pause not—let each with kindly deeds be rife.
Bathe him in dew from Lethe's waters drawn.
Soon will the cramp-racked limbs be lithe as willow,
If new-refreshed he sleep to meet the dawn.
Fulfil the fairest elfin-rite,
Give him again to the holy light."

And so on; until the morning:

" Now the hours are spent and over,
Weal and woe are swept away.
Dream of health! Thou wilt recover! " . . .

The Addanc therefore represents unconsciousness—
darkness—the *forgetting* of spiritual realities in which the
uninitiated soul really lives every night during sleep.
The Sun-Hero Hu needed no stone or armour of
invisibility to conquer the Avanc, because he was
" master of the stars ", i.e. fully conscious of the
stages not only of falling asleep but also of waking,
which are so delicately suggested in Goethe's four
groups of aerial spirits that herald the tumult of the
rising sun. And Hu could bring music to the consciousness of waking man and teach it to him, because he
himself could hear in sleep the harmonies of the
spheres, and his passage from waking to sleeping and
sleeping to waking was unbroken by any obliteration
of consciousness. This was always the summit of
initiation experience.

Those who could be " awake in sleep " recognised
that their spiritual consciousness travelled outwards—
from the ordinary waking state—through three planetary regions or spheres, those of Mars, Jupiter, and
Saturn; and that on returning again to the ordinary
waking state they were aware that they were passing
spiritually through the polar opposites of these
spheres: Venus (Mars), Mercury (Jupiter) and Moon

(Saturn). It is interesting to find that the Druids spoke of three Bulls and three Cows as " consorts of the Sun "; and, since the mysteries of conscious sleep were an essential part of the Druid wisdom, we may, I think, assume that they were " imagining " the three planetary companions of the Sun-like soul of the initiated sleeper: three Bulls to lead it heavenwards, three Cows to bring it back to earthly waking life.

The secret underlying all the ancient Mysteries in some form or other—but especially and clearly in the Hibernian Mysteries and in the essential characteristics of Hu and Ceridwen—was this passing out and in of the soul and spirit of the human being, not only in sleeping and waking, but also in the greater rhythm of dying and being born. It was the secret of *Incarnation* and *Resurrection*. And for this reason, the greatest Incarnation the world has ever known, that of Christ Himself—the Sun-Logos—which, though clearly foreseen, was still wrapped in the obscurity of the future, was not an incredible or incomprehensible event in the wisdom of Hibernia, and its offshoots.

The legend of Hu and the Avanc is so mysterious, and at the same time so simple in its storied form, that it is impossible to approach it without a certain feeling of awe. We feel that, though it seems to emerge as a legend comparatively late, it is nevertheless " unborn ", because interwoven—and universal—in all that is most ancient in spiritual knowledge.

Ceridwen, on the other hand, stands out more clearly in the silver-toned pictures of mythology, in all the dramatic happenings of the life of souls seeking for enlightenment, as they wander through Nature's enchanted and shimmering forests to that trysting-place where Hu would at last meet them and lead them to the Heights.

CHAPTER VIII

DRUID SCIENCE

". . . For whether they looked upward they saw the Divine Vision,
Or whether they looked downward still they saw the Divine Vision
Surrounding them on all sides beyond sin and death and hell."
(BLAKE.)

NEARLY all that has been written about the Druids is based on what has come to us through Greek and Roman historians, and on various collections of Bardic documents and poems; and we glean a little here and there from fairy-tales and old customs, but see in these no more than the relics of an ancient superstition. The difficulties attendant upon all archæological research are increased in the case of the Druids because there is so little in the way of material evidence of their cultural life. Moreover most of the documentary evidence was produced during a time when the great Druid-Hibernian wisdom was in its decadence, when its glory was past and its vision clouded; when the Islands were distraught by invasions and strife and violence and the sanctuaries were profaned. Only the Bards—and of these but a few—could pass on, in song and rune, some of the wisdom of the past, and conceal it in allegory and image. But there still remain the solitary stone pillars, stone circles, stone altars, holed stones—all of immense antiquity and to be found all over the world. But their use, and what they meant to the mind of man, is

what baffles us, particularly as the relics of the knowledge we possess of different ancient peoples, point
to a variety of uses and meanings. What did they
stand for in the cult of the ancient Druids?

We shall never begin to *feel*—if we cannot know by
so-called historical evidence—what they meant so long
as we believe that the ancient people's intelligence was,
though crude and undeveloped, similar to our own.
The habit of our time, ingrained into us during at
least a century or two of materialistic thought, is to
base all our reasoning on the principles of physical
science; and in historical research we carry our own
modern mentality back with us in our adventures into
the past; we picture to ourselves " primitive man "
and our guesses at the external forms of his civilisations,
aided by the discoveries of archæologists, are accurate
enough; but we cannot easily change *ourselves* so as
to enter into his consciousness and place our changed
selves into his environment and so judge of it from that
standpoint.

So what are we to do? Is it possible to " unravel ",
so to say, the web of our own modern constitution of
soul, stepping first out of our sheath of self-conscious
egohood, then out of our sheath of intellectual " brain-
thinking ", then out of our inborn sympathies and
antipathies, right into a condition of fresh, untarnished,
natural insight? Nature would appear wonderful to
us if we could do this! If we had no modern science and
no logic and no arrogance of opinion, and no astonishment at death, and no other conscience than the potent
visible effects of our deeds; if sleep were an awakening,
and if personal memory came to us only in the repetitions and solemn sentences of the writing of the stars,
and if " history " was a reading in the blood of our
ancestors pulsing in our veins; yes, and if our head

felt like a model of the whole earth carried on our shoulders in the rhythmic balance of our movements; and if our heart was an image of the Sun and our lungs the wings of the Moon protecting it . . . the whole Universe would be a mighty gesture of the Spirit— we should move in dreams and visions of the Gods, and the Earth would be our writing tablet upon which to inscribe, in stone and wood, our immortal deeds.

Then, if we pledged ourselves, not to the service of the " Lords of the Dark Face " who would lead us into a worship of the powerful Nature-forces of destruction and mal-creation, but to those leaders of the Temple Mysteries who represented the true path of human evolution—we should learn, little by little, to draw these inchoate dreams more and more into our own personal sphere of experience—we should begin to separate ourselves a little more from the flowing universal life in which we were immersed, and order would begin to prevail in the " veil of chaos " in which we had been enwrapped. We should find, to begin with, how all knowledge and search for knowledge fell into its two categories—knowledge of the outer world, and knowledge of the self, the inner world.

Our self would no longer be mingled in Nature's Imaginations; but, standing a little apart from them, yet still with the open eyes of visionary insight, we should begin to penetrate, one by one, the secrets of our existence; and the knowledge of the substances and creatures of the Earth would come to us, *through the Sun risen in our heart's thinking*. And looking on the other hand into ourselves—now separated a little from the bewildering bestowals of Nature—we should say to ourselves: " Revere the blood of thy ancestors. Prepare thyself for the search of thy fathers; shall they not teach thee and tell thee, and utter words out of their heart?"

In these two phases of human consciousness, that of the at-one-ness with Nature, and that of the partial separation from her, we surmise (but this is here only broadly indicated) the possibility of two kinds of human memory in ancient times.

In the first phase, outer Nature would have to supply us with the power of remembering—we should have to put, so to say, a book-marker in the page. And these book-markers were *stones*. Countless memorials, countless book-markers, were placed by man wherever he wished to impress upon his soul some memorable event. For he could not then find it within; but only in the moving, shimmering, shining, spirit-peopled landscape; and the landscape would itself paint for him again the pictures of the event whenever he returned to the stone he had placed there. And others would see it too, with their clairvoyant eyes, for it would be mirrored in the atmosphere.

To-day in country places abroad how often we find little shrines of stone or wood set up, with the crudely painted picture of some catastrophe or some blessed happening! And we have too our more stately monuments. But in the ancient civilisations of the world there was no need to paint the picture or make a written record, it was written or painted in the æther, and clairvoyant sight beheld it. . . . " Let us build here an altar to the Lord "—that was a later development of the ancient stones of memory.

The Atlantean inhabitants who first set foot upon the Western coasts of Britain surely set up such stones as these. Some of their initiated leaders served the Oracle of Saturn, or " Cronos ", if we interpret our material aright. I think we could assume that they knew a great deal about the laws of Time, of cycles and epochs, and their correspondence with the different organs and processes of the body in the order of their evolution within the evolution of the world. But the vision of the future, in the sense of the continuation of the life-forces of the Earth and humanity, was dim; they recognised a still unknown future as *hidden in the past*. And for this reason the Saturn-oracles became, in a spiritual sense, involved in a process of dying.

Legends sometimes suggest this; as, for instance, that the solitary stones of memory were once living people who became petrified. The Druidic *circles*, coming later, represented more a culmination of the Mysteries of the revolutions or rotations of Time-cycles, because the Druids served the Sun, and their initiates studied the Sun as the great Life-bearer, irradiating the future and permeating all knowledge with inner light. They were most interested in the relation—a threefold one—between Sun, Earth, and Moon.

There is something in all these ancient stones that seems to make them eternal, defying Time and defying the destruction that man brings to nearly everything he touches. Their " pictures " still hover round them; we cannot see them, but we feel their presence; and through this preserving power that is inherent in them and communicated to their surroundings, we may some day awake to their original message.

To this aspect of primeval memory we must add that other aspect which was connected with the blood, and with a communal or group instinct for the veneration of particular individuals. This memory was nurtured by speech, the record of events was in this way " handed on ", and so became a more inner and individual faculty, but sustained by the whole tribe or family, and was, naturally, deeply imbued with

feeling. The " vendetta " or " avenging by blood "
is the last remnant of this tribal or ancestral way of
feeling the Ego through memory.

It was only the initiated who could develop an independent sense of their Ego, and so, being less
dependent both upon Nature and hereditary instinct,
could attain the spiritual isolation necessary for being
teachers or Kings of men. Stones could be for them,
not " idols ", not even symbols, but awakeners of their
humanity, as well as stimulators of their clairvoyance.

There is a great difference between the old sanctuaries of the Mysteries that were built either underground or enclosed and shut off from the heavens, and
those, like the Druid circles and alignments, that were
open to the sky. The difference, to put it in a few
words, was that the former preserved all those Mysteries which taught the relation of Man to the Divine;
and the latter, the relation of the Divine to Man.

The very form of the Egyptian Pyramids, for example, as Temples of initiation, suggests esoterically, the
idea of humanity, as a physical, psychic, and spiritual
Being, its apex, or " origin ", in the heavens, spreading
downwards from the world of Spirit to cover the
Earth. But the *interior* of the great Pyramid was a
" house of death ", where the spiritual re-birth of
initiation could take place, and whence man could
go out from the physical body in the death-trance of
initiation and return, in a higher consciousness, to
the place of his origin—that is, to a vision of the
spiritual world.

The word " pyramid " itself is derived from
Egyptian words meaning (in their full interpretation)
" a going out of the Temple of the body to Heaven "—
or " a going out by day ". This can be understood in
two ways; what the *initiated* man experienced in

going out of the body " by day "—that is, while still living—was the same in essence as what the dead experienced, who " went out " not *by* day, but *from* the day (or " by night "); namely, from life to death.[33]

So in the greatest stone monument of the whole world we have a picture, seen from the external aspect of its form, of the Cosmic Man descending from heaven; and from its internal aspect, as a Temple of initiation and House of Death—it tells us of man, as a human being on the Earth, placed during the initiatory rites into the darkness and narrow enclosure of a tomb, dying to the earthly consciousness, and becoming once more, through this mystical death, fully conscious of his spiritual origin. To be " initiated " means, in more senses than one, to " know the beginnings ".

I have mentioned this because, for many people, the Druid stones are in some way suggestive of death. And some of them were burial places as well as Mystery sanctuaries. But it is very difficult for us to-day to realise that in pre-Christian times a " death " was possible during life. Such mystic deaths could not be experienced except within an enclosure. The spirit of man, in its own world, is " as great as the Universe "; in incarnation it is shrunken, and dies to its true nature by its imprisonment in the body; and *from* the body—its temple or enclosure—it can be set free, either in initiation through the three days' death-like trance of ancient times, when it wandered to begin with among the dead and knew the *spiritual Earth*; or completely, then as well as now, in the actual dying of the physical body.

The Egyptian *Book of the Dead* sets all this forth in detail.

" Seeing the Sun at midnight," a well-known phrase connected with all initiations, implies that the initiate had the power to perceive, not the physical Sun, but the active radiance of the solar forces (the deeds of exalted spiritual entities) which work upon all forms of life, even in the depths of the night. They are the vital solar essence out of which human beings receive their self-consciousness, the knowledge that they have an Ego, because this Ego is in contact, through the physical matter of the body, with Life itself; and so the initiate was led by this vision to the knowledge of the laws of Life belonging to the other kingdoms of Nature also, the plants and animals; in other words, it was the spiritual source of science.

To be able to be aware of life in this way was something quite apart from the usual three-dimensional experience of the world. It was entirely an *intuitive* experience. Darkness, or " midnight ", implies the cessation of the ordinary activity of the waking senses. In Druidical times an artificially produced darkness, or shadow, could bring about, if the right mood of soul—an *initiated* mood of soul— were present, a vision of the natural processes and spiritual processes dependent upon the " concealed " rays of the spiritual Sun. The only author, so far as I am aware, who has indicated that there is a connection between the midnight Sun of the Mysteries and the Druid stones, was Rudolf Steiner.* He asserts that the significance of the trilithons, for example, lay in the shadows that they cast, as will be presently described.

Imagine a dark mirror, and in this dark mirror reflected the *qualities* of living Nature. This would not be describable in ordinary language, but the initiated Priest, looking into the shadows of the stones, would have a direct inner perception of them. Inspiration

---

* *The Evolution of the World and Humanity.* Anthroposophical Publishing Company.

would complete the experience—an understanding of
the intuitive perceptions. And then again, it would be
necessary to " translate " the inspirations into ordered
ideas, thoughts, and deeds. The first thing was the
intuitive clairvoyant perception of " something "
in the space where the physical light of the Sun was
excluded.

A great difference between the earlier Mysteries and
the later was that in later times people had no longer
the same capacity for receiving spiritual intuitions
directly into their consciousness, but required the
assistance of something external; in the case of the
Druids, the shadows cast by the stones.

Under certain conditions and at certain seasons they
" consulted " the shadows cast by the horizontal stone
of the trilithons, which was penetrable by the spiritual
(not the physical) rays of the sun, which passed through
the stone into the Earth. It is not possible to give a
scientific term for these rays. What they saw in them,
clairvoyantly, was the same as what was experienced
by the soul in sleep more or less unconsciously, or
during the mystical death of initiation: knowledge
of the spiritual laws of the Earth.

When the stones were arranged in circles their
shadows showed them the same rays but modified by
the interplaying influences of the zodiacal constellations.[34] The astronomical knowledge possessed by
the Druids, learnt by means of this kind of clairvoyance, was taught from century to century. The
setting up of the stones is now seen to have been
faultlessly accurate.

It is quite possible, even for quite matter-of-fact
people to-day, to see a certain lively and mobile
" dark radiance " in the space between their own
bodies and their shadows when standing, say at noon,

with their backs to the Sun. But no matter-of-fact person to-day would be able to learn anything from that! Goethe, however, knew something of the secrets of shadow, and wrote of them in his *Farbenlehre*,† and gives a hint of this in the second part of *Faust*, when Faust is awakened from his sleep at dawn by the elemental spirits. He cannot bear the full radiance of the direct sunlight:

" Then bursts from yonder depths whose days ne'er dwindle
  Excess of flame—we stand as smit with thunder . . ."

And he cries:

" Nay, then, the Sun shall bide behind my shoulders! "

So he turns his back to the Sun and sees the rainbow gleaming in the foaming cataract, and finds in it the image of human effort and the reflection of Life itself:

" Think, and more clearly wilt thou grasp it, seeing
  Life in the many-hued reflected splendour." *

There was more, however, to be seen in the shadows than what could be instructive about the laws of Nature. The Druids could perceive other radiations that travelled upwards, as though coming through from the other side of the Earth. These were connected with the reflected Moon-rays. Under certain conditions these could be instructive with regard to moral and immoral influences, and what was learnt through these means could be applied by the Druids in the ordering of the social life of the people.

All this seems at first sight somewhat fantastic. But not if we are able to free ourselves from our present-day habits of thought and honestly make the attempt to

* *Faust*, Part II, Act I.
† Goethe's Theory of Colour.

recognise the vast difference between our modern consciousness and faculties and the consciousness and faculties of three or four thousand years ago. After all, all our archæological research proves this difference; only, our habit is to look for the similarities.

The two aspects of initiation knowledge previously mentioned, namely, the science of the outer world on the one hand and the moral perceptions of the inner world of soul and body on the other hand, were combined in Druidism through the Druid initiation and the Bardic initiation.

The former was more especially concerned with Nature; the latter more especially with the human being, in his life of soul. The flowing together of these two paths of knowledge was, one might say, a natural outcome of the junction of the two great streams of wisdom represented by the " Fathers " on the one hand and the Celtic Druids on the other; and which had their original united source, prepared beforehand, in the Mysteries of Hibernia.

All consciousness arises in man through the opposition of integrative and disintegrative processes in the interplay between nervous energy and metabolism. St. Paul knew this: " In life we are in the midst of death." This is a physical as well as a moral truth. The Bards were acquainted more with the element of death; the Druids more with the element of life. The Bards, in " dying " to the physical world by overcoming the lower ego-hood,* reached the wisdom bestowed—as has been described—by the " Virgin of Light " which they brought down into their earthly consciousness as music and as knowledge of the laws of speech: they attained to the recognition of a pure Ego-hood in man that is able to grant full value

* Similar to the Orphic initiation of ancient Greece.

to all other Egos—understanding the *Word* as it passes from one to another. They knew the Courage out of which Love is born; so they knew the influences bestowed by Mars, the representative of Power and aggression, and their transformation into the gentleness of Love,* the Mercury-Messenger between Heaven and Earth. The Druids, in discovering Life, learnt how no life is possible that is not the product of dying, and no death is fruitful that is not sanctified by sacrifice: in these lie the secrets of man's toil upon the Earth, of seed-times and harvests, and of all the institutions of civil rights—of justice and mercy. So they knew the influences of the Spiritual Sun.

Is this a very idealistic representation of the Mysteries of Druidism, and not at all compatible with what historians tell us of the barbarism of the people of the ancient Druid lands? But it must be remembered that the mass of the people lived in a certain state of indifference as regards " worldly " concerns and the importance of the bodily life, because *all* were to some extent dreaming in the last phases of clairvoyant perception in the midst of a Nature both turbulent and wild or seductive and lovely, whose veil might at any moment be withdrawn to reveal a world shining with the glory of departed ancestors, and the " lordly ones of the hills ". . . .

To become an initiate in the Mysteries at that time was to become enlightened in respect of the *physical world*; and for this a higher clairvoyant perception of the *spiritual* nature of the Universe was necessary, because this gave a clearer understanding of the claims and purposes of physical life. In our own day it is exactly the opposite: initiation is to bring knowledge of the *spiritual* life.

* See chapter on the Bards.

In ancient Egypt there was a decided cleavage between the general population and the powerful groups whose task it was to cultivate the Mysteries and guide civilisation in the way that the spirit of the age demanded, and this was kept inviolably secret. Therefore there existed a distinct esoteric and exoteric knowledge, and this was the case in greater or lesser degree all over the world. To belong to the Temple groups was to be of " royal " descent —not necessarily physically but certainly in a mystical sense.

All exoteric rulers were also initiates. The priestly caste represented the " divine Fathers "[35] who appeared in the visions of the Temple cults, and they stood " behind " the Kings. Government was hierarchical in the true sense.

The Bardic cult, when at its height, corresponded, as regards the scope and direction of its initiatory revelations, to the oldest phases of the Egyptian Mysteries, but about a thousand years later than the latter. But the Druid cult (working together with the later Bardic wisdom) was, if one can put it so, more up to date and more " democratic "; that is, it had to serve a consciousness among the general mass of the people, more akin to that which the Pharaoh Akhenaten (Amenhotep IV) strove to reach when he abolished the old Amen Mysteries and inaugurated the worship of Aten, the Sun as the Giver of Life; and for this he replaced the enclosed and darkened Temples by the sun-filled courts and sanctuaries of his holy city.[36]

But now let us see what science of Nature could be obtained by the Druid Priests when they gazed into the scintillating darkness of the shadows of their stones. We will not here attempt to describe any ritual, but will simply outline the observations that were made, remembering that season and time of day have all to be taken into consideration as necessary conditions for the various observations; also that the astronomical knowledge of the Druids, carefully applied, was an accumulation from many ages of study and revelation, continually renewed and amplified.

The most important sciences were those connected with agriculture and healing; and healing was recognised as an ever-increasing necessity, in order to combat the dark powers (represented by Avagddhu in the Ceridwen myth) which were believed to be always ascending into man out of the Earth-depths. The *becoming physical* of man they saw as a great spiritual battle between the forces of light and darkness. The more intense the physical intelligence the greater became the possibilities of ill-health.

Working out of the prevalent idea of a threefold structure and life of the world, the Druids distinguished the opposition, in plant life, of the hardening and " salt " processes in the roots, as against the sublimation or burning—the " sulphur " processes—in the blossoms; and the " mercurial " element—that is, a rhythmic upbuilding of substance, the flowing of saps, in the balanced structure of stem and leaves. The whole picture of plant-growth was, to them, a copy of planetary movements and stellar " geometry "; and they felt the forces of polarity, so essential a part of any threefold order, in the opposition of Moon and Sun: the Moon, which reflects the Sunlight, brought about the *substantial* development of the plant, its material expansion, while the Sun was not only the bestower of life but also the destroyer of the substance, converting it, through the forces inherent in fertilisation, into renewed life. The Moon

worked from below through root-formation and
general substantiality; the Sun from above, by
sublimation *ending* the expansion of physical substance
and bringing about decay for the purpose of re-
construction. " Except the seed fall into the ground
and die, it abideth alone."

But every plant has its own characteristics, visible in
the nature of its surroundings and in its specialised
form and mode of growth. If we were to try and describe the Druid art of healing in general terms more
adapted to our present understanding, I think we
should have to imagine that the Druids had an insight
into the nature of the relation between man and the
plants which might be described as follows:

The root contains the greatest amount of mineral
salts, it is the hardest and most earthy part. In man,
it is his head which corresponds to the root. In the
leaves and stems there is the living flow of saps and
the assimilation of " life " not unlike man's system
of breathing and the rhythm of his circulation. In
the blossom, in scent and colour and the pollen-dust,
the saps are expending themselves and becoming
dissolved into the light and warmth of the atmosphere
—or better said, into a " cosmic " existence. And in
the human metabolism there is also a sublimation—
the continual arising and passing away into the
" fire "—of the streaming saps of life. As the plant
lifts its creative forces heavenwards in the ripening
seed, so man bestows his creative forces on the Earth.
He is a heavenly plant inverted in the Cosmos, rooted
above, and blossoming below.

Thinking of plant and man in this imaginative way
one must go further and see that this suggests that roots
would heal illnesses connected with the head, the
brain and nervous system; leaves and stems in the

rhythmic processes; blossoms and fruits in the digestive system. For in each member of the plant's organism forces lie waiting to be released, and to be used to re-establish harmony in disturbances of the corresponding processes in the human organism.

A strong moral element pervaded all ancient methods of healing because the connection between the life of the soul and that of the body was more clearly perceived than it is to-day.

The mistletoe was especially an object of veneration to the Druids because of its peculiar nature. It grows, not on the soil, but " in the air ", and lives on the life of a tree.

The form of its growth represents a force of expansion working in a wonderfully regulated manner; by the constant division of every stem into two it tends to build a sort of circular form, an image of the world of air that surrounds the Earth. It resembles the branching of the bronchial tubes. This quality endows it with a force that is opposed to everything that is of a hardening or contracting nature. It is life-giving. And it flowers, not in the spring, but in the autumn when other things are decaying. Used in a particular way its extract could heal many illnesses. Not only that, but it could have an effect on the consciousness, lifting it above the bodily senses and so facilitating— in those times—the power of clairvoyance. So it was used in connection with the rites of the Mysteries.

The " Golden Bough " which the Grecian Sybil instructed Aeneas to discover was the mistletoe. It enabled him to enter the world of the dead, by changing his consciousness, so that he could converse there with the shade of his father.

The Soma juice of the Indian Mysteries was no doubt the extract of some particular plant; but it is also an expression denoting the whole fluid element in the world, including the saps of plants and all other forms of moisture. If a man " entered into this fluid " or it " entered into him ", he could know, in the Mysteries, the secrets of Birth—not merely his own, but the birth of the world out of the watery womb of an earlier world.

The knowledge and appreciation of the value of all " moisture "—as in the saps of plants, the inner secretions of the body, etc., was always, in antiquity, associated in some form with the emblematic worship of the Bull. The Bull, in Orphic rites, was said to be " torn in pieces ", as a necessary preparation for the purification of the candidate; but this is surely a reference to the principle of moisture[37]—the Water of Life—which is distributed over the whole creation, and was a reminder of the " mystic birth " of the initiate (as well as the physical birth). Every Mystery School in ancient times knew how to use, not only plants, but minerals, in curing physical illnesses in relation to their psychic and spiritual causes.

An essential part of the oldest Druid methods of healing was the knowledge of how to change the character of the root, leaf, and blossom so that they would not work too one-sidedly. A " salt " process in the roots needed to be restrained; or a fluid process to be reduced by dessication; or a " fire " process to be increased, and so on. We would call it boiling, dissolving, extracting, drying, roasting, etc.

The Druids could see, for instance, how severe frost so enchanced the mineralising " moon " forces in the roots that, in their imaginative vision, it appeared gigantic, demonic, and threatening; or how the heat of summer released great expanding fire-elementals that could overpower all normal " earthly " tendencies

. . . and so on. The legends sometimes represent this as all kinds of meetings and conflicts with giants, or elemental spirits.

The *moral effects* of the contracting and expanding tendencies in the world in winter and summer could also be guided by the Druids in the way in which the social life of the people was regulated. All human moods and sensibilities in connection with the changing seasons were far stronger than ours are to-day. In summer the " frenzy " of expanding consciousness could be brought into line with the ordered beauty of the harmoniously sprouting green of the plants, by rhythmic dances, music, and processions; and in the winter the contracting and hardening effects of the cold could be modified by a more inner kind of activity —a kind of education was arranged. We still possess fragments of this idea in the old poetic riddles and conundrums. Or, for instance, even the freezing waters could be made a means of instruction; because —human bodies being less sensitive than ours are to-day while the fine sensibility of touch was greater— the hands and limbs could be taught to feel the plastic modifications of the water in its freezing and melting, and in this way the constructive forces working in the human body could be experienced; and strange as it may appear, it was really necessary for the people of ancient times to learn to *feel* their bodies in connection with the earth.[38]

A far-off memory of this old custom survives in the Hallow-e'en games, when melted lead is thrown into cool water, and its fanciful shapes suggest the coming year's " fate ". And there are many other such relics of ancient observances connected with the seasons, once taught by the leaders of the Druid Mysteries to show how man, *in all reality*, lives within the cosmic influences of the Universe, and can thrive best when this fact is recognised.

But now let us turn to the Druid stones again, and see in what way they can be said to be connected with death, as well as life.

The greater secrets of existence could only be experienced if the body underwent a sort of temporary " petrifaction " in the mystic death of initiation, releasing, or casting from itself like a " shadow " the spiritual light of consciousness. (The Egyptians called a certain principle of the soul, *khaibit*, or *shadow*.) But the centre of the consciousness, the " I ", has not lost, though it was no longer associated with the entranced body; and so a reading in, or interpreting of, the surrounding astral light could take place. This is the central event of all the old initiations, as is well known.

Monoliths, the single pillar-stones of antiquity, could always be a reminder for the beholder, of this inherent quality of freedom of the " light ", from (or within) the " darkness " of matter. Such a stone could be the image, through its immobility and its shadow-casting of the ethereal light, of the mystery of the human being himself—with his consciousness expanding to the stars as a " soul-shadow of light ", and the " darkness " of his material body like a stone. . . . In such a consciousness a man could be likened to a God.

It is not difficult to imagine how in some cases great stones set in the open landscape could become foci where spiritual beings could be " conversed " with. " The Kaffirs," says Wood-Martin, " a tribe of the Hindu Kush, say of the stones they worship: ' This stands for God; but we know not His shape '; and therefore they leave the rock untouched by chisel." Totemism, on the other hand, according to Sir James

Fraser, is the worship of the Higher Self of a human being, represented in the individual and varied forms of the *carved* stones.

In very remote times intercourse between the sexes was carried out in a dream-like state of consciousness, and the dream of the occurrence took the form that the human beings concerned were throwing stones behind them on to the ground.[39]   We know, too, that there are countless legends of men and women being " turned into stone " by wizards or fairies; and the " wizards " of our own minds—fear or ecstasy or passion—will do the same for us even to-day! But none of these legends could have arisen if it had not been felt, deeply and intensely, how the soul of man is an alien guest in the physical body, and could take its flight from the solid world and leave the body entranced and motionless.

The densest part of the body is the skeleton. Initiation in the higher degrees has always been able to bestow a certain power over the body, endowing it with more vitality; but it was not possible to know the whole extent of the " dying " process which is continually going on in the body, and whose ultimate climax is represented by the hard bones. But some knowledge concerning the death-in-life of the body, and so of all illness, was a necessary complement to that side of the Druid wisdom which taught about the healing properties of Nature and their application.

Druid initiation at a certain stage was veritably experienced in the " shadow of death "—in caves, in stone cells, in dark underground labyrinths. These dark enclosures represented the prison of the body where the spirit lay captive. It is recorded how different heroes had to undergo imprisonment; and Arthur is said to have been imprisoned three times.

Once in the cell of Oeth and Anoeth, whose names mean " wrath and the remission of wrath "; once in company with Wen Bendragon, the " lady of the source of generation "; and once under the " flat stone of Echemeint " which covered the " cell of Ceridwen ". These are all experiences connected with *dying*.[40] The first suggests the recognition of sin and purification—a dying of the lower self; the second suggests the becoming acquainted with the divine origin of the soul which is born out of the spiritual to " die " or forget its origin when born in the material world; and the third suggests the sacrifice of all earthly desire in returning to the womb of the World-Soul.

Here and there are traditions and proofs of the existence of underground passages or cells under the Druid cromlechs or circles, some of them used as actual burial places, or as " prisons " in the sense referred to above. The neophyte, in devoting himself to the studies he had to undertake, and so " wandering " in the labyrinths of the body, learning to look into himself with clairvoyant sight, had to accomplish this task symbolically also by a real sojourn in some " dark cell without light ". And in his actual wandering in the darkness, alone, and facing unknown terrors, he met a Messenger carrying a basket. The Messenger—doubtless one of the Priests of the cult— represented one of the four leading principles in all initiations and in all wisdom concerning the evolution of the world, namely, the *science of number*. The Messenger was the great " mathematician ", who taught the neophyte the relation between all parts of the body and the hierarchies of Divine Powers. (A similar knowledge of the body is described in the *Book of the Dead*, but in another way.) The Messenger carried in his basket the symbols of number, weight, and measure; for what the neophyte had to be prepared for was the spiritual " building of the Temple of the body "—the bringing down of heavenly wisdom *into physical life*; so that he could become a *living stone* in the holy structure of the world.

This side of Druid culture was especially related to the Bull-symbolism which has been described. In some respects it resembled the Mithraic Mysteries. The conquest of the "Bull" and its taming meant the gaining of a deep knowledge of the physical body in its relation to the divine creative Powers. Even the effects in the body of seasonal changes, of geographical and geological influences upon it, were studied. Mithras is represented in old sculptures as slaying the Bull in a cave. But Hu the Mighty was supreme master of the Bull's *living* majesty.

From all this we can gain some idea of how sublime a thing was the true Druid's conception of Life, and his search for those things that cast, over all life, the shadow of death. And it is not so difficult to understand how, in the degradation and decay that showed themselves at the close of the great Druid era, human sacrifice could now and then take place as a distortion of the older and loftier ways of initiation.

Let us try to imagine how the Druid may have regarded human sacrifice in the age of decadence. He may have said to himself something like the following:

" Everywhere in Nature, and in the body of man, there is a continual sacrifice of life, but it is an unconscious one. The life-sacrifice going on in every human being can be made fully conscious to an initiate by the powers that the Priests can exert.

But to the *un*initiated we can say, when a victim
is slain, that a physical human life shall be offered
up to the Sun, the Giver of physical life to Nature.
We, who are initiated, see in the victim's death the
sublime restoration of a unit of *spiritual* life back
to its Source. This unit of spiritual life is borne by
the blood in the body; but the blood is also an
immemorial link, through ancestors, to the very
beginning of all human life on the Earth. . . . No
man, who is uninitiated, can as yet realise his own
spiritual Ego and voluntarily sacrifice his lower self;
nor can he command the processes of death in his
own body; but we can *show forth* this dual sacrifice
to the people, who cannot do it for themselves, in a
ceremony of propitiation to the Life-Giver Himself!
The blood-link through the ages must be intact and
virgin, not passed on into a new generation, but
complete in itself and chaste. And when the knife
flashes and the blood streams upon the earth, it is for
us the highest and most exalted of all experiences,
for we behold and witness, in overwhelming
magnificence, the reunion of that freed essence of
life which has been imprisoned in matter, with the
radiance and splendour of the Universal Life-
Spirit! . . ."

It is entirely conceivable how, with the decadence
and final extinction of the higher faculty of clairvoyance, this and other more " magical " expedients
were introduced here and there; the spilling of blood
was a potent factor in assisting a temporary and
artificial restoration of the old powers of vision and
prophecy; and self-deception as to motive and
principle would become ever more and more insidious.

And so there drew towards its close, in the tragedy of failing vision and the clamour of awakening self-consciousness and intellect, the last afterglow of the twilight of a noble and all-embracing Mystery-wisdom.

I am very sure it is true that our puny souls are too crippled and starved by the cold winds of our cleverness to rise higher than the grey lichens that cover the now silent and lonely altars of the Druids. We may listen to the strange music of the winds that blow about them and feel the stirring of some dim sadness; and that is all . . . " They lure us to the streams where the world ends."

A few among us, perhaps, can raise their eyes to the surrounding hills and see the fleeting rose-red furrows of some titanic brow above eyes that burn with the immortal fire; or, looking down at the quiet earth, beside a grey pillar, may see it suddenly transparent and crystalline, opening to a vortex of ice-blue vapour that spouts gigantic incomprehensible jets of power out of the depths. And then some movements in the grass, or the flight of a bird, suddenly closes the open door . . . and we forget, and go our ways still starved and small, and a little disdainful.

But we make to ourselves pictures of the ancient men —their dress and jewels, their mien, their speech. . . . We are like Ferad-artho the warrior who, requesting a description of the hero Fingal from his messenger, asks: " Is the king as tall as the rock of my cave? Is his spear a fir of Cluna? Is he a rough-winged blast on the mountain which takes the green oak by the head and tears it from its hill? Glitters Lubar within his stride when he sends his stately steps along?" But the answer is different from what we expect: " Nor is he tall as that rock; nor glitter streams within his strides;

but his soul is a mighty flood like the strength of Ullin's seas."*

But to find this greatness and this strength we must ask first after the ancient Beauty—for, as Matthew Arnold says: " To see things in their beauty is to see them in their truth."

Why is it that so many Bards were blind? They had looked on Beauty and had not been afraid of Truth. They knew that " men shall die who have an ear for harmonies ". They had seen " the souls of words in their immortal shape and colour "; they had known the " blazing in lightning and the roaring in thunder " of the Bulls of Heaven; they had been in the realm of the celestial Man Himself, wandering through the great folds of the " robe of His strength "—Who yet was to be as the Jew unto Israel. . . . Their blindness was the true seeing. But our blindness is the stark sleep of those whose feet have strayed to the uttermost ends of unwisdom.

And a voice calls to us on the wind: " We have passed away, like flames that have shone for a season."

And another cries:

" Beside the stone of Mora I shall fall asleep. The winds whistling in my grey hair shall not awaken me. Depart on thy wings, O wind! Thou canst not disturb the sleep of the Bard. The night is long, but his eyes are heavy. Depart, thou rustling blast. . . . Shalt thou then remain, thou aged Bard, when the mighty have failed? —But my fame shall remain, and grow like the oak of Morven, which lifts its broad head to the storm, and rejoices in the course of the wind! . . ."

* Ossian's poems.

PART II
AFTER CHRIST

CHAPTER IX

THE LEGEND OF ODRUN

" Like a Lord of Fire, a pure guest comes to the house. They offer him this greeting: Bring Water, O Death, Son of the Sun! "
(From the *Upanishads*.)

THE chief purpose of these pages is to try to show something of the ways by which the immortal spirit of man refreshes itself ever and again at the hidden fountains of wisdom; and how the sparkle or the sweetness or the bitterness runs through the eternal fountain according to the will of worlds; and how it was the bitterness that had to flow through it for two thousand years, while men struggled in the darkness to comprehend the Light that has come down into the Earth.

Five hundred years after the great turning-point of time that marked the beginning of the Christian era, lived one in whose personal life the battle between Light and Darkness was fulfilled; because it was his destiny to stand where East and West—the spiritual Brothers who are always united in the Mysteries, but separated by the hand of man—met and wrestled together. And this was Saint Columba, the " Royal Bright Star " of the blessed island of Hu, Iona. But we can never understand the mission of St. Columba and his pupils unless we first go back again to the Mysteries of Hibernia and beyond, and seek there for the key to it.

We will begin, however, by devoting a chapter to a legend of St. Columba's own time which contains a great secret, but one which very few in these days will be willing to listen to or accept. Nevertheless the secrets shall be told—if not fully (and that is impossible for the end of it is still to come)—at any rate in part. It is not woven out of fire, or air, or water, or earth, but out of the prints of the footsteps of God when He walked in the Garden in the cool of the day. It is really as old as that—as old as Paradise.

The story of St. Columba and the monk Odrun— sometimes called Oran or Odran—has been told and re-told by nearly everybody who has ever written about Iona. But it is not mentioned by St. Adamnan who wrote Columba's biography, and who was born only twenty-seven years after the Saint's death. All that we can discover about the meaning of this legend may possibly explain why it was omitted by Adamnan. The very name Oran or Odrun—a great rune or rann, meaning a secret or mystery—itself suggests one of the reasons *at that time* for its omission from a published writing.

Columba and his monks found themselves continually hampered in the work of building the first church on Iona by hosts of inimical demons. As fast as any part of a wall was built, it collapsed. After a time it was revealed to the Saint that his church would not stand unless a human victim was buried alive under its foundations. " It is good," said Columba, " that our roots should go down into the earth here."

One of the monks, Odrun, offered—or was commanded by St. Columba as some say—to be the sacrificial victim. Accordingly he was buried alive. After three days Columba desired once more to look upon Odrun, and so the soil was removed from where

he lay.   But to Columba's astonishment, Odrun,
" raising his swimming eyes " said: " There is no
wonder in Death, and Hell is not as it is reported to
be."   Columba, horrified at the disclosure of such
secrets, ordered the earth to be quickly shovelled back
again, saying:

" Earth, earth, on the mouth of Odrun, that he may
blab no more."

This extraordinary drama is recounted by Wood-
Martin in his book *Elder Faiths of Ireland and Pre-
Christian Tradition* in all seriousness as probably afford-
ing additional evidence of the prevalence of human
sacrifice; showing that he has very little penetration
into the character of the Saint of Iona, and still less
into the possible deeper significance of such a legend.
So unimaginative is this writer that he at once goes on
to speak of the killing of fowls, etc., as a last trace of
" this barbaric custom ".

The " experiment ", as Wood-Martin calls it, required—and this is important—to be carried out by
one who was a friend of Columba's.   To be the
" friend " of an initiate (as Columba certainly was) is
not without significance.   And Odrun was his friend.
Those who are companions in the Mysteries share a
communion of the spirit which nothing can break;
and investigation into any aspect of the Mysteries was
always, in olden times, based upon a certain co-
operation between such individuals.   The founding of
any Christian community, at that time, was an event
deeply rooted within the New Mysteries of Christ, and
so was always opposed by the demonic powers that
work against the true evolution of man.

Great questions—things of enormous importance—
send their echoes far into the future from this legend of
Odrun!   And Odrun, who by reason of his special

qualifications shared with Columba the mastery of the secret we shall presently try to describe, went through the three days' mystic death of initiation, and was afterwards commanded to silence; for the old Mysteries of Hibernia were to be gradually closed. This was the "great secrets" of Odrun's death. And only by closing them for a time (for they will return in a new form as exoteric knowledge) was it possible for *esoteric* Christianity to be guarded in all its purity, while still *retaining them as its hidden foundation.* . . . " Our roots must pass into the Earth here "; there, in Iona, the Isle of the Holy Spirit. Then the church could be built.

To begin with, we can all of us who know the north-western shores of Britain and the Isles, make one link at least between that legend and our hearts—a link of sea-foam and mists, wild winds and storms and soft-murmuring seas and gentle sunshine; we remember the caves and hollows of the rocks; the old grey stones and weathered crosses in the heather; and above all the tales of sadness and of longing and of strange sleep; the lonely wanderers on the hills; the sense of a phantom darkness that steals over the soul from the heart of the sunsets. Death, or the shadow of Death, goes about softly, hidden in many guises, and calling with the music of the " sea-madness "; " Come away to Tir-nan-og! " Tir-nan-og is the name of the mysterious West. It is the land of the ever-young where,

" The blackbird lilts, the robin chirps, the linnet wearies never. . . ."

It is the land where every human soul goes every night in deep and dreamless sleep.

In deep sleep the soul is free of the body; it is no longer cumbered by the heaviness that steals into the body by day; it forgets sickness and sorrow; it looks back at the body and sees it as a wounded thing; but sees it too as a haven of shadows where the too great brightness of Tir-nan-og may be forgotten in its turn. In Tir-nan-og

" Summer and spring go hand in hand, in the radiant weather,
Brown autumn leaves and winter snow come floating down together."

It is just that: life and death. The soul in sleep sees the interweaving of life and death, going in and out, in the body that is its temporary house. And the soul, returning in the morning, partakes ethereally of both, and so is divided against itself; and waking, must know, like Faust:

" Two souls, alas! within my breast abide.
The one to quit the other ever burning.
This, in a lusty passion of delight,
Cleaves to the world with organs tightly clinging;
Fain from the dust would the other wing its flight
To realms of loftier sires . . ."

The soul itself is one; but the body shows itself to the soul as a dark mirror, and in this mirror *the soul sees its " Double "*, and knows that it must be its companion till death. . . .

" Like a Lord of Fire ", the soul, as a pure guest, comes to its house; and its inmates " offer him this greeting: ' Bring Water, O Death, Son of the Sun.' "

In these words lie the immense paradox of our life. Death, that lives always in the house of the body, is truly a " Son of the Sun "! We partake daily and hourly of his offering. Our daily dying is the true nourishment of our life.

Everywhere in Celtic literature and folk-lore there are traces of this presence of death in life. It is a death

that calls to the living out of a realm of beauty and
ecstasy; yet the voices of the unnameable hosts do not
cry from Heaven but from the Earth—from the
mountains and the hollows of the hills, from the
streams, or—from the *crystal*—the invisible transparency of an emerald and sapphire world, deep down
under the ancient waters. And so it seems that

> " . . . the unappeasable host
> Is comelier than candles at Mother Mary's feet."

But,

> " . . . if any gaze on óur rushing band
> We come between him and the deed of his hand,
> We come between him and the hope of his heart,"*

for the shadow-soul of man that lives in the depths
would fain keep him away from his ultimate fulfilment,
from his own thought, his own love, and his own deed.

*The burial of Odrun is the sacrifice of the old dream-
pictures of a submerged Paradise upon which man was no
longer worthy to look. It is the end of the great Mysteries of
the West and the concealment of the secrets of the " Double ".*

But now let us consider this problem in another
mood.

It has already been mentioned† how America was
well known to the ancients as a region of the Earth
where the magnetic-electric currents influenced human
bodies and souls to a greater extent than elsewhere;
and where certain forms of illness could best be studied.
There was a regular traffic, long, long before the time
of Christ, between what is now Norway and the
American continent. Knowledge as to *how* the
magnetism of the Earth worked upon man's bodily
processes was considered as of the greatest importance,

---

* Both quotations are from poems by W. B. Yeats.

† Chapter II.

and was actually the original basis upon which all ancient medical science was founded.

At the same time these forces were known to be associated with good and evil powers in man, and that they are " at home " in that part of our nature which we call to-day the subconscious. It is important to realise that the Earth is not a " dead " thing, but living, and every part of the Earth pours out into its surroundings various influences, not only magnetic, which do not cause the ethnological varieties of type in humanity, though they may influence them.

Every human soul is heaven-born. It clothes itself in an earthly body. But from the living Earth there rays back into us a " shadow-soul " or " Double " which is nourished by electrical forces which—the Earth being what it is—are engendered in the body in the nervous system through the *destruction* which our conscious life of thought and feeling and will brings about there. All organic diseases are said to have their origin in this sphere of what might be called " vital death ". The ancients discovered that these influences of the magnetic currents of the Earth working into the subconscious processes of the body, were particularly strong in America, and afforded the best possibilities for the study of organic diseases.

Such characteristics of the Earth, of which only a brief mention can be made here, do not expend their forces only in the physical body but penetrate the mind. At the close of Atlantean times and on into the third post-Atlantean epoch of civilisation the subconscious life of man appears to have had quite a different character from that of our own age; it possessed a kind of affinity with Nature and her forces, as a strong " elemental " power of will and an elemental intelligence of a lower (but most intense) kind. *Magic* was possible through the use of these deep-seated powers when they were raised into consciousness.

Obviously, if humanity was ever to develop apart from Nature, if human beings were to become *self-conscious*, able to distinguish " good and evil ", able to separate themselves from Nature so as to observe her, and to devote themselves at the same time to the education of the higher soul, then the " Double ", with the forces it could bestow (and these included a certain dominion over electricity and magnetism, a power to work with them *from within outwards*) must be allowed to sink wholly into the realm of the sub-conscious; but only for a time. We shall see later how these influences are at work in our own day.[41]

The science of the " Double " must have formed an important part of the teachings of certain schools of the Mysteries, especially those that were dedicated to Saturn. We have already spoken of these, and how they were established in parts of Britain after the last Atlantean catastrophes. They are mentioned by Plutarch and others.

Ireland was always regarded as a remarkable country. There is a legend which tells how very different a place *Paradise* is, where Lucifer dwells and whence man had been driven forth, from all the rest of the world which is populated by fallen human beings; but that Ireland is not a part of the ordinary world, for it is an image, placed in the Earth by God, of the ancient Paradise, before Lucifer entered into it. It was only when this " image " of Paradise was separated off from the original and *became Ireland,* that Lucifer could enter into the real Paradise. So Ireland is the only spot on Earth free from the influence of Lucifer.

This legend no doubt issued from some school of initiation where it was known that the earthly forces of the " Double " were opposed by the character of the people dwelling in Ireland; in other words that these forces were at their best there, not their worst; and it must also have been known that the colonisation of Ireland by people from Asia Minor—planned, as has been mentioned, by wise men of the Grecian Mystery schools during the third epoch—could develop, with the Irish, into a race having certain definite qualities of temperament.

It was known to the old initiates that forces radiating through the soil of Ireland tended to damp down intellectual and egoistic characteristics; they work against the capacity of decisiveness and " self-possession". Steiner says that the initiates who sent colonists there chose people whom they knew to be especially able to absorb the peculiar influences of the Irish earth.

Atlantean wanderers, who had worshipped in their Mysteries the " Great Spirit ", Ruler both of the heavenly heights and of the earthly depths, had remained in Ireland, where the secret wisdom concerning the geographical psychic influences could be guarded from evil effects. They founded Saturn Mysteries, and could make use in a very high degree of the old clairvoyance. To this population, thousands of years later, were added colonists from Asia Minor and other places. There was also the advent of the Celts from Europe with their (Druid) Sun-Moon wisdom. These had a more " detached " relationship to Nature. What lived in Ireland from that time onwards was a deeply contemplative spiritual knowledge—magical still—but rich in knowledge and healing. Their initiates awaited, with prophetic insight, the coming of Christ. (Ch. III.)

So here a soil was prepared where the early Christian missionaries could sow their most beautiful seeds. Here was a people whose closeness to Nature, in the best sense, could enable them to understand the salvation of Nature through Christ; whose lack of egoism and decisiveness was something inborn that could lessen the opposition to a new teaching, and make it easy to " lose all ", to become " homeless men ". And permeating the entire background of their life was the atmosphere of the greatest Mystery centre of the whole world.

America was still the great source of this knowledge. The people of Britain and Europe, feeling their way towards the foundation of our own much later epoch of culture, must have had an overwhelming desire to come into closer touch with the secrets that other parts of the Earth had to offer; and most especially to find their way to that far-off Western land where power over these secrets, and the knowledge of a great healing art, and of the forces of Nature that could illumine the dark avenues of mortality and immortality, could be obtained.

It must not be forgotten how every civilisation, in early times, depended upon a knowledge of the Earth in all its various aspects that was still a *Mystery-knowledge*. But also how, on the other hand, the more that such wisdom was attained, the stronger grew the inner spiritual conflict between external knowledge and mysticism. All knowledge in ancient times meant a progress in the direction of materialism and a growing sense of isolation from the old spiritual guidance. But if materialism were to remain allied to powers that were in their nature dark and elemental, the progress would not be towards the good in evolution but towards the evil.

The early Irish monks were people who had absorbed all that Nature could bestow upon them of the peculiar characteristics of their land. Many of them had been nurtured in the shadow of Druid temples. St. Columba himself was the pupil of a Bard. And they knew well all that the people of the Islands experienced when they felt the enchantments, the longings, and the terrors, that were like dreams in the depths of their souls of the elemental powers of the " Double ". Through their blood they remembered the sunken lands, the magic and the glory of old Atlantis. And through their very simplicity the true souls of them sought *escape* from the enchantments and the shadows, in the strength of the Sun of Righteousness.

Ireland, and all Britain, were not isolated from Europe. They lay on the direct route of the expeditions that were sent to the far West to study the science and medicine of the " magnetic lands ". But this study was of necessity bound up with the old powers of clairvoyance, and the wisdom that was sought from the American Indians was, with rarest exceptions, already degraded and adulterated.

The Christian missionaries of Ireland had to know the nature of their neighbour-souls who were saturated with the ancient traditions; and they had to know the sciences and arts of their time. But, on the other hand, through their initiated Christian leaders, they knew that a decisive turning-point in human evolution had already come. From Greece and Rome they had become familiar with the fact that the new *intellect* was already born and had to be developed. And they must have known it too by their intercourse with Druid initiates, under whose centuries-old régimes music had long ago paved the way for a new kind of thinking and intelligence and reason.

It was abundantly clear to them therefore that the last remnants of the ancient wisdom of Atlantis, especially where it concerned the inner nature of the Earth, must die. On the other hand, they recognised in it an element of purity and greatness that *could not* die; for it had been a mighty preparation for the culminating Mystery of all—the *Mystery of Golgotha*. Now light streamed into the shadowy West from the East. The West had the strength of the Earth, the formative power, the inner gesture of the Spirit, that could carry this Light in the chalice of Nature as an offering of hope back to Europe and the East— selflessly.

But their mission, not theirs only, but that of their successors too, would fail, unless the Mysteries of the Depths could be shut off for a time from the stream of Christianity.

The strong forces of the " Double " permeated the wisdom of the far West through and through, imparting to men an elemental will, an unselfconscious power, allied to the magnetism of the Earth and the destructive processes of reflex nervous activity. Through this inner alliance, forces could be introduced into civilisation which, *without any clairvoyance* and in opposition to the free development of self-conscious Ego-hood—would in time cause a universal sickness of both soul and body.

This is perhaps hard to understand. But the loss of natural clairvoyance (the inherited clairvoyance of ancient times) throws a human being back on to himself; he must rely, not on the Gods for his flashes of inspiration and instruction, but on his own heart, and his own head. And he must find the way from his ancestors—that is from a group ego-hood—to individuality; and so from his own centre create a new relationship to other human beings—but one that is universal. The shadow-soul that indwells him, that fills him with the powers of an unconscious instinctive and inherited ego-hood and a " blind " will, must *not* retain its mastery.

There is an inexorable onwardness in the purpose of the human spirit. It begins its pilgrimage in the immemorial past under the visible guidance of higher powers; it grows blind; gropes in the darkness; finds at last its own inner light, and after bitter struggles will gain the power to radiate it over the whole Earth.

And now we guess the meaning of the legend of Odrun, the " great secret ". It tells us of the " Twilight of the Gods " in a form that embodies the peculiar sombreness of a Dionysian magical element.

The drama of Odrun is a world-drama. " Our roots must pass into the Earth here," says Columba. The root of Christianity sinks deep into the rock of the ancient Mysteries; and Odrun is the secret of their union, the secret of Death in Life, and of Life ever rising out of Death. He does not die, for he has embraced the Earth, the Body of the Lord, and goes down into the dark with a last message: " There is no wonder in Death, and Hell is not as it is reported to be." He sees in all its clarity the meaning of the Earth. *But it is too soon.* Columba, in the legend, gives orders that the still living body of Odrun shall be covered over again: " Earth, Earth, on the mouth of Odrun that he may blab no more! "

With these words is foreshadowed the immediate mission of Western Christianity: to work with the aid of Rome for the abolition of the voyages to America. And this was accomplished, not only by Papal edicts, but by the destruction of all records, so far as it was possible. In eight hundred years all was forgotten. And so America was " discovered "—at the end of the fifteenth century—and strangely enough by one who bore the same name as he who had been chiefly instrumental in causing its existence to become concealed. It was re-discovered *through greed of gold*, a short time after the commencement (calculated by the sun's entrance into the constellation of Pisces) of our own epoch of civilisation—the age of materialism.

Till then, a spiritual wall, one might say, was erected between Europe and America. The only records kept of these things—with the exception of a few authentic documents and innumerable legends—were preserved within the circles of various secret brotherhoods, who kept faith with their self-imposed silence until the end of the nineteenth century.

At the same time that the early Irish monks were preparing for the final closing of the doors of the ancient temples with their secrets of magnetism, something was being created by the Soul of the Celtic people which was to shed an undying radiance over the grey cromlechs and the misty hills, and far over many lands. It was the legend of Bride, who nourished the infant Christ in the warmth of her breast. To her, He was the *King of the Elements*. She sang of Him:

> " I am but a little child,
> But my garment shall be laid
> On the Lord of the World.
> Yea, surely it shall be that He,
> The King of the Elements Himself,
> Shall lean against my bosom
> And I will give Him peace."

If we can read ever so slightly the soul of the Celtic people, we shall see in the birth of the legend of Odrun and the birth of the legend of Bride—in the form in which they appeared in the early centuries of our era—no matter if they had a far remoter pagan origin—how each legend supports the other.

Bride, who is the *soul* of the ancient Mysteries—wanders in loveliness for ever under the canopy of Heaven, wrapped in her mantle of bluest æther, and the vision of her calls every human heart away from the dark companionship of his shadow-soul, and saves every one from that sinister dominion.

Christ, the King of the Elements, is nourished by the Woman-Soul, in whose breast the milk of eternal wisdom ever flows. She is the Virgin-Sophia, the Virgin of Light whom the Bards once met among the stars. Companion of Christ, she came down to Earth with Him, and wanders over all the graves of Odrun with the Child in her arms. . . .

But she too has her shadow: the *forgotten* Mysteries. And this shadow lives in all the sadness of Celtic twilight tales, when hearts wake again to longing for the forbidden lands, or for the shining hosts of the Sidhe, or the caves of the hoary Sleepers; but it is a longing filled with dread and hopelessness and the expectation of death. And when the wanderer meets the " shadow " of Bride, she is the Woman of Tears, or the Woman of the Crossways. . . .

" Sometimes ", says Fiona Macleod, " she is seen as the Washer of the Ford, a tall gaunt woman, chanting the death-dirge as she washes the shroud of him who sees her; and sometimes she may grow great and terrible, and inhabit darkness, and the end is come."

He tells too of the " Woman of Tears "—who " had her feet far down among the roots and trees, and stars thickening in her hair as they gather in the vastness

and blackness of the sky on a night of frost." Her form
fills all the world where wisdom dwells. But she is
sorrowful and terrible, for the hearts of men know her
no more in her ancient loveliness. And she tells the
wayfarer who she is:

> " I am she who loveth Loneliness,
> And Solitude is my breath.
> I have my feet on graves,
> And the resurrection of the dead is my food.
>
> .   .   .   .
>
> For I am a Queen,
> Queen of all things on earth and in the sea,
> And in the white palaces of the stars
> Built on the dark walls of Time
> Above the Abyss."

Odrun, Bride, and the Woman of Tears! What a
history is written there! . . . It tells of the great climax
when the old has ended and the new has scarcely
dawned. It bids us look back to the " golden age "—
even long before " Odrun " existed—and forward to
the bitter age of doubt in which we dwell.

In looking back we see how the ancient Egyptian
initiates taught their pupils about the transcendent
vision of a still unearthly humanity that was free from
passion and desire and knew neither sickness nor
death; and in the temple sleep the Priests conjured
this vision before them, so that they saw the holy
Mother of the human race with her child in her arms
that was Sun-born, and not conceived through any
human contact:

> " There stood before them the Woman with child
> who is a Virgin; she was called Holy Isis. Her veil
> has no mortal raised, for she is the Figure which was
> there when Death had not yet come into the world.

She is the one who is rooted in the Eternal, she is the great principle of Healing to which Humanity will again attain when it absorbs anew the spiritual wisdom."*

And now hear the tale of Mary MacArthur (told by Fiona Macleod in *The Gaelic Heart*), who saw the " woman of beauty ", and heard her say:

" I am older than Brighid of the Mantle, Mary, and it is you that should know that. I put songs and music on the wind before ever the bells of the chapels were rung in the West or heard in the East. . . . And I have been a breath in your heart. And the day has its feet to it that will see me coming into the hearts of men and women like a flame upon dry grass, like a flame of wind in a great wood. For the time of change is at hand . . . though not for you, old withered leaf on the dry branch; though for you too, when you come to us and see all things in the pools of life yonder."

This Woman, who is " older than Bride " and " clothed with the Sun ", is the Virgin Wisdom of the world, who gives birth to all men. She has reigned in every religion in every age. She has been called Demeter, Isis, Ceridwen, Herta, Kwan Yin, Kwannon, Sophia, Bride. . . . Dante calls her the " daughter of God ". Brunetto Latini, the teacher of Dante, saw her weaving the world in the mountain of Mystery. From her hand man is able to receive, even to-day, a healing gift for every ill that exists, if he knows how to seek with spiritual insight, in the kingdoms of the plants and the minerals—and in his own soul. That is

* Steiner.

her comforting assurance that all is well, during the dark centuries when the supreme vision of her is not granted save to a few, and cannot be granted to all, until the Child she carries is recognised as the Spirit of the redeemed Earth.

In concluding this " Rune of the Depths ", so sweetened by its companion legends, let me tell of one other legend whose origin is unknown to me. Its character is entirely different. It is a relic of some heart's deep brooding, born of the sea-foam and far horizons of the Western Isles—intangible and beautiful, it is the vision of a vision:

> " A certain solitary, whose dwelling-place was on a hill-side of the mainland, not very far from Iona, sat one day in meditation gazing over the calm sea. Presently he saw, rising up majestically in the airy clouds, the glorified golden-hued form of St. Columba. The Saint too was in meditation, and created in his thoughts a picture which, by reason of the holy power in him that sent it forth, became endowed with immortality and purpose. It was a picture of the Virgin with the Christ-Child in her arms. It floated away from the Islands, came towards the mainland, and spread in lovely colours far and wide over the world. Yet it was more than a picture for it seemed to utter its meaning: ' I am Mary Sophia, sent forth in this image over all the Earth to bring healing to men who will lose the power to see me as I really am. I will live in their *Art* till their thoughts raise me again to the Kingdom of the Heavens which are within them on Earth.' "

Columba had buried Odrun, but his heart showed him the heavenly compensation.

As the centuries went on, and the esoteric Christianity sank under the burden of the power of Rome, many devoted themselves to the strengthening of this Imagination; but it grew gradually weaker in proportion as the sublime figure of the Virgin became " popularised " in Art. But a wonderful thing happened. Raphael, above all other painters, received the vision in the purest form possible in his time, and his Sistine Madonna still has the power to heal. He painted it, this greatest of all pictures, *within a few years of the re-discovery of America*. He placed on record, as it were, *the counteracting force to the forces of the Double*. Novalis, in the *Disciple of Sais*, says of great works of Art: " It is as though they might show me the path to a place where, slumbering, lies the Virgin for whom my spirit yearns."

Can we, in this age whose mission it is to come to grips with the problem of evil, find the divine and pure Wisdom, Mary-Sophia? Where is she to be found? Has she been banished so far and so irrevocably in our laboratories, and in the abstract mathematical calculations of Space? Has her voice been stifled by our ideas that man's body is a mechanical contrivance, doomed to an unfree existence upon a dying Earth?

Is it possible for the faith of the old Celtic peoples, expressed in the lovely *Sheiling Hymn*, to become a living reality for the humanity of the twentieth century?

" Thou Father! Thou Son! Thou Spirit Holy!
Be the Three-One with us day and night,
And on the crested wave, or on the mountain side,
Our Mother is there, and Her arm is under our head.
Our Mother is there, and Her arm is under our head."

CHAPTER X

ST. COLUMBA

" The souls of the Living are the Beauty of the World."
(BACON.)

IT is essential, if we are to understand the prevailing
mood of mankind at the time of the dawn of
Christianity, to recognise that there existed in the
greater part of the world a profound expectancy of
some tremendous super-sensible event, vital to the
continuation of human evolution on the Earth.

This was no vague foreboding. It was not only the
Hebrew Prophets who foretold this event, but in many
and various ways it had for ages been foreseen in the
Mysteries. There it was known that the old power of
being able to see into the spiritual world was doomed
to disappear, and that a new power must come that
would be able to replace it. For if there was nothing
to heal the unbalance in the souls of men so sorrow-
fully perceived by the initiates, then weakness and
sickness would more and more overpower human
bodies and the souls would grow more and more
empty of content. The realisation of this gradually
entered into the whole " sense of Life " which Nature
was still able to bestow upon those who could approach
her through the Mysteries. There was not a single
phenomenon of Nature that had not spoken to men's
hearts of an all-embracing force of Life. To every
human being the vision of elemental spirits, nature-
spirits, the whole floating tapestry of supernatural

beauty, had been like a refreshment, a quickening of vitality. Now all this was vanishing away. But whither? Into the dark recesses of an ever-growing subconscious life of the soul—out of sight, out of hearing . . . Baldur was dead. How could he live again?

We must try to feel how great had been this dependence upon Nature as the Revealer. If we can, then we shall more easily understand how many of the early Christians and how many of the so-called heathen could be aware that with the advent of Christ something had happened to the whole Earth. It was not a mere mystical enthusiasm that could call forth such words as these:

> " . . . the heavens burst asunder,
> All the flashing planets
> Fall out of their places . . .
> And the stars also
> Shower down from heaven
> Headlong through the roaring lift
> Lashed by all the winds."

Christ was a Cosmic God:

> " Son of the Dawn
> Son of the clouds
> Son of the planets
> Son of the stars
> Son of the elements
> Son of the heavens
> Son of the Moon
> Son of the Sun,"

and by His advent Nature was shaken to its foundations. There are so many witnesses in the early days of Christianity who tell us of this change. Were they all mere dreamers?

The sign of the Logos was no longer to be found in the escape from the body in the death-like trance of the old Temple rites, but in the Communion, the transubstantiation of the elements. The Sun-Being had entered the Earth, and *risen in it*. The Communion itself is but a symbol of this fact. But it is a symbol which becomes reality when human consciousness can raise itself to the level where all earthly substance, the " Bread " and " Wine ", is perceived as spiritual substance. Such a consciousness was still possible to the early Christians. But the perception that the Earth had changed the course of its evolution presented many spiritual problems. The legend of Odrun shows us one of them. And we shall try to look at the whole life of St. Columba from this point of view. But first let us see how this passing through from one stage to another in human development reveals itself in the souls of two remarkable personalities between the fourth and eighth centuries A.D.

St. John Chrysostom (388 A.D.), in the famous Christmas sermon, says of this new initiation, or Communion:

" This Table (the Altar) takes the place of the manger; for here too the Body of the Lord will rest, not, as of yore, clad in swaddling clothes " (i.e. not only as a " birth-mystery ") " but bright with the radiance of the Holy Spirit. Those who are initiated know whereof I speak . . . Picture to yourselves what it means to behold the Sun that has come down from Heaven to dwell on Earth, letting His radiance shine out from this place over *all* men." (As the initiate perceives the Act of Consecration.) " But if the Light that is *visible* cannot shine without arousing wonder in the hearts of all who behold it, only consider what it signifies to see the radiance of the *Sun of Righteousness*

streaming forth from our own flesh and sending
Light into the soul."

It is difficult for modern man to realise the intensity
of the feeling of joy and release experienced by the
spiritual seers of that critical time in the fourth
century A.D. when the danger that had been foreseen
for human souls had been proved impotent! Men
had lived through an age of " cosmic lamentation "
for the loss of the life-giving visions which Nature
had everywhere bestowed upon them. But then they
came to know that " Nature, once radiant as Paradise
must become dark and silent as death around us,
but the eternal power of Life triumphant ripens in
Nature's graveyard."

An echo of the sadness and sorrow of these earlier
Christian centuries still sounds in the beautiful poem
Christ, by the Saxon poet Cynewulf in the eighth
century. He is speaking retrospectively, approaching
in his poem the description of the Birth of Jesus, and he
says:

"Verily in distress we utter these words, we
entreat Him Who created man that He may not
elect to declare the doom of hapless man, of us, who
sit in prison sorrowing for the Sun's joyous journey,
until the Lord of Life reveal Light to us, become a
Guardian to our soul, and gird the feeble mind
with glory."

And a little further on he appeals to Christ as the
Rising Sun and cries:

"So now thine own handiwork in distress be-
seeches Thee boldly to send us the Bright Sun and

to Come Thyself that Thou mayest bring light to those who long erstwhile have sat here covered with darkness and in gloom, enfolded by sins in eternal night, and who have had to endure the dark shadow of death."

It is impossible to understand such a mood of soul as this, which was felt by countless human beings, unless we can trace, through poetry and legend and tradition and in many other ways, how great was the darkness when the old clairvoyance had almost entirely vanished and the " twilight of the Gods " had deepened into night. Light remained only with the initiates who, like St. John Chrysostom—St. John of the " golden mouth "—could see the " radiance of the Sun of Righteousness ".

I have quoted these passages from St. John Crysostom and Cynewulf because in a wonderful way they weave together a texture of Light and Darkness which is somehow native to the majestic figure of St. Columba, and, one might say, build a sort of aura in which we can well perceive him.

St. Columba lived his whole life in the heart of the conflict between Light and Darkness—not merely in the sense in which everyone can feel these opposites in his own soul, but also in the way in which he was drawn into the events of his time. He was placed both by inheritance and destiny in the very centre of the echo of those mighty spiritual voices that had uttered, in Hibernia, the secrets of the Earth-depths and many mysteries of the ancient art of healing; but also, his face was turned Eastwards to carry into Europe the Light of Christ.

St. Columba was born at Gartan in Ireland—that " waterfall land " as he called it—in the year 521, on the 7th of December. He was the son of a chieftain of the clan O'Donnell, and descended from Niall, King of Ireland.

A little while before his birth his mother had a vision of the Angel Gabriel, who brought to her a " mantle of marvellous beauty in which lovely colours of all flowers seemed as it were depicted ", as his biographer Adamnan tells us; " and after a brief interval the Angel asks for it back, and took it from her hands, and raising and spreading it out sent it forth into the empty air. She however, saddened by its being taken away, thus speaks to that Man of venerable aspect: ' Why dost thou thus quickly take away from me this lovely mantle? ' He immediately replies: ' For the reason that this mantle belongs to one of such grandeur and honourable station that thou canst keep it no longer by thee ! ' " And then Adamnan describes how this mantle increased in size till it seemed to cover all the plains and mountains; and the Angel said to her that she should bring forth a son " so illustrious that, like one of the Prophets of God, he will be numbered among them, and is predestined by God to be a leader of innumerable souls to the heavenly country."

Wherever in olden times such birth-legends are told, they are an intimation that the child to be born is destined to be an initiate. A seer could perceive that when an ordinary human being was born, his spirit corresponded to the capacity of the body to receive it; but in the case of one who was to be more than an " ordinary " human being, a radiance surrounded him which revealed that there was something greater, which, so to say, could not find room in that body. Such a birth would be regarded as a birth not only in the physical world but in the spiritual world too.

So in trying to describe something of the life of St. Columba it is not so much the external course of it, how he lived as a monk and missionary, that is important but rather what concerns the more concealed nature of his work as a Christian seer; and this has already been touched upon in the last chapter.

There are conflicting accounts with regard to the reason of Columba's leaving Ireland for Iona, which he did in the year 563, when he had reached the age of forty-two. It has been said that the primary cause of his departure was a quarrel, on more than one count, between him and his clan and the supporters of Diarmit, King of Ireland, resulting altogether in three great battles. Columba's friend and confessor St. Laisren, told him that as a penance for his share in these events he must leave Ireland, and in some other land save as many souls for Christ as had been slain in the battles.

But a legend tells that it was the Archangel Michael who really banished him from Ireland. The old *Irish Life* merely states that: " When he had sown faith and religion; when numerous multitudes had been baptised by him; when he had founded churches and establishments . . . then the determination that he had determined from the beginning of his life came into his mind—namely to go on a pilgrimage. He then meditated going across the sea to preach the word of God to the men of Alba and the Britons and Saxons. . . . He went in good spirits until he reached the place the name of which is to-day I-colm-kill." That is, Iona.

No one who has voyaged on a quiet day of summer beside the blue mountains of Mull, his ship threading its placid way between the little islets of rosy felspar— coming nearer and nearer to the holy Iona—will ever

forget it. The very name Iona rings in our ears with the
sea-sound of many mysteries. *Hu*, it was also called, or
Hii, or *Ioua*—the sacred vowels of the three " Rays of
Light ". It is *Jona*—John—the name of those who die
and are raised. And Iona, says Adamnan, is in Greek
Peristera and in Latin *Columba*, the Dove. The sound of
I-O-N-A sighs over the waters. The white wings of the
" Dove of the Eternal " are in the clouds and foam.

It is told how Columba continued his voyage from
island to island until he reached his destined home,
from whose highest point there was no longer any
sight of Ireland, the ancient Paradise. Steadfastly
he turned his face away from that great centre of the
old Mysteries and directed all his love and all his
strength towards the East. " *Cul-re-Erin* "—(my back
turned to Ireland) —" shall be my mystical name! "
he cries. Beyond the shores of Ireland stretched two
thousand miles of ocean and the lands of the forbidden
West. Only once, in 585, did he return to visit Ireland, to see some of the monasteries he had founded
there. And in addition to these foundation his missionary work spread over the Orkneys, the Shetlands,
the Hebrides, and the Faroe Islands, even to Iceland,
and far over the North and South of Britain.

We cannot think of Columba only as a saintly monk.
It is obvious from all that has been recorded of him
that he had the qualities of a statesman. The manage-
ment of his enormous diocese, the tact and wisdom
which he displayed in his dealings with men and affairs
are evidence of this. He was far-seeing and purposeful,
strong and passionate, and at the same time loving,
humble, and tender.

We cannot picture him apart from the Nature that
surrounded him—the granite of the Earth, the
tempests, or the still waters, when all the islets lie

like pale roses on the sea's sunlit surface; and behind
them the long purple line of the mountains of Mull
and the distant mainland. All this he loved for he was
a poet, and a Bard too.

All contrasts are typical of Columba. And in looking
at his life as a whole, sharply divided as it is between
the Irish and Iona periods, one is drawn more and
more towards the acceptance of what is so persistent a
tradition, his banishment—not his voluntary departure—from Ireland as a result of the share he had had
in the wars of his people.

In his early education he had been taught in monastic schools, but he had also been closely associated with
Bardism, and his poetic gifts had been cultivated under
the Bard Master Gemman of Leinster. He was of
course no stranger to the Druidic rites and teachings,
as the legend of Odrun indicates, and he knew from
them their art of healing. Moreover he was of royal
blood, and must have lived in close sympathy with
all that concerned his warlike kinsmen. Clans and
ecclesiastical authority often came into conflict. And
it accords with the whole picture of Columba's later
life if we think of him as having lived in the midst
of these opposites, not only in his external activities
but also in his inner life—in his appreciation of the
greatness of the Druidic Mysteries and the significance
of their origin, and on the other hand of the new way
of Christian initiation and his own tremendous
mission as one of its leaders. Out of this there must
have grown in him, by very reason of these opposites,
a profound humility and a radiant illumination.

It is a spiritual law that in the first thirty-five years
of human life much has to be developed and worked
through that is like a coming to terms with the
inherited forces of family and race as against the free

forces of the individual spirit. And after that, the working out of the now *liberated* destiny that leads on into the future. The change may be one that is only felt inwardly in the soul; or it may be reinforced by a predestined change in outer circumstances. And so it was with Columba, exiled from Ireland. In the Preface to his hymn *Altus* we find these words:

"The hymn was written because he was desirous of praising God. For seven years he was searching out this hymn, *in the Black Cell without light* (my italics)—that is, beseeching forgiveness for the battle of Cull Dremhne which he had gained over Diarmit son of Cerball, and the other battles which were gained on his account."

There is some confusion of dates here, for it was actually only *two* years between the battle of Dremhne and Columba's voyage to Iona, and the Black Cell is said to have been in Derry in Ireland. But it is more than likely that the seven-year period refers to a period of initiation, a time of development in self-knowledge, which was in process both before and after the first battle, and culminated after his banishment. The "black cell without light" may well have been the bitter darkness that every soul knows on the Threshold of enlightenment.

St. Adamnan divides his *Life* into three parts: the more external activities, the miracles, and the visions of Angels. I have dealt as much as is necessary here with the first of these. Adamnan arranges the other two parts as he does because he is desirous, I think, of showing how the whole life of the initiate is based on the adjustment of the polarity of the forces in which he was to experience the fulfilment of his mission— the *earthly* and the *heavenly*.

The miracles attributed to St. Columba are first
of all related to the Earth and its elements. Before
considering them, even if we allow for possible
exaggerations, it is well to remember how much, in
those times, man's whole relation to Nature was still
conditioned by his psychic sensitiveness towards
all that was concealed behind the outer natural
phenomena; and in regard to miracles of healing,
the relation between soul and soul must certainly
have been altogether different from what it is to-day,
so that healing of the sick could be accomplished by
the exercise of psycho-mental influences of one human
being upon another. Even, in some cases, the growth
and virtues of plants could be affected. We have
only to read some of the oldest herbals, for instance—
or fragments from Albertus Magnus and others—to see
that the most extraordinary claims were still made even
centuries later, and quite seriously. But however carefully we might follow some of the old magical recipes
to-day, they would no longer " work "; because *we* are
different. But we will let Columba's miracles speak
for themselves.

In the *Gospel of St. John*, by Rudolf Steiner, the
occult foundations of the first miracle performed by
Christ, the changing of the water into wine, are
described. The miracle, he says, had a significance
for the whole future development of humanity. It
was based on certain accepted customs: water was
used at Jewish marriages between people who were
connected by blood; wine, when they were not so
connected; and the marriage at Cana was of the latter
kind. The drinking of wine has a certain effect.
It creates a kind of feeling of independence in the
Ego. What was indicated by the changing of water
into wine was that the time had come for the widening

out of relationships between human beings, that they
had to become free from the dependence upon mere
group ego-hood and raise themselves to a sense of the
brotherhood of all humanity.

Steiner also shows how the whole sequence of the
following miracles reveals the increasing power of
the Saviour which culminates in the raising of Lazarus.
And in St. Adamnan's *Life*—though the greater miracles are interspersed with all sorts of lesser ones—the
general trend of the succession of them follows a
similar process of enhancement. Considering that
it is the life of an initiate that Adamnan is describing,
it is interesting that the first miracle he records is a
changing of water into wine for the Eucharist:
"Thus Christ the Lord showed His first proof of
miraculous power through His disciple, just as He
wrought it Himself when He made a beginning
of miracles in Cana of Galilee." And he concludes the
account of it with these words: "May this divine
miracle which was manifested through our Columba,
shine like a lamp in the Introduction of this little book,
so that we may then pass on to the other great miracles
that were manifested through him."

One who had such a mission as Columba had, must
bear in his soul an understanding for the need of free-
ing men from the old attachment to blood-ties, and
awakening them to a sense of world-brotherhood. He
could "change water into wine".

A great many of Columba's miracles in Iona, taking
them in the order given, were worked in what Adamnan calls the "lower species", the element of Water.
The Saint averts a pestilence which is falling in the
moisture of the air from the clouds; he heals cases of
sickness by administering water that he has blessed;
he draws water out of a rock; he cleanses a poisoned

spring; and from the juices of a plant which is bitter he takes away the bitterness; and so on.

Next, we find his miracles in the element of Air—calming the storms at sea when his monks are in danger in their boats; changing the direction of the wind; and through the air his staff (which he had left behind him in the monastery) is miraculously wafted to him.

And then his powers are directed to the multiplying or purifying of food, and to the exorcising of demons; he is working in the element of warmth, or Fire.

Later, we find that he is not working directly into the elements, but into the *souls of men*, in events that have to do with their destiny; he administers justice in miraculous ways. And finally, there is the greatest miracle of all, the raising of a dead youth to life. Adamnan, in his enthusiasm for detail, only approximately follows the sequence of the "increase of power". But it is there; and we can understand much that lies concealed in his simple narrative if we follow it with the aid of some knowledge of the typical events that show themselves, in different ways, in the lives of great initiates.

At the time that Adamnan was writing his book miracles had already become much more "miraculous" than formerly, and something must be allowed for inaccuracies. But his account of the miracles at least reveals the power of Columba's love which really brings about the *action* of the psychic relationship between his own and Nature's forces, and between his own soul and the souls of others, intensified step by step until it touches at last even the mystery of death. And this is the culmination of the changing of water into wine—that love, pouring directly from the Ego itself, can conquer death.

But all this is only the one side of Columba's life—
the carrying of Light into Darkness. The third Book
of the *Life* is devoted to the description of the visions
of Angels. Now Columba is not only carrying Light
into the Darkness, but his own Darkness—all that
belongs to his human nature—is lifted into the Light
of the spiritual world. His intercourse with the
Angels, where he seeks to attain to it for the sake of
helping his fellow men, is constantly reached only
after intense struggle—he has to pass through that
region in the spiritual world itself where the war
between Light and Darkness—Angels and Demons—
is desperately waged. Again and again, in spiritual
vision, he follows the souls of those who have died
and encounters their purgatorial demons; or, when
unable to go in person to the aid of the living who
are in some kind of danger, he fights valiantly for
them in spirit on the side of the Angels. But in the calm
silences of his secret devotions and meditations the un-
dimmed Radiance falls upon him, bright and dazzling
in the holy night.

On one such night one of the monks crept into the
chapel to pray, while Columba was engaged in his
devotions in the oratory adjoining, the door between
having been left a little ajar:

"But the brightness of that same celestial light
bursting through the inner door of that chamber,
filled the interior of that other little house where
Virgno was doing his best to hide himself, and not
without a certain degree of intense fear. And as no
one can gaze with direct and undazzled eyes upon
the summer and noonday sun, so also Virgno who
saw it, could by no means bear that celestial
brightness because that incomparable flood of

light much dazzled the sight of his eyes. He was so greatly frightened at the sight of this terrible and lightning-like splendour, that no strength remained in him." . . .[42]

We are not without a hint here and there in Adamnan's *Life*, and elsewhere, of the connection between the diseases and plagues of that time and the secrets of the " magnetic earth " that were described in the last chapter. The most important of these hints is of course in the legend of Odrun. But here we have an account of the Saint's battle against the demons of a certain disease, who were armed with *iron darts*—a curious statement, and only to be understood in the light of what has been said about the magnetic forces of the " Double ", against which the Irish initiates were said to be able to exert their special influence. The mention of " iron darts " is certainly not merely a picturesque touch. The story is worth quoting in full:

" When he began to pray suddenly he sees a very black host of demons fighting against him with iron darts; and as had been revealed to the holy man by the Spirit, they wished to invade his monastery and with their darts to kill many of the brethren. But he, one man against innumerable foes—and such foes— taking the armour of the Apostle Paul, fought in brave conflict. And so for the greater part of the day the war was waged on both sides, neither could they, innumerable as they were, vanquish the one; nor was he strong enough alone to drive them from his island, until the Angels of God, as the Saint afterwards related to a few persons, came to his aid, and for fear of them the demons, terror-stricken, quitted the place. And on the same day the Saint, returning to the monastery after the flight of the demons from the island, speaks this word about the same hostile bands, saying: ' Those deadly foes . . . who have this day been put to flight from the boundaries of this territory to the Ethican land shall there, like savage invaders, attack the monasteries of the Brethren and bring about pestilential diseases, by the virulence of which many shall be attacked and die! ' " He afterwards added that the prayers of the monks there had greatly mitigated the attack. And this was proved correct, only one monk having died.

This story is of some importance because it is one of the many links that are to be found in the chain of evidence relating magnetism to illness, the old secret of the " Double ", about which a little more will be told in another chapter.

The time was drawing very near when all connection with this knowledge would have to cease. Only a clear intellectual consciousness, shut off from the old clairvoyance, was in the future to be admitted to a rediscovery of the secrets of electricity and magnetism— things which we have around us in all abundance to-day not as " secrets " but as inventions—as the very structure of our modern civilisation.

One feels that the spiritual guidance of the world worked in a grand and magnificent way in leading the religious life of that time out of the old into the new, during the first few centuries after Christ. This change had to flow in two directions, from East to West and from West to East; and in such representative figures as St. Columba, the two streams met.

In all the accounts that we have of Columba his intercourse with the Angels is strongly emphasised. In

certain esoteric teachings it is said that these Beings
have a special relation to the human intellect; that
they are the " Thinkers " in the Cosmos, and influence
the brain, and in this capacity they are said to have
prepared the way for the coming age of intellectual
culture. And as we have seen, *light* has always been
associated with thought, and darkness with ignorance.
The Angels are said to be those Beings whose mission,
in the creation and sustaining of the world is the interweaving of Light with Darkness, of intelligence with
ignorance. The characteristic of the Angels is what,
in ourselves, we call the " longing to attain ": the
desire for Light produces in the Angels the desire
for Darkness—in the sense that out of the higher
spiritual state, where all Beings are *inwardly illuminated*,
there issue the Angels, seeking Darkness that they
may bear it into the Light. This it is, woven into
the souls of men, that urges them to be born on Earth,
and *on Earth*, in the Darkness, to find their own
illumination. And what human souls can find on
Earth of inner Light is then carried by them after
death into the spiritual world.

But it is in a very special way that the mission of St.
Columba seems like a human reflection of the angelic
mission. He was closely connected, by birth and
education and destiny, with the old pagan wisdom; he
had quite certainly learnt in Ireland, and as a seer,
what the Druids knew about the nature of the Earth-
depths; the legend of Odrun shows this clearly. He
had learnt from them, and from the whole atmosphere
of his native land, many things about death and sickness and healing. He knew how death is interwoven
with life. On the other hand, one feels that his capacity
to penetrate with the clear vision of a Christian initiate
into the spiritual world—how his whole life is irradiated

by the power which could come to those to whom
" Resurrection " was a daily experience—gave him
illumination with regard to the " other side " of birth:
the instreaming glory of the deathless spirit. What
lived in him was a union of the Western and the
Eastern Mysteries.

St. John Chrysostom, from whose Christmas sermon
a passage was quoted at the beginning of this chapter,
says further how nothing of the Mystery of Christ,
neither His Passion, nor Death, nor Resurrection, nor
Ascension, could have taken place " *if He had not first
been born.*" St. Paul, on the other hand, says that
nothing in Christianity would have any meaning *if
He had not died and been raised from the dead.*

To be born is to die to the spiritual world, and meet
on Earth the " false form of Death ". To die on Earth
is to be born into the spiritual world. That is the
" true Death ".

So Columba, standing on the threshold between East
and West at the beginning of the Christianising of
Europe by the Western stream flowing through Celtic
Christianity, lived out in his own life as an Initiate
what was a fragment of World-destiny.

Vividly the picture of him stands out against
the dim background of the ancient wisdom. We see
him, a tall, majestic, and commanding presence—fiery
and passionate, tender and loving, with a voice that
could be gentle with healing and peace, or mighty with
prophetic utterance. In his soul, the dark shadow of
profound penitence and humility; in his Self, the sunlight of Eternity—so that men called him the " Royal
Bright Star ".

And outwardly around him the wild and turbulent
seas; or the calm and bright-sparkling seas; the crying
gulls, the solitudes, the scent of the heather on the Hill

of the Angels; the constant activities of the monks, their sailings and fishings and herding of sheep and cattle; the never-ceasing planning and building; the innumerable voyages in cold and heat, in storm or becalmed. . . . And behind it all the woven tapestry of Light and Darkness in which the jewel of his life gleamed in heavenly lustre.

For him, all darkness in Nature was irradiated by the light of Christ. So that we can write for him too the lovely words of the *Rune of St. Patrick*:

> " At Tara to-day in this fateful hour
> I place all Heaven with its power,
> And the Sun with its brightness,
> And the snow with its whiteness,
> And Fire with all the strength it hath,
> And lightning with its rapid wrath,
> And the winds with their swiftness along the path,
> And the sea with its deepness,
> And the rocks with their steepness,
> And the Earth with its starkness:
> All these I place
> By God's almighty help and grace,
> Between myself and the powers of Darkness."

CHAPTER XI

ST. JOHN AND ST. LUKE

" The first and oldest of things illuminate the last; and immaterial principles are present in material things."

(IAMBLICUS.)

A CERTAIN aspect of the old Mystery wisdom which continued on into early Christian times was known as the Gnosis. The Christian Gnostic scriptures which have come down to us in the *Pistis Sophia* tell of the descent or fall of the original " Virgin " wisdom into darkness, and its salvation by Christ. It is called Sophia, the Virgin of Light. There are passages which refer to the power of the Virgin of Light to redeem mankind from the " counterfeiting spirit ", which we have described as the " Double ".*

In the Third Book of *Pistis Sophia* the nature of man is described as consisting of the " power ", or spirit, the " soul ", and the " counterfeiting spirit ". First there is a description of how all these powers are feeble in the body of the new-born child, without " any of them sensing anything, whether good or evil, because of the load of forgetfulness which is very heavy ". And then how the food of the Earth, being eaten, increases the strength of the three incarnating principles, until little by little " the power and the soul and the counterfeiting spirit grow, and every one of them senseth according to his nature: the power senseth to seek after the light of the height; the soul on the other hand

* Chapter IX.

senseth to seek after the region of righteousness which is mixed; the counterfeiting spirit on the other hand seeketh after all evils and lusts and all sins; the body on the contrary senseth nothing unless it taketh up force out of matter."

But there is a fourth principle too, one which is in alliance with the counterfeiting spirit, and this is the " destiny ". This has already been mentioned as the geographical influence of the Earth at the place of birth which tinctures or predetermines the character of the individual's physical and sentient nature, through the " Double ".

The teaching continues (and it is beautiful to read) that the counterfeiting spirit—or rather its effects—becomes, if the soul has not been able to release itself from its influence, the *judge* of the soul after death in the presence of the Virgin of Light; that is, in the presence of divine Wisdom. But the soul that has freed itself and has absorbed wisdom " becometh a great light-stream, shining exceedingly. . . . It becometh entirely wings of light, and penetrateth all the regions of the rulers and all the orders of the Light, until it reacheth to the region of its kingdom up to which it hath received Mysteries."

The whole content of the Gnosis is really a teaching about the spiritual Universe—as spheres or " Mysteries ", with their corresponding hierarchies of Beings; and the *contraction* of the spiritual Universe into the being of man at birth; hence of the descent of the Logos, the Christ, through these spheres to Earth, and His Ascension, or subsequent " expansion ". He takes humanity by the same path—descending, and ascending. The Gnosis presents the idea of the Cosmic Christ; the same idea, in essence, as was contained in the revelations received in all the ancient

Mysteries, under other names. This aspect of Christ shines radiantly through the Gospel of St. John.

The " Virgin " has always stood for the archetype of the Soul, clothed in the light of wisdom. The " wise " and the " foolish " virgins of the parable in the Gospels represent the souls who perceive the world with spiritual insight, and those who do not. The Eternal Feminine is for ever sought by the human soul as the only guide to the Spirit.

What all the old Mystery schools tried in their various ways to bring before their pupils was a fundamental absolute truth of human existence, the " virgin birth " of the soul. The Woman with the Child in her arms is a picture that has no date, for it belongs to the realm of the Archetypes. It has always been there since the beginning of human incarnations, and always as the sign of protection from the dominion of the material world.

The connection of the different Mystery schools of the past with Christianity can be traced also through the remarkable symbols that tradition ascribes to the writers of each of the four Gospels, the Man, the Lion, the Bull and the Eagle.

Each Gospel has been written out of different sources of inspiration which are represented by these symbols. In the earlier chapters of this book emphasis has been laid upon the importance of the Bull-symbolism, which abounds not only in the Egyptian cult of Apis, the Bull, but also in Druidism, where Hu is often identified with a Bull, or else is attended by Bulls. Wherever this is the case the wisdom taught in these cults had a great deal to do with the secrets of the *physical body* in its relation to the spiritual world—as a creation of the spiritual world; it was a physical science based entirely on spiritual knowledge. The body was studied

as an image of the macrocosm; the organs in their
relation to the planets, the structure of the body in its
relation to the fixed stars, the processes of the organs,
inner secretions and so on, in their relation to the
elements, the seasons, etc. And the stars, the elements,
the Earth, Sun and Moon, were not regarded only *as
such*, but could be experienced in clairvoyant states
of consciousness as colonies of Gods, who had sacrificed
their own being in the creation of the body.

Looking at the Universe, Earth, and Man in this
way, the ancients believed that during æons of time
devoted by the divine Beings to the creation of man,
certain archetypal forms had arisen as Thoughts of
the Creators, which later developed on the one hand
as the three archetypes of all the animal species, the
fourth being the archetype of the complete man; their
clairvoyant imagination showed them how *in* man the
animal forms were absorbed and metamorphosed into
human qualities and human physical processes.

If we look at the bovine creatures, we certainly
recognise in them a sort of abandonment to the digestive
processes, and to the heaviness or gravity of the Earth;
they seem to correspond to the lower part of human
nature. But to the ancients this was not " lower " in
the sense of inferiority but the contrary; for they saw
in the digestive processes an image of the metamorphosis of material things into spiritual things—
a sort of image of the Creation, in reverse order. It
was a majestic revelation;* for the nourishment of
man presented an image of his *humanity;* they saw
him partake of the products of the Earth and change
them into life, and through life the spiritual activity
of thought, feeling, and will is sustained. The Bull-
archetype was an image of the most profound and the

---

* The Mysteries of Mithras were especially connected with this.

most unconscious and fundamental working of the
human *will* throughout the whole living organism,
and especially as it works in man's power to procreate
his own kind.

In the same way the Lion-archetype was conceived
as a spiritual power that brought about especially
the creation of the heart and the rhythmic system of
breathing and circulation; and as a human *quality*
(in its positive aspect) revealed itself as courage and
enthusiasm and love.   The spiritual Lion-archetype
suggests a tremendous cosmic fire of energy and
splendour.   The Eagle—soaring above the world—
belongs to the majesty of the force of Resurrection.
As a *thinker*, man aspires to the stars.

Mark   Matthew   Luke   John

Selected Figures from Angelico de Fiesole's Life of Christ.

The Human Archetype, the Man, represented the
harmony of these three.   All four were seen in clairvoyant vision as spiritual Beings.   There is plenty of
evidence of this.   Some schools of initiation revealed

the wisdom of the Bull, some that of the Lion, some that of the Eagle, and others the Mysteries of Man.

The four Gospels are presented by the writers under these four aspects, which were at that time still recognised orientations of inspiration. Matthew is inspired by the Human Mysteries, Mark by the Cosmic Mysteries of the Lion, Luke by the Earth-Mysteries of the Bull, John by the power of the Resurrection, the Eagle.

There is a peculiar harmony—due to their polarity—between the inspiration of Luke and that of John. The Gospel of Luke (the Bull) is the Gospel of healing and peace descending to the Earth. John reveals what is highest and at the same time most profound—the *recreation* of the human being through the power of the Logos, Who says: "*I am the Resurrection and the Life!* . . ."*

Now let us look again at the old Mysteries of Hibernia. The pupil stands before the two enigmatic statues, the one male, the other female; the one awakens him to the vastness of the creation; he sees the infinite perspective of the past which rises before him at first as a dying world, in every detail of which his own being is immersed and dissolved and scattered and lost. He feels: I am one with the whole Universe —I was born of God. And then he sees into himself. He looks at the awful profundity of his own soul, deep into the fires of his body, into the flashing beauty of his imaginations; and he sees them overwhelmed by Life, which withers in the onrushing of the future and of eternity. He is torn asunder. He sees himself on the one hand soaring like the Eagle into cosmic heights, and on the other sinking like the Bull under the weight of his earthly nature. And then the Answerer appears.

* The raising of Lazarus. The first Christian initiation.

And from Him he receives the power of the Word which reveals Resurrection from death and the Healing of all sickness of soul and body.

The Druid Mysteries that arose on the foundations of the Hibernian, were tinctured especially by that aspect of them that revealed the nature of man as an earthly being. The female element showed itself in them in the dark conflicts of the soul in its imprisonment in the body, as in the legends of Ceridwen; and so the revelation of the divine to which the initiate was led by Ceridwen, and which appeared in the form of the God Hu, was pictured under the imagery of the *glorified body*, whose spiritual archetype had the form and attributes of the " Bull ". Such an ascension to spiritual knowledge of the Universe from *out of the body* implied also the attainment of inspiration with regard to the healing of the body. The Druids were physicians. So too, were the Egyptians.

But the necessity of healing arose, not from the revelation of resurrection, but from the revelation of all that precedes it—the descent from Heaven.

The writer of the Gospel of Luke was one who was inspired out of these sources of initiation knowledge.

Those who were initiated into the Bull Mysteries did not remain ignorant of the secrets of the "Double". Knowing the Earth (and that is the physical body too) they understood what the Earth bestows upon the human being in determining certain physical factors by means of which he fulfils, partly at least, his *destiny*.

Illness—organic illnesses arising from sub-earthly forces in the " Double ", and working through the destructive processes in the nervous system—is one of the companions of destiny. And destiny is daily fulfilled through the actions of the will. This is a

profound mystery of human life. Healing (whether of
the soul or of the body) works into destiny as a divine
grace; and passing from one to another human being
through compassion, creates a sharing of destiny
which magically unites mankind.

The seal of Destiny is Birth; and the image of the
Woman with the Child in her arms appears (the
inevitable picture of the logical sequence of these
thoughts) as that supreme saving and healing element,
the protection against isolation in egotism—the bond
that unites all men under a destiny that is *shared*—
the destiny of Birth. This conception places the
Woman and the Child into a sphere of imagination that
is no longer earthly, but heavenly. She is an Archetype,
unborn and deathless, a Virgin, bringing her Child—
the human soul—from the Sun.

And so she appeared at a later stage in the degrees of
initiation as the opposite pole to the sickness which
comes from the shadow-realm of the sub-earthly. And
in the Gospel she is to be found incorporated in Mary,
the Mother of Jesus. In no other Gospel is the immortal birth-story so magically told as in the Gospel
of Luke the Physician. And this is one of the reasons
why we can also feel in the Gospel of Luke something
like an echo of the wisdom of Buddha: that sickness
and old age and death are sorrow, but that compassion
throws down the barriers of separation and brings
liberation from them.

The other aspect of the Hibernian Mysteries which is
reflected in Druidism is not what is only connected
with the *soul*, but what is connected with the *spirit*,
namely, the creation of the world, and its opposite
pole Resurrection from the Death of the world. In
this the masculine element, power, rules. This is
the male statue of Hibernia.

The Father-God—the " Great Spirit "—of the old Western Mysteries, was felt as embracing the entire Universe, so that His nature was equally manifest in the fact of death as in the fact of life. Everything was " in the Father ", and the Father was in everything. So it is true to say that " Death is the Father ". We come from the Father; and we return to Him, through that part of Him which is Death and which is His extreme manifestation in the world of matter. Man has " contracted " the whole Universe—the very Being of the Father—into his body at birth; at death the body is dissolved, and as a spirit man expands again into the Universe, but in the full experience of his " I am ".

The three days' mystic death, or deep trance, of the old initiations represented a foretaste of this expansion. Only, in initiation, there was a return to the body, and the memory of the spiritual universe and the knowledge gained in this transient " death " remained in the consciousness of the initiate.

In Druidism the experience of the Ceridwen Mystery was the experience of the deep entry of the soul into the body—birth. That of the Hu (or Hesus) Mystery was the leaving of the body, death, but at the same time its " glorification ". In other words, the real nature of the body as an image of the Creation, and therefore " glorious ", was realised.

In the Gospel of St. John we find the likeness to this experience in the initiation (or raising) of Lazarus. Only, in the Gospel, the initiation is carried to a higher degree because Christ Himself is the Initiator, and places the impulse and power of Resurrection (received from the Father) into the words " I am " (that is, through Christ into Lazarus himself) " I am the Resurrection and the Life." And subsequently the writer of the Gospel shows, by his insight into special sayings of Christ, that *he understands the Mysteries of the Father.*[43]

This suggested connection between Lazarus and the God Hu-Jesus in his character as the revealer of the " glorified body ", and who, as a real human being, was the Initiator of the ancient Cymric race, and was later perceived clairvoyantly in the Mysteries as a being of god-like beauty and power as has been described—is not merely a haphazard connection.   It reveals the direct continuation of a certain type of initiation.

Centuries later the spiritual impulse of the old Celtic Mysteries, working throughout in a more or less concealed manner, *and meeting, through the missionary work of the Irish monks in middle Europe with the Johannine " gnostic " Christianity,* gave rise, in the fourteenth century, to the foundation of the secret school of Christian Rosenkreuz, the Brotherhood of the Rosy Cross, also called " *John Christians* ".

This Brotherhood adopted a certain symbol, a black cross encircled by seven red roses.   In its outer form it is similar to the encircled cross of Celtic origin.   (See Frontispiece.)   The black cross is the body, purified, through the purification of the soul, of all lower desires; the roses are the stations of the Cross—each member of the human nature becoming stage by stage a blossom of the Spirit.   But *cosmologically*, the roses represent the seven stages of the evolution, purification and ultimate resurrection of the Earth itself.

The two statues of Hibernia showed, in the most ancient form, an eventual union between the two ways of spiritual knowledge, as mirrored in the Gospels of John and Luke, the " outer " and the " inner ", the " above " and the " below ";   and the Christian symbol of the Rosy Cross is the symbol of their union. Both these Evangelists point to the cosmic nature of Christ-Jesus; St. Luke through His genealogy, which he traces to *God*; St. John, in the language of the Mysteries, points to the *Logos* Who is " made Flesh ", and Who has the power of Resurrection.[44]

In the Gospel of Luke the crucifixion of Christ between the two thieves is dramatically described in a way that is not recorded by the other Evangelists. On either side of the Holy One are the two great enigmas of human existence—even as they stood before the neophyte as the two statues in the Mysteries of Hibernia, and even as the two Sphinxes guarded the altar in the Temple of the Sun in Egypt—but revealed now in quite a different way. And Luke records, as the last words from the Cross: " Father, into Thy hands I commend my Spirit." This is entirely in accordance with the spirit of Luke's way of inspiration.

In the Gospel of John we find something quite different. The Mother of Jesus, *Mary-Sophia*, is to be united with the beloved disciple: " Woman, behold thy son! " John takes the divine Wisdom of the world into his heart. And the last words from the Cross are: " It is finished."

What is finished? Not the mission of Christ, because its fulfilment is hardly begun. But the " contraction " of the whole spiritual Universe into the material creation of man and the Earth—that was finished.[45] The " expansion " was to begin; the redemption of the divine Wisdom by *man* was to begin. The Book of Revelation looking far into the future was its first-fruits.

Luke feels himself gazing into the Depths where he touches the secret of the still unrepentant thief; he feels the ground-note of Cosmic Destiny there (hence his lovely account of the Birth of the Child), and knows how healing can come to it; and he recognises the Spirit in its relation to the Father-Death, that is, to the physical body and its mortality; and its ultimate reunion with the Father of the Heights.

John gazes with Eagle-vision into the infinite future evolution of the world, and writes of the past: " It is finished."

Luke brings into his Gospel the echoes of the Great Mysteries of the West.

John crosses over from past to future, because he has the secret of the Creative Word which *continues*: " I am with you always, even unto the end of the world." He sees the future because he has understood the Beginning. He is united with the divine Wisdom Sophia-Mary, whose symbol, from the Father, is the Dove. The Eagle of vision becomes the " Dove of the Eternal ".

John, through the " John Christians ", carries into the future the Mysteries of the Word from East to West. Out of this there arose what became known in the ninth century as the Wisdom of the Grail, whose Knights had the emblem of the Dove on their armour. But first, as already stated, it had to be united with the stream of the Celtic Mysteries of the West, brought Eastward to Europe by the pupils of St. Columba. And this union is already foreshadowed in the words of the daughter of the West, Bride: " *My garment* " (Western Mysteries) " *shall be laid on the Lord of the World.*"

And so there came about, in the fourteenth century, not only the ripe fruit of the meeting of these *two* aspects of the old Mysteries as the esoteric teaching of the Rose and the Cross, but in this secret Brotherhood all other aspects as well were drawn together to form a nucleus of teaching which has survived beneath the surface of civilisation into our own time, and will be able to make itself known little by little.

The preparation for this Brotherhood, of the fourteenth century, germinating in history about five hundred years earlier, is told in the beautiful legend of Floris and Blanchefleur, the Rose and the Lily, which shall have a little chapter all to itself.

CHAPTER XII

THE LEGEND OF THE ROSE AND THE LILY

THIS is a summary of the legend of Fleur and Blanchefleur, or Floris and Blanchefleur—the flower with red petals and the white flower—the legend of the Rose and the Lily. There are several versions of the original poem, the earliest one published in France about 1160.[46]

This charming story has an oriental flavour, but undoubtedly originates in its published form in the West of Europe. It is a most wonderful example of the way in which deep spiritual impulses underlying the history of the world could be given out in legendary form.

There were two child lovers, whose love was pure and steadfast and outlived all tribulation. The children were real people. Blanchefleur, the " Lily ", was the grandmother of Charles the Great on the mother's side.[47] Floris, the " Rose ", according to the legend, was the son of Fenix, King of Spain, and the heir, through his uncle, of the kingdom of Hungary. History, however, reveals that he is *Charibert of Laon*.

Circumstances brought the mother of Blanchefleur and the mother of Floris together, and the children were born " on one day, in one house, in one hour ". It was on Palm Sunday. When the King of Spain observed how they loved each other, he wished to kill Floris, but the Queen pacified his anger. Nevertheless, she decided that they must be separated, and Floris

was to be sent to school in Andalusia. He consented
to go on condition that Blanchefleur was sent after him.
But she never arrived. For the Queen had sold her,
in return for a precious Cup, to merchants from
Babylon. The Cup was said to have been made by
Vulcan himself, and on it was engraved the meeting
of Paris with Athene, Juno, and Venus. Blanchefleur
was bought from the merchants by an Eastern ruler,
Amiral, and imprisoned in a tower. Meanwhile,
Floris returned from school and was told that Blanchefleur was dead. Her grave was shown to him, with the
wondrous shrine that covered it.

On the shrine was carved a representation of Floris
himself offering Blanchefleur a Rose, while she offered
him a Lily of burnished gold. The shrine had many
other marvels: the elements themselves lived in it as
wind and perfume and healing balsams that streamed
from the tomb and gave movement and life to the
carvings. When Floris was told that Blanchefleur was
dead he threatened to kill himself, so great was his
sorrow. So there was nothing for it but to tell him what
had really happened, and when he heard it he determined to go in search of her. The horse that carried him
was half red and half white, the colours divided by a
line of black; and on its body were the words: " Only
he is worthy to ride me who is worthy of a crown."

Floris, after many adventures, reached his goal in a
land governed by seven kings. And there he found the
tower where Blanchefleur was imprisoned. There is a
graphic description of the marvels of this tower that
was illumined by a fiery carbuncle, and supplied with
springs of living water by a silver pipe in which the
water circulated up and down. Four watchers guarded
the tower, and seventy damsels lived in it. Floris
succeeded in obtaining access to Blanchefleur by

hiding himself, clothed in a red garment, in an enormous basket of red roses. But Amiral, the ruler of the tower, discovered him asleep with Blanchefleur and threatened them both with death. After extraordinary scenes, when each again and again begged to be slain in place of the other, Amiral had pity on them, and the sword fell from his hand. Floris and Blanchefleur were wedded, and lived till they were a hundred years old. They died " in the same hour and on the same day ".

This legend really tells us of one of the occasions in the history of the world when an attempt is made to unite the ancient and pure mystery wisdom with advancing Christian and " intellectual " civilisation. This intention was based on a profound knowledge of spiritual evolution, namely, that in the inspired wisdom of the past lay the key to the future development of the Christian impulse. In the eighth century the soul of Europe, which was in danger of being overwhelmed by the intellectual culture-stream of Arabia, longed for the " Lily " that was still fragrant in the East, while the Christianity of the West, nurtured on the soil of the Irish Mysteries, sought to unite itself with the " Lily " and the " Rose " in the quest of the Holy Grail. Four hundred years later, we find this longing in another form—for Platonism to be united with Aristotelianism; in short, everywhere where there are two things that are spiritually at one, and have to overcome their predestined temporary separation.

Charibert of Laon, the real Floris of the legend, journeyed to the East out of a similar impulse to that of Julian the Apostate—the desire to find the treasures of the old Persian Mystery-wisdom at the Court of the Caliphs. It was felt that the still untarnished remnants of Eastern wisdom should be the real bride of the Rose-soul of Western culture—before it could be ravished by the scientific intellectualism of Arabia.

What the soul of Europe sought, when the legend of the Rose and the Lily came to birth in the eighth century, and still seeks, is that inspired insight into the meaning of the Incarnation, Death, Resurrection and Ascension of Christ, which was almost quite lost after the first centuries of our era. The mystical Christianity that in the Middle Ages was still nourished by Platonic thought and the last echoes of Eastern wisdom, retained a perception of the meaning of the power of Christ to transform Nature; but the advancing intellectualism of the age required, not only to " feel " its reality but to grasp it in thought and idea; and this required the Aristotelian method of Scholastics. But in " thinking ", it may be that inspiration is gradually lost.

The alchemists of the secret brotherhoods alone, while they reverently handled the substances of Nature, could still experience something of the old rejoicing in the holiness of the Earth.

CHAPTER XIII

THE DAWN OF A NEW AGE

" Then from the dawn it seemed there came, but faint
As from beyond the limit of the world,
Like the last echo born of a great cry,
Sounds, as if some fair city were one voice
Around a King returning from his wars.

Thereat once more he moved about, and clomb
Ev'n to the highest he could climb, and saw,
Straining his eyes beneath an arch of hand,
Or thought he saw, the speck that bare the King,
Down that long water opening on the deep
Somewhere far off, pass on and on, and go
From less to less and vanish into light.
And the new sun arose bringing the new year."
(TENNYSON. *The Passing of Arthur.*)

I

AS we draw near the end of our wandering beside
this stream of ancient wisdom, let us look
where the last rays of the setting sun shed a glory
upon it before it sinks from our sight underground.

One of the greatest of the Druid centres was where
the Cathedral of Chartres now stands. The original
church was raised above a crypt where rested an
ancient pre-Christian Druid statue of the Virgin with
the Child in her arms. Her eyes were closed. Proph-
etically, the Mother of the World was represented
as having already passed into her long sleep, waiting,
like the old Heroes of the West, to be awakened by
the touch of a new Initiate, and so fulfil the age-old
prophecy that Isis-Sophia would come again and

kindle the light of cosmic wisdom once more in the
eyes of men. " *Notre Dame de Sous-terre* " the old
builders called her—the Virgin of the under-earth.

But also, this figure was a prophecy for a nearer
future. A tradition tells how many centuries before
the Incarnation, the Druids in Chartres received a
revelation that a Virgin would appear who would
bear a Child, and this Child would bring salvation to
the world. So they built an altar in her honour, and
wrote upon it *Virgini parituræ*, " the Virgin who will
give birth ". And on the altar they placed a statue
of her with the Child on her lap, and founded a cult
and offered sacrifices to her.

Similar temples consecrated to the Virgin arose in
many parts of Gaul. Tradition tells us further that
when at last the Druids found that many strange
wonders were taking place—as we have already told
in the Irish legend of Conchubar—they knew that
the Saviour had been born; and they made a hymn
O gloriosa Domina, and publicly worshipped the
Virgin in the Grotto where her statue had been placed,
and where the Cathedral of Chartres now stands.

The statue has disappeared; but the inspiration of
her presence remained; and for hundreds of years
Chartres was perhaps the greatest centre of culture and
learning and the spiritual life to be found in the whole
world.

But it has a special interest for us in connection with
our subject, because Chartres was the place above all
others where the last echoes of the Mystery-wisdom of
the Greeks lingered on in the Christianity of the great
Platonists, until the end of the twelfth century. It is as
though they could still touch with spiritual hands and
see with spiritual eyes the splendid ethereal Imaginations which the ancient Druid seers had moulded in

the vapours of their incense and coloured with rainbow tints from the Cauldron of Ceridwen: and this atmosphere nourished what awoke in their own souls as they studied the Platonic philosophy and dreamed of the golden Persephone.

How much more significance *places* have than we ever imagine to-day! How little we realise with what care and what vision they were chosen, so that the living Earth should pour into the atmosphere what was needed for a particular cult—whether of moisture, or dryness, or heat, or cold, whether of iron or copper or lead or sparkling silica, or the " magnet's invisible passion "!

See how beautifully Platonic thought, breathed into Christianity, could feel itself at home amid the ethereal imaginations of the vanished Druid Mysteries. Rudolf Steiner summarises this:

. . . " God lies hidden spellbound in the world, and you need His own power to find Him. You must awaken that power in yourself. . . . Where is God? This was the question asked by the soul of the Mystic. God is not existent, but Nature exists. And in Nature He must be found. There He has found an enchanted grave. It was in a higher sense that the Mystic understood the words ' God is love '. For God has exalted that love to its climax, He has sacrificed Himself in infinite love, He has poured Himself out, is scattered in the manifoldness of Nature. Things in Nature live, and He does not live. He slumbers within them. We are able to awaken Him; if we are to give Him existence, we must deliver Him by the creative power within us.

" The candidate now looks into himself. As latent creative power as yet without existence,

the Divine is living in his soul.   In the soul is a
sacred place where the spellbound god may wake
to liberty.   The soul is the mother who is able to
conceive the god by Nature.   If the soul allows
herself to be impregnated by Nature, she will
give birth to the Divine.   God is born from the
marriage of the soul with Nature, no longer a
" hidden ", but a manifest god.   He has life, a
perceptible life, wandering amongst men.   He is the
god freed from enchantment, the offspring of the
God who was hidden by a spell.   He is not the great
God, who was and is and is to come, but yet he
may be taken, in a certain sense, as a revelation of
Him.   The Father remains at rest in the unseen;
the Son is born to Man out of his own soul.   Mystical
knowledge is thus an actual event in the cosmic
process.   It is the birth of the Divine.   It is an event
as real as any natural event, only enacted upon a
higher plane. . . .   The uninitiated man has no
feeling for the Father of that god, for that Father
slumbers under a spell.   The son appears to be born
of a Virgin, the soul having seemingly given birth
to him without impregnation.   All her other children
are conceived by the sense-world.   Their father
may be seen and touched, having the life of sense.
The Divine Son alone is begotten of the hidden,
eternal, Divine Father Himself."*

In the centuries preceding the culmination of the
" glory of Chartres " many beautiful things were
written about the Virgin.   It seemed as though a
heavenly radiance shone out all over Europe from Her
throne there.   Fulbertus, Bishop of Chartres in the
tenth century, wrote of Her:

* *Christianity as Mystical Fact.*

" She who is to give birth to the greatest King
    The Sun of Righteousness
  Maria, Star of the Sea, approaches her rising to-day,
  Rejoice, ye faithful, and behold the Light divine! "

Fulbertus' whole life was influenced by his devotion to the Virgin; it was more than devotion in its intensity and rapture. His worship of the " Star of the Sea " communicated itself to everything that went out from the School of Chartres over the whole of Europe. It is said of him that he was the first to discover the real date of the birth of the Virgin Mary, as September 8th, and that he founded a permanent festival in honour of it.

Up to about the thirteenth century the Virgin was thought of more as the Queen of Heaven—throned in majesty among the stars. " Later, she drew nearer and nearer to the more immediate life of human feeling . . . in the thirteenth and fourteenth centuries becoming more and more an image of human womanly love and charm. Then she entered completely into the realm of human feeling. The *Minnedienst* (Minnesingers) is rooted in this Mary-worship."*

So in Chartres, saturated with the atmosphere of the Mysteries of the West and of Greece, and crowned with the star-radiance of the Virgin of the World, a Christianity and a learning could be nurtured during the tenth, eleventh and twelfth centuries that still carried in its heart the afterglow of a vanishing and inspired wisdom.

The legend of the Rose and the Lily, told in the last chapter, was a secret record of the search for a way—undertaken already in the ninth century—of uniting esoteric Christianity, still imbued with the best elements of the old Mysteries (the " Lily ") with the

---

* Karl Heyer: *Das Wunder von Chartres.*

" Rose "; that is, with that part of the *spiritual* life of man which is destined to be the builder of external civilisations. But the twelfth century demanded an intellectual development in which this spiritual union was not possible. Outwardly, the strife between Church and State was for a time the pivot around which all political events turned.

The Lily is not so perfect a flower as the Rose.

The Angel Gabriel carried the Lily to the Virgin as the sign of the coming of the Rose; the most perfect flower, Love, was to blossom not in the Heavens like the white Lily of an unearthly wisdom, but on the Earth. This was the lesson mankind had to learn.

In the secret schools of the Order of the Holy Grail, the pupils were taught that though they had gained all wisdom, and might see themselves in vision in the white garment of the Lily, yet its perfume was not pure, and the Lily must become like the Rose, red with the blood of the heart's love. Lily and Rose must be one.

The legend of Floris and Blanchefleur is a legend that tells deep secrets also of England and France. Here, in the early Middle Ages, was the stage where the drama was concentrated, of the first beginnings of the epic struggle to bring to the soul of Europe a realisation that the Rose, already wandering for centuries on the Earth seeking to be united with the Lily, and fearful of its ravishment by a merely material intellectualism, must at last gather the Lily to its heart and create an earthly civilisation that could *prepare* the world for universal love, born out of the lap of wisdom.

In Britain the Rose became the national emblem. It sprang originally from Wales—last stronghold of Druidism—from the house of Owen Tudor. The

Fleur de Lys (Lily) of France, the national emblem from the twelfth century, is really the *Fleurs de Luce*—the Flowers of the Light: the three petals of the heraldic lily are the *Three Rays of Light*, once sacred to the Druids of Gaul and Britain as the threefold utterance of the Name of God.*

The Rose, as symbol within symbol, is Druidic too; it is the fiery girdle of the Druids' Divinity Hu-Jesus of whom we have already told. But *then*, the " Rose " was still in the Heavens. Only when Christ's love—the true Rose—permeated the Earth and transformed Nature, could the ancient Mystery wisdom with its " flowers of the light " be united with the earthly symbol of the Rose, as the symbol of self-knowledge and selflessness. This is the herald of a future in which *human* wisdom will be founded on Divine Love.

The history of England and the history of France were woven inseparably together until the early part of the fifteenth century. It was only then that the Folk-Soul of the English people could begin its own independent existence under the earthly symbol of the Rose.

But the *spiritual* link is never broken: the Rose is everywhere on Earth; the Lily is everywhere in Heaven. Nevertheless: " *Heaven and Earth have kissed each other*," as the Psalmist sang.

When all men recognise that, there will be peace.

2

If we look at the England of that time we see a remarkable development going on, the struggle for the accomplishment of the real birth of the English Folk-Soul, incarnating into, and striving to bring into a harmony, all the various elements of its composition.

* Chapter I.

We said just now that places were important. It seemed as though the actual " earth " of Western Britain were still so alive under the cloud that had fallen over its ancient sanctuaries, that it had a repellent power—built around itself a spiritual wall, against which, in Ireland and in Wales, no arrogant conqueror could prevail. The " English " and the " Britons ", the latter with their predominating Celtic blood, were not yet welded together. The former were advancing towards a real self-conscious Ego-hood; the latter were still a people into whom their " earth " breathed the old indeterminate dreamlike qualities, a heritage for which they fought like those who are fired by a blood-feud, with passion and conviction and incomparable heroism. They were a hard problem for the fiery Norman Kings; but a problem which, for the time being, could wait, while the complicated internal history of Europe in its hither and thither between rebellious crowned heads and papal supremacy was absorbing all attention, while Popes excommunicated Emperors and Emperors deposed Popes. . . .

One can get the strangest impression if one looks on the one hand at the seething turmoil of nations in the throes of making, and on the other hand at the under-currents of the spiritual life—the secret brotherhoods, the noble schools of learning standing at the cross-roads between Platonic and Aristotelian modes of thought; and in the West, the mystical legendary life of soul, that waited for its longed-for fulfilment and believed utterly in the return of King Arthur and a re-birth of some half-understood and half-forgotten glory. Neither Danes (except for a single century), nor Saxons, nor Romans, nor Normans, had succeeded in prevailing against the Celtic-Gaelic soul.

There were three human beings in the twelfth century who seem to have been focal points in the consummation of the immediate destiny of England, spiritually and externally, and so bringing about something like the actual birth of the English folk-soul at the very moment when the old epoch of civilisation (the fourth, which had lived itself out under the predominating influence of Greece and Rome) was entering into its final century of preparation for the fifth—our own Anglo-Saxon-Germanic age of culture.

These three human beings were bound together in a strange knot of personal, and world, destiny. They were Henry II, Thomas à Becket, and John of Salisbury; and they played out their drama in the last half of the twelfth century.

They seem like separate embodiments of the three qualities of the soul of a people: Henry, the force of Will, John of Salisbury the power of Thought; Becket, the sacrificial element of the life of Feeling, caught up between the other two, swayed by both, and dominating both, yet spiritually freed from both by his martyrdom.

This is not a " history " book; but let us look at a few pictures connected with these three souls, which may help to suggest to the reader something of the underlying character and significance of this century in relation to what has already been described in earlier chapters.

The age was the age of the great struggle of the Church to free itself from secular control and all its attendant evils, a struggle so brilliantly inaugurated by Gregory VII. The monastic systems of that time had a great civilising influence in the midst of the endless quarrels of kings and barons, Normans and Saxons, and the oppressions of the poor; and the

allegiance of the people either to the Church or to the
State must have been quite as much a question for
them of comparative comfort or comparative misery
as a question of religion or loyalty. And two outstanding events enormously strengthened the ascen-
dancy of the Church; one was the excommunication
of Henry IV (of Germany) for daring to depose the
Pope, and his subsequent submission and spectacular
penance: the romantic story of his standing in the
snow barefoot for three days, whether true or not,
at least emphasises the prevailing dominant idea of the
all-importance of penitence and of exhibiting it,
publicly. A hundred years later Henry II of England
made his great act of penance too, stripped and flogged
at the altar of Canterbury for the murder of Thomas à
Becket. Thomas's death really set the final seal to the
end of the last degenerate efforts on the part of the
secular power to hold to what had long since vanished,
the ancient belief in the divine overshadowing of
kings—once a reality in the initiation of all rulers—
and its acceptance of them as " Kings and Priests
unto God ".

It is the final passing of the dominance of the Sword
as a sign of *divine*, not brutal, authority, to the dominance of the Word, and the degeneration of the authority
of the Sword. The " Sword " was once an emblem
of the Sun—it was the Sun-ray, or the " golden
plough " for the furrowing of the Earth—a symbol
created by the ancient wisdom that could behold the
glory of Nature and love her as her champion and
fight for the peace of her.

The same problem faces the eleventh and twelfth
centuries—but quite metamorphosed—as in the great
enigmas of the Hibernian statues, and in the legend of
the Lily and the Rose; but being played out now on

the stage of the external life, by the Will, the Thought, and the Feeling of the European soul, in the personalities of Henry II, John of Salisbury, and Becket.

3

" Learning " was the greatest of all professions; and learning was inevitably allied to the ecclesiastical life. The Church alone showed the way to its supreme achievement.

John of Salisbury is said to have represented the very flower of English learning. He began life, like Thomas, as a secretary at the Court of Archbishop Theobald at Canterbury (1154); Thomas turned his attention to specialising in canon law, became first of all Chancellor of England, and at last Archbishop; but John followed the path of philosophy, his other appointments being in some sense secondary to the dominating passion of his soul, learning. Their friendship was a life-long one. John dedicated his books to, and wrote them for, Thomas; was always his counsellor; always, with his calm foresight endeavouring to restrain Thomas's ardour and impetuosity; always trying to bring about, in later years, a reconciliation between Becket and the King; sharing his exile with his friend; being present with him at least on the day of his death—but, as it seems, fleeing at the last from the sight of its atrocious fulfilment.

There is a little story of John as a child which throws some light on the continued existence, within the Church, of decadent methods of clairvoyance, and reveals the " Thinker " in John very delightfully; it is typical of what was so urgent an element in the culture of the Middle Ages—the flight from all remnants of the old clairvoyance towards the development of the intellectual soul and reliance on individual reasoning. John tells the story himself in his *Poli-craticus*:*

"It happened that he" (his priestly tutor) "made me and a boy somewhat bigger than I, after some unholy preliminaries, sit at his feet and apply ourselves to this sacrilegious business of 'scrying', so that what he sought to know might by our means be revealed to him, either in nails smeared with some consecrated oil or chrism, or in the smooth polished body of a basin. When then, some names having been invoked, which, child as I was, I judged from the horror I felt at hearing them, to be the names of evil spirits . . . I for my part proved myself so blind a scryer that I could see nothing there but the nails or basin or other familiar objects. So I was after this considered useless for this sort of employment, and was sentenced as one whose presence was a hindrance to these sacrilegious proceedings, never to come near when such were in hand; and as often as it was intended to engage therein I was shut out as an impediment to any sort of divining. So gracious was the Lord to me in my tender age."

Further on in the book he expresses himself quite plainly on the subject of omens and magical practices and dreams, but with careful and thoughtful discrimination concerning the value or worthlessness of all the many different kinds of such things which were so familiar to most people at that time.

A wonderful clarity of thought shines out like a lamp over John's whole life, and is what makes him an outstanding representative of the culture whose most perfect expression was to be found in the great School

* *John of Salisbury*. By Clement C. J. Webb.

of Chartres—where he afterwards ended his days as
Bishop—and when the whole climax of the old age and
the preparation for the new, in the realm of Thought,
culminated in the passing over from the rule of the
Platonists to the rule of the Aristotelians.

To understand this moment in history, and the
personality of John of Salisbury, is to understand more
clearly the other aspects of this threefold human drama
which we shall come to presently.

For a long time after the closing of the old Mysteries
their echoes remained; but in what way? In such
a way that there was still a vivid awareness of the
living dead.

Right on into the twelfth and thirteenth centuries
men who were striving to adapt themselves to the more
intense intellectual form of thinking, felt themselves
" haunted " by the thoughts of the dead that came to
them vividly and with immense reality. The great
battle that was waged by the leading thinkers of the
Scholastic period against the long-dead Averroes,
whose doctrines concerning " universal " immortality
they strove to refute, is only to be accounted for by
this fact (evident in many other ways), namely, that
the spiritual consciousness could still gain access to
the so-called dead in the spiritual world even if only
in a shadowy way. We may think the writings of that
period dry and uninteresting, but every thought had
been won by struggle, the struggle for a *free* self-
conscious expression. The Platonists of the earlier
years of the Chartres period had not yet reached the
climax of the endeavour to " claim thoughts as their
own property " as against the impersonal, universal
view of thought held by such philosophers as Averroes.

The Platonic philosophers (and " philosophers "
were not " dreamers ", but active men) were still

nourished by the echoes of the old " cosmic thinking "
—(they felt thoughts *coming to them* from spiritual
realms rather than from their own heads)—which
linked them still with the past ages of Mystery-wisdom.
But even they could only look back upon the greatness
of that wisdom as upon a phantom. The Cistercians
were those who felt this influence the most deeply.
The Dominicans were more under the influence of
Aristotelian methods.

It is hardly possible, I believe, for us even faintly to
imagine the enthusiasm that men of that time carried
into their ideas. We have discussions enough in these
days, and opinions, and we " think " with a certain
nonchalance and attach far more importance to the
effects of our thoughts than to Thought itself. But
then, to think, to have certain views of life and the
world, was dramatic in the extreme, and it could
culminate as real tragedy in any human soul that was
caught up in the vital spiritual warfare of thought—
amid the echoes of the Mysteries, the voices of the
dead, the whole enormous birth-throes that heralded
individuality in thought and in the hope of immortality.

John, like Bernard of Chartres, Theodoric of
Chartres, Bernadus Sylvestris, William of Conches,
and Abelard of Bath, tried to harmonise Plato and
Aristotle:

" They based their philosophy on Plato, but at the
same time endeavoured, in order not to come into
opposition with Aristotelian authority, to harmonise
the views of both these thinkers. John of Salisbury
regarded Plato and Aristotle with equal love, seeing
in Plato the scientific advocate of an ideal world-
conception, and in Aristotle the master and method-
creator of scientific research."[48]

Clerval describes the teachers of Chartres as "Christian philosophers", pupils of Plato in regard to doctrine, and of Aristotle in regard to method.

Rudolf Steiner says:

"The world-conception of Aristotle is not really opposed to that of Plato. The difference between them consists rather in the *way* in which both men are captured by different sides of Reality—the world of ideas, and the world of the senses. For Plato, the world of the senses is only a preliminary stage from which one rises to the world of Ideas; the former has no other importance except as the means for reaching the latter. With Aristotle it is the opposite: he desired first to explain the world of sense, and *through* this explanation, to reach the Ideas. One can say that actually the two philosophers share the same view; only they are interested in it from opposite sides."

Karl Heyer points out* that he who only sees a chasm between these two philosophers is really destroying the *continuity of the spiritual evolution of man*, while he who sees the harmony between them upholds that continuity. "The later intellectual conception of the world had to be joined—as by a process of growth—to the earlier *vision* of the world." "Both streams are a world-historical unity in the spiritual life of mankind. Platonism looks back to a pre-existence, the time before birth, but also indicates the need for an eschatology. In Plato, a mighty human Past is sounding to its end; in Aristotle, are the great impulses for the Future. Plato looks to the East; Aristotle to the West, revealing how the ancient

* Ibid.

visionary wisdom must be replaced by concepts of Thought."

I have written at some length of these things because the turn of the eleventh and twelfth centuries was in every way the moment of the final passing—as represented in the great leaders of external culture if not yet fully in all domains of life—of the long-continued afterglow of the old Mysteries. And it is necessary to emphasise the suggestion contained in the words " the continuity of the spiritual evolution of man ". No matter what apparent chasms are rent in the sequence of external historical events, the spiritual evolution of man passes in reality quite harmoniously from stage to stage; and at every point it is possible to trace, in single individuals, real foci where all the threads are visibly gathered together, representatively, in qualities either of will, or thought, or of feeling.

And so we find that what first showed itself only in secret in the Mysteries, becomes externalised, undergoes continual transformation, but is always there as the message of the " Way, the Truth, and the Life ".

4

In Henry II, intimate friend, companion, and bitter enemy of Thomas à Becket, we see in another form the external reactions of this hidden progress. John is always—like our own powers of thinking—a mediator between the turbulence of the will and the fluctuations of feeling, till he too rouses the enmity of the King and is, at one point, in danger of his own life.

It is not my task here to enter into the details of Henry's reign, or to describe his life at length. All that can be read elsewhere. We picture him as " a man of iron physique, with broad shoulders, red hair, large head and curiously harsh voice. He inherited from his father an insistent restlessness, and from his mother courage, firmness of purpose, and the Norman genius for rule . . . He was well-read for a man of his day, eager in his conversation, generally indifferent to religion, with intervals of terrified superstition. His nature was cold and cautious, but even kings share human inconsistency, and his determined policy was frequently interrupted by violent fits of passion. He loved order and discipline, and it was this passion that enabled a king who never spoke a word of English, and spent a comparatively short time of his reign on English soil, to become the actual father of English law."*

His life was in many ways a deeply tragic one. One imagines him as a man born before his time, as one predestined to represent the unripe but vigorous forces of the Ego—(ripened only in our own day)—plunged into its first immature contact with the unbridled will-forces of a nation struggling into birth. He represented in his own being a picture of the titanic effect of mankind to overcome the old hereditary instincts—subconsciously—and prepare the way for the " I am ". He endured at times the bitter solitude of soul that this engenders. He was a man without a nation, though he ruled over vast territories in one, and was the crowned King of another. He fought for the creation of a new Folk-Soul. And his destiny, time and again, brought him to the events that made this possible. John of Salisbury was the instrument that brought one of these events to his hand.

It was during one of John's many visits to the Pope Adrian that, as he tells us himself:

* Sydney Dark's *St. Thomas of Canterbury.*

" It was at *my request* " (my italics) " that he granted
to the illustrious King of the English, Henry the
Second, the hereditary possession of Ireland, as
his still extant letters attest; for all islands are
reputed to belong by a long-established right to
the Church of Rome, to which they were granted
by Constantine, who established and endowed it.
He sent moreover by me to the King a golden ring,
adorned by a fine emerald, in token of his investiture
with the government of Ireland; and this ring is
still, by the King's command, preserved in the
public treasury."*

Twenty years later Henry was ready to subdue the
unsubduable Ireland, and before the end of his reign
the " ancient Paradise " was organised (as well as
might be) by Henry's juridical genius and was in the
restless occupation of the Norman barons. Another
milestone was reached and passed.

But before this another event had stamped its tragic
seal into his passionate life. At Christmas time, in
the year 1170, his furious outburst against Becket—
his cry that not one of his courtiers " will deliver me
from this low-born priest "—bore its bitter fruit, and
Becket's blood was shed on the altar-steps of Canterbury Cathedral, " for the preservation of God's
Church—not Henry's ", as the dying Becket cried.

Europe was horrified enough. But Henry was pursued as if by Furies. He could not rest. " He may
rather be said to fly than go by horse or boat," it was
said of him. He fled from England to Ireland, from
Ireland to Wales, from Wales to France.... And at last,
in 1174, he walked barefoot to Canterbury, knelt and
kissed the place where Becket had died. He went

* From the *Metalogicon*, of John of Salisbury.

down into the crypt, removed his cloak, revealing his hair-cloth shirt, and kneeling with his head and shoulders on the tomb " received five strokes from each of the bishops, and three strokes from each of the eighty monks who were present ". And all night he stayed there, fasting.

For the time, at least, his fiery will was brought into subjection, not to the Ego in him, but to Thomas— to the heart.

I do not want to weigh and criticise nor attempt to balance up the conflicting historical opinions concerning either Becket or Henry; but only to present pictures. Before we come to the final one, let us try to see Becket as he appears in the circle of the destiny of this trilogy of human beings.

5

The personality of Thomas à Becket presents a great problem; and the opinions that have been expressed about him vary considerably. But he is a problem to us first because the age in which he lived was at the cross-roads, and secondly because we have lost the capacity to feel that vital and intense devotion, that consuming fire, which entered into all questions of feeling and of religion, and especially of thought and philosophy, at that time.

Becket and Henry II had been friends and companions even in their youth, and Becket's destiny from the beginning had seemed to point to a life of secular activity rather than to that of celebrated Churchman. As Chancellor of England he was the confidant and loyal friend of the King, and his responsibility towards the well-being of the Church was, after all, implicit rather than necessarily explicit. But he knew that the King was fully determined to maintain or assert his authority, if necessary, against all papal rulings, over ecclesiastical appointments and jurisdiction. When Henry made up his mind that Becket should be Archbishop of Canterbury, expecting that he would remain on his side, and not on that of the Pope, Thomas saw himself faced by the inevitable crisis which his appointment must bring about: as highest representative in England of the Roman Church, he must be loyal to that Church and so to the Pope, and to be loyal to the Pope meant accepting the bitterness of a broken friendship and the loss of every worldly advantage that accrued from it.

Some historians see in Thomas's acceptance of the See of Canterbury an act of treachery against and betrayal of his friend the King. But that is an " arm-chair " judgment. Thomas repeatedly warned the King what his course of action would have to be; and he began by resigning his Chancellorship against the King's wish, who desired him to occupy both the secular and the spiritual positions together.

We must try, I think, to see in this astonishing crisis in Thomas's life something that is fully representative of the spiritual undercurrents that flow—generally quietly and unknown to us—through every single human life of normal span. Thomas was forty-four years old when he had to make this momentous decision. We have already suggested that in these three human beings are to be found, in Henry the Will, in John the Thought, and in Becket the Feeling of the changing age. Feeling is of the heart, and in the heart there springs always the hidden fountain of spiritual guidance that leads men to the fulfilment of their real destiny. It works so that for the first half of human life there is all that which is bound up with circumstances: with heredity, with environment, the building of qualities of character, the predestined meetings with all those persons and influences which are necessary factors in the creation of any really *significant* human life. (And I am speaking only of these.)

The second period is the period of fulfilment. When the destiny of a nation, of a cause, of an age, concentrates itself in some individual, all this is emphasised a thousandfold. Look in history, and you will find it!

Columba, leader of an earlier transition, entered his stage of fulfilment at the age of forty-two, when he went from Ireland to Iona.

Dante has immortalised this secret of human life in the opening words of his *Divina Commedia*: " Nel mezzo del cammin di nostra vita " . . . He was thirty-seven when his whole life was reversed and he began his twenty years of exile, without which the world's greatest work of art would never have been created.

That the crisis occurs a few years earlier or later than the age of forty-two is no contradiction of this spiritual law, for the years between thirty-five and forty-two— the middle of our span of seventy—constitute the period of inner and subconscious preparation for the " fulfilment ".

With the remarkable reversal of the course of his life, Becket began to play his part in *world*-destiny. This destiny, at that time, was in the hands of the Roman Church. But why? Because that stream of the spiritual life of Europe was the instrument, already prepared in the ninth century, whereby the development of purely intellectual thought, and through it, the later rise of natural science, was given its most inviolable foundation.

It had to be so. Every remnant of the old Mystery
teachings, whether concerning Nature or the esoteric
(and so-called heretical) doctrines of Christianity, or
the deeper secrets of the subconscious life of the soul,
had slowly and relentlessly to be thrust into the background; for the old clairvoyance had almost quite
died out and something else had to replace it. Nevertheless, the Mystery-Wisdom remained, but concealed
below the surface of life, fostered by small circles of
people who were persecuted or suppressed if they were
discovered; until the majority of them, in their turn,
became decadent and insincere, and only a few
were left to preserve what they could of the ancient
wisdom for the future. The age of materialism was
heralding its approach.

Had Becket a gift of seership?—no uncommon thing
still, even in those days; and no uncommon thing for
men suddenly, in the middle of their path of life, to
forefeel the future, not clearly perhaps, but with that
instinctive wisdom that still had ears for the " words
out of the heart ".

His decision—the heart against the dominant will
and against the clarity of thought—awoke in him the
dormant Ego—the " voice crying in the solitude "—
and he knew himself. He became a lover of humanity
and a servant of God. He knew well enough what he
had to expect, but pursued his way to the very end,
still with the old fire and ardour—and sometimes
petulant anger—that had so endeared him to the
King.

John of Salisbury tried to smooth things over between the King and Thomas. But his part in the
drama was, I think, one that flowed more evenly
and perhaps unconsciously through the realm of
thought that, in its temperatures and movements,

was like the air in which the spirit of the coming age could breathe. Henry was the instrument in the construction of its body.

The end of Thomas's exile in 1170 and his return to England under the truce of a diplomatically arranged reconciliation with the King, deceived nobody, and certainly not Thomas, who was convinced that he was doomed.

He came home to die. It is in the life and death of Thomas à Becket that we know the perfume of the Lily that has become the Rose—the selfless release of the spirit from the body—the power of self selflessly abandoned in the cause of love.

6

The final scene of this world-drama with its three human actors is still to tell.

Again I say that this is not a history book, and so we are free to admire the genius of tradition which gives us the last picture, at the close of the last decade but one of the twelfth century.

Becket was dead; his memory was immortalised by the love he had aroused in the hearts of the people. John was made Bishop of Chartres ten years after the tragedy of Canterbury, and was still living. Henry, tormented by remorse, saddened by the rebellion and later by the death of his sons, broken by wars in France, was near his end. His son John had been driven from his insecure kingship of Ireland. Wales was not yet subdued. The soul of the Welsh people was fervently awaiting the return of King Arthur, and was impregnable in its faith. . . . Let us see how the eye of modern scholarship looks at our last picture whose tale is told by the historian Giraldus Cambrensis and others,[49] and has been retold many times in various accounts of the history of Glastonbury. It is the story of the discovery of the tomb and the bodies of King Arthur and Gwenevere.

[50] " The monks of Glastonbury pretended that their founder was Joseph of Arimathea, whom they represented, as already mentioned, as the *first* to convert the people of this country to Christianity. According to their fabulous assertions the claims of the Church of Rome to supremacy in matters relating to the faith in this realm had no foundation in history; and this fell in well with the views of Henry II whose differences with the Papacy culminated in the murder of Becket. The King is said to have had the pretensions of Glastonbury examined and approved; for they struck not only at Rome but also at St. David's and the traditions of the Welsh, who were a source of annoyance to Henry. So in 1189 the said monks required the King's favour by discovering at Glastonbury the tombs of Arthur and Gwenevere. This discovery was calculated to discourage the troublesome Welshmen who were credited with looking forward to the return of Arthur to lead them to victory over all their enemies."

Whatever part the monks of Glastonbury or Henry himself are said to have played in this event is unimportant. What *is* important is that here is the sure touch of the hand of destiny; that here the curtain is finally rung down on the ancient Mysteries of Britain— and of the world. For the word goes forth that *Arthur is dead.* . . .

From John of Salisbury's childish horror of the " scrying " priest; from the dawn of his friendship with

Becket; from the emerald ring that he brought as the seal of Ireland's fate; from Henry's genius for organisation and law-making and his thirst for power to carry them out untrammelled by the Holy See; from Becket's decision and the tragedy of his broken friendship and his martyrdom—step by step the foundations of a new age are secretly laid in sorrow; and finally unveiled when the stones are turned back in Avalon and the light falls on the golden hair of Gwenevere and turns it into dust.

CHAPTER XIV

CONCLUSION

" Spiritual knowledge is transmuted *through its own nature* into love. . . . Wisdom is the necessary condition for love; love is the fruit of wisdom, reborn in the Ego."

(STEINER.)

I

THE Mysteries have in reality never died out. They have only changed.

If the reader has been able to guess at this from these few chapters, they will not have been written in vain. But we must be quite clear as to the nature of the metamorphosis through which the consciousness of humanity has passed up to our present time. What was once experienced as inviolably secret in the ancient sanctuaries as the spiritual vision of that which Lessing has called the " education of the human race ", has now become physical fact.

The problem of Hibernia—which was the parent of every Mystery school in ancient times—meets us in almost every problem and situation of our modern life. We have daily to come to grips with it. The raising of Lazarus—an evidence of the reality of spiritual enlightenment—was the last witness of the old *method* of initiation; and it was enacted openly. It was a clear assertion that there are no more secrets; and the beginning of the Gospel of John tells us why: The Word, the Creator of the Earth, formerly sought and found in the old Mysteries during a condition of soul

that was an *escape* from the body, this Eternal Word,
had been " made Flesh "; and it had to be recognised
by the disciples of Christ that His Incarnation changed
everything; because: " as many as received Him,
to them He gave the power to become Sons of God,[51]
even to them that believe on His Name."

The significance of this sentence lies in the words
" *He gave the power* ".

Formerly it was the great Priest-initiates who
bestowed this power by inducing a supernormal state
of consciousness in the neophyte; they performed
upon him a secret spiritual-magical action. They were
Magi in the true sense; but now their time was at an
end. Man had to find the way to spiritual enlightenment by voluntarily awakening his own forces of
Ego-hood: by " finding himself "—the " God within ".

But this could not happen suddenly for all people;
only for the few who in the early centuries of our era
were the first teachers and bearers of the Christian
way of initiation. The process of completing a *general*
metamorphosis of human consciousness is one that
must last even thousands of years; we are hardly at the
beginning of it, since man has to find Faith before he
can find Knowledge. This need not be wondered at,
considering that the old Mysteries ruled the world
for thousands of years too. But they ruled it as the
creators of earthly knowledge. The new Mysteries
must rule the world as the re-awakeners of spiritual
knowledge—to " bring all things to our remembrance ".

The history of this development resembles the history
of any single human life: from infancy, while the
course of childhood and adolescence and manhood
to full ego-consciousness is a gradual condensation or
contraction of divine creative powers into a single

entity; then a time of "living on the Earth as man", through maturity and old age, and at last the final expansion of the human spirit once more in the home of its origin. . . . The history of the Mysteries, and therewith the history of the general evolution of the consciousness of humanity, seems to pass through similar phases.

During the middle phase of "living on the Earth as Man", in the full possession of human faculties—and this phase covers our own time—does it not fall to the lot of each one of us to be brought face to face at some time or another with the real problem of our individual existence? Do we not ask: What am I? Whence have I come, and whither am I going? . . . Few in these days can find the Answerer! And the reason is partly because we have learnt that no individual life stands alone; it might not be so difficult to solve our *own* problems; but what is ours, is also humanity's. And that is the difficulty. Moreover, that awareness that we have of the whole world is itself a new revelation, brought about by modern discoveries. It is no longer an abstract conception, but an ever-present fact of our daily existence. The idea of "world-destiny" has taken the place of national or even of individual destiny. One has the feeling that now, for the first time, the entire world of humanity has *incarnated*; and over the entire world there rises from below, as in the case of single individuals too, the "shadow" of incarnation, the "counterfeiting spirit". And this too has been given a world-body, through the advent, throughout civilisation, of *electricity in the Machine*.

It is as though one could see, very far away, almost in another world, the tiny miniature picture—clear in its details and bathed in an unearthly spiritual radiance—of the lonely neophyte in Hibernia, in the presence of the towering and inscrutable symbols of cosmic Being and Becoming; while here and now, and close at hand, gigantic and overshadowing and omnipresent, the same symbols vastly delineated from horizon to horizon—that have now emptied themselves and scattered their divine offspring in every corner of the physical earth, as *human questions* in titanic conflict with the powers of the Depths.

Humanity is at the Threshold of the Incarnated Mysteries.

Let us glance at this evolution from a historical standpoint.

We need not here attempt to go further back than to the period which has been described as the third (post-Atlantean) epoch of culture, which found its highest manifestation among the Egyptian, Chaldean and Babylonian peoples; and during which we also find the early Hibernian-Druid Mysteries with their resulting culture in the West; and in the latter part of this epoch the segregation of the Hebrews under the leadership of Moses.

In the earlier part of this epoch, some three thousand years B.C., the rulership of the Priest-Kings was accepted as a self-evident rulership of divine beings: the Pharaohs were initiates conversant with the spiritual hierarchies above humanity who instructed them, through inspiration, in the Temples. When Priest-Kings issued from the Temples and went among the people, the very colours and forms of their clothing were ritually adapted to correspond with the colours and forms of supernatural vision. This was not a " vain show ", for the " light " of initiation could be perceived upon them by everybody according to the capacity of his or her normal and usual clairvoyance;

and the dress was therefore an expression of something that was a reality.

There is evidence of this in the Old Testament: . . .

> " When he came down from the mount, Moses wist not that the skin of his face shone while he talked with them. And when Aaron and all the children of Israel saw Moses, behold, the skin of his face shone; and they were afraid to come nigh him. . . . And till Moses had done speaking with them, he put a vail on his face. But when Moses went in before the Lord to speak with Him, he took the vail off, until he came out. . . . And the children of Israel saw the face of Moses, that the skin of Moses' face shone: and Moses put the vail upon his face again. . . ."[52]

So one can say of that age—at least up to the last third of it—that the spiritual world and spiritual beings were *present* in the physical world. The spiritual could be perceived interwoven in the physical. Human beings were not entirely limited to a physical consciousness.

In the next period (if we follow the precession of the equinoxes as marking the flowering of the culture epochs) is the Græco-Roman; and according to this method of calculation, it rises about the year 747 B.C. In this age it is not difficult to trace how *Theosophia* gives place to *Philosophia*; the spiritual consciousness begins to withdraw into an intellectual consciousness, and the earlier experiences of the presence of spiritual beings are " represented " rather than actual. Temple rites assume more and more a symbolic character, and surround the spiritual experiences as though with a veil. So in that period we have the great mystical dramas played before the celebration of the higher Mysteries. And we have too the great human tragedies, the noblest ever written. The spiritual world comes to be spoken of as a " world of shades "; while the inner content of the Mysteries passes in veiled forms into the philosophical literature of the Platonists and others, and clothes its ancient beauty in language that expresses the loftiest imaginable *thinking*.

The Romans had taken a step further than the Greeks away from spiritual experiences. Their mission was to establish human consciousness entirely upon the physical plane in an ideal of citizenship. The Mystery Schools, such as they then were, were gradually obliterated; and in this great transitional moment everything hung in the balance.

" The greater part of the Christian community— (about the fourth century A.D.)—opposed as it was by Roman unspirituality, still held fast to the esoteric Christianity of which it only gradually lost the understanding.   Slowly there grew up an immense fear of the Spirit, so much so that at the Ecumenical Council of 869 the Spirit was dogmatically set aside, and more and more the Life and Death of Christ was robbed, as time went on, of its supernatural character."[53]

". . . The rise of the Roman Empire took place under the still-continuing influence of spiritual forces that had held sway in earlier epochs of culture. . . . It was not until the commencement of Christianity that, in the time of the Cæsars, a veritable abyss of godlessness became manifest; and it was only *because* of the presence of Christianity—even though it was subject to persecution—in the very midst of the Roman people, that an actual step forward in evolution was rendered possible. History shows this fact of the progressive force of Christianity; although it was not fully understood, yet it *worked*, for its force was quite independent of human capacity to understand it."

The direct influence of the Græco-Roman period of culture ended in the fifteenth century; the revolutions of Time marked the commencement of our own epoch, the fifth of the post-Atlantean series, in the year 1413. Anyone can study the history of Europe during the fourteenth and fifteenth centuries and see how the Græco-Roman influence is still present; or can observe the way in which the Christian impulse, in its outer form, becomes—even through the instrument of the sword—the shaper of Europe. But the *undercurrents* of the religious life, the flowing of esoteric Christianity from Ireland over as far as Austria, the secret workings of the John-Christians in Middle Europe, the inner history of the Templars, of the Knights of the Holy Grail—all this is more difficult to trace, and more important than what it throws to the surface.

What appears on the surface is temporal. What works in secret is eternal.

The Græco-Roman age is the pivot upon which the great cycles of the evolution of the civilisations turned; and it was in this epoch that Christ appeared on Earth.

2

Now look once more at Merlin's legendary apple-orchard, with its 147 trees of " delicious fruit "; and at all the legends in all parts of the world that in one way and another are built up upon the number seven, or upon the number three with its repetitions and variations! Feel how in really ancient times, but most particularly in the East, there is no such thing as history as we understand it—as a succession or " straight line " of events; but Time appears as " revolutions " or recurrent cycles.

We say that history repeats itself; and in a sense that is true. But it no more repeats itself than one day or one season repeats itself. The days of the week, the months, recur—but they are never the same; the hands of the clock move over the same circle of symbols, but who could say they bring the same messages of birth and life and death? Nevertheless, all these things are in their way repetitions.

Humanity as a whole has looked at history from two different points of view. The old Eastern conception of Time was wholly a conception of repetitions —embodying the three principles of growth, maturity and decay; and in the decay lay the germ of a renewal of the similar. The conception of reincarnation in the East was fundamentally bound up with this. There was no beginning and no ending—but a " Wheel of Births ". There was no sense of history, history as a progressive succession of events, but cycles, revolutions of Time, subject to the " Wheel of the Law ".

Even as late as the time of the Orphic Tablets, the escape of the *initiate* from the dominion of remorseless cyclic repetitions is most beautifully expressed:

" I have flown out of the sorrowful weary Wheel.
  I have passed with eager feet to the Circle desired.
  I have entered into the bosom of Despoina Queen of the
      Underworld.
  I have passed with eager feet from the Circle desired.
  Happy and blessed one, thou shalt be God instead of
      mortal."

But the " sorrowful weary Wheel " gives place to other Circles—the heavenly ones—where the soul, after death, passes *to* and *from* (see above) the Circle *desired*—ever ascending.

How often in poetry is the simile of the Wheel used to express the inexorable endlessness in Time on Earth? . . . to " enter the ceaseless rings and never be quiet again ".*

But if we look at a later period, or to begin with to the impulses flowing through the Hebrew race, we find quite another conception of Time, a historical one. Steiner† points out this difference very clearly:

". . . One continuous path leads through the seven days of creation, through the period of the Patriarchs; from Abraham down through Isaac and Jacob. All is growth, all is history. Where is anything recapitulated? The first day of creation is not repeated in the second, even in the most abstract way; the Patriarchs are not recapitulated in the Prophets, the time of the Kings is not repeated in the Judges, and so on. Then follows the time of the captivity. . . . Through the whole of the Old Testament time is brought forward as a real factor in what takes place, quite apart from what is recapitulated. . . . The Old Testament offers the first great example of an historical aspect of things. . . . The East looks upon evolution as being like the yearly repetition of the growth of a plant. Thus in each epoch the several great Initiates appear and repeat what had taken place before, and the fact of this repetition is what is generally quoted. It was particularly emphasised in abstract fashion that

* Walt Whitman.

† *The Gospel of St. Mark.* Anthroposophical Publishing Company.

each Initiate was only a particular form of the One, who continues to evolve from epoch to epoch. . . . This leaning towards the One, the abstract devotion to the similar, is the reason of the non-historical aspect of all the conceptions of the pre-Christian ages—with the exception of the historical accounts given in the Old Testament. . . ."

These two views suggests that a new conception of history can perhaps dawn in our age, which shall combine these two: a conception that accepts the revolutions of Time in the periodic changes in civilisation, but sees them moving onward in accordance with the inherent nature of all that is *sevenfold*: three moving onward towards maturity (as in the life of every human being), then the focal point; and then the fruit of the earlier three.

If we accept this theory, then we cannot but see in the *fourth* (Græco-Roman) epoch of civilisation a great and significant turning-point, containing as it does the cosmic event foretold in the three preceding ages, the descent of the Logos, Who gives the impulse for the birth of a new world out of the old.

In Merlin's imagination of the orchard, he extends the sevenfold principle into the greater time-cycles, and so introduces fully the universal ancient conception of the revolutions of Time as born out of the creation and mobility of the seven planets of our system.

The prophet Ezekiel, when the heavens opened to his vision, saw four of the cosmic periods of Earth-evolutions that have passed—one of them now is passing—in the image of the four " living creatures " and their Wheels:

" The appearance of the wheels and their work was like unto the colour of a beryl: and they four had one likeness: and their appearance and their work was as it were a wheel in the middle of a wheel.

" When they went, they went upon their four sides: and they turned not when they went.

" As for their rings, they were so high that they were dreadful; and their rings were full of eyes round about them four.

" And when the living creatures went, the wheels went by them: and when the living creatures were lifted up from the earth, the wheels were lifted up.

" Withersoever the spirit was to go, they went, thither was their spirit to go; and the wheels were lifted up over against them: for the spirit of the living creature was in the wheels."*

And to St. John all the seven were revealed, the three, the one, and the three—the past, the present, and the future; he saw them under different aspects in the seven churches, the seven Angels, the seven seals, and the seven trumpets, and the seven Stars in the Hand of Him Who said that He was Alpha and Omega.

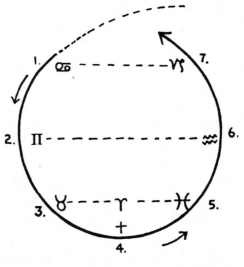

But to return to what is nearer to us. If the " earlier " is matured in the " later ", then it is clear that

* Ezekiel i, 16–20.

the cyclic revolutions, under the dominion of onward-moving Time, must bear some relation to one another —the later must be *in some sense* repetitions of the earlier; just as the latter part of human life is a working out of the earlier part—no matter what apparent irregularities may have intervened.

If this is so then the third would reappear transformed in the fifth, the second in the sixth, and the first in the seventh: " the first shall be last, and the last first ".

The Egyptian-Hibernian-Druid age would reveal itself again, but *metamorphosed*, in our own time. And, as though to suggest this possibility to us, it is only in the last century or so that we have " discovered " the Egyptian culture; and also only in the last century or so that what was inherent in a peculiar and secret way in the Mystery-wisdom of that time, as knowledge of magnetism and electricity, has emerged into the open, and become the dominating influence of our present age.

Again, the sacredness of the dead body to the Egyptians and their practice of mummification— the cult of the immortality of the human *form*— reappears before us to-day, but as intimate and intricate physical and morphological science, all of which is based, fundamentally, on a study, not of the living, but of the dead; but directed towards the promotion of life.

One could multiply such instances. The point is, however, not the repetition of the *similar*—(we canot, being different, repeat the Grecian culture for instance, though we may *imitate* it)—but the repetition of similar things in an evolved conception of the world; a repetition that reflects in a more advanced form the corresponding lower step in the evolution of the human race.

The whole of the Egyptian-Chaldean epoch was overshadowed by the essence of the wisdom of Hibernia—in the sphere of esoteric spirituality—for it was the *background* of the other Mysteries. In our own time its paradoxical problems are present in material facts.

3

Certainly an immense paradox was concealed in the symbolic presentation of the male and female statues in the Hibernian initiation; the paradox that though what appears in feminine *form* in the world is passive, yet the supersensible nature that lies behind it is *active*. On the other hand, what appears in masculine form presents outwardly the active principle, and inwardly the passive one. One must receive, the other give. But the aspect that is revealed on the physical plane is reversed on the spiritual plane.

In greater or lesser degree this paradox is always present in the sexes. Every man has the woman within him; every woman the man. This is well known. But it is also a fundamental principle of world-evolution, giving rise to a kind of cosmic conflict which urges evolution onwards towards its fulfilment. The fulfilment consists in the harmonising of these male-female principles.

We find them in nations, in epochs of civilisation, as in individuals—sometimes the spiritually active (feminine) and sometimes the spiritually passive (masculine) predominates. The physical masculine element, which is that of " Becoming " in the evolution of man on Earth, must gradually absorb more and more of the cosmic feminine, the active spiritual principle.

Expressed in another way, it is what is meant in the evolution of the " Rose and the Lily ".

We could follow this aspect of evolution if we wished to, in its many historical developments. Merely to make statements about it here would, however, be abstract and unreal.

Nevertheless it can be said that the whole question of Celticism in our own time presents this polarity too. There is, stirring beneath the surface of things, a secret urge towards the establishment of a new Celtic spirit—a desire for the birth of a purely external political " Celticism ". But this would only fall into line with much that is spiritually retrograde in our modern civilisation. The old Gods can no longer be invoked with impunity; the Folk-souls of the past have another mission to-day. Men are afraid of the real future, and seek refuge among the phantoms of other ages, into which they breathe the breath of their desire.

And this is the other pole: the Celtic Folk-soul is no longer the soul of *a people*, but the soul of a spiritual awakening of mankind. The blue mantle of Bride is his banner shaken out over the expectant heavens. " King Arthur " will not be roused by the blast of the horn of any national egotism, though it may shake the Earth; he will awake only at the touch of the " Woman of Beauty " who will " come into the hearts of men and women like a flame upon dry grass, like a flame of wind in a great wood ".

The Celtic Mysteries of old are the signature of our immortality. They are the ladder upon which Christian faith may mount to the stars. The Celtic Spirit that prepared the way for the Holy Grail is the Forerunner of all those Announcers of Christ, whose great procession will *follow* His " second coming ", when He is admitted at last into the hearts of the nation-souls of the world. In no external way should we dare to call this Celtic Spirit down into the councils of humanity, but only as a spiritual fertilising power.

The saying of St. Bride rings through the centuries as a cosmic utterance: " My mantle shall be laid on the Lord of the World "; for the Lord of the World is, in reality, the Christ, suffering in the darkness of human ignorance, on the *Earth*. And the real fulfilment of the words of Bride is to be found in the saying of St. Paul: " Not I, but Christ in me."

This foreshadows the marriage of the Rose and the Lily.

The late Rudyard Kipling felt, in his own inimitable way, the separation between the material building of a great civilisation and its spiritual background when he wrote his poem " *The Sons of Martha*."*

But Kipling did not see—perhaps—that these two opposites must not for ever run parallel; he did not sense the solution of the problem of their union. But he instinctively touches the very heart of it in the *Dedication* at the beginning of *The Years Between*. Read the poems; and you will see how this immense problem of outer material development—which contains the seeds of death—in opposition to inner spiritual force—in which lies the seed of the future— sends its scorpion-sting into the heart of a modern Bard. For Kipling was a " Bard " through the very fact that he could voice this problem in a poem which is the last modern expression of those anguished questionings of the human soul that once filled the dark Temples of Hibernia.

* Printed in the collection entitled *The Years Between*.

4

There is another side of the ancient Mystery-
wisdom of Hibernia which, in its metamorphosed
form, is pressing upon humanity to-day.

The secret of the " Double " has been touched upon.
But what is this secret in reality? . . . Long ago the
Earth was regarded as a living Being. Every part of
the Earth was felt to be alive, sending out quite
special forces (not everywhere the same) from its
different geographical areas, which directly influenced
the human beings who lived there; not determining
the ethnological varieties of the human race—for
these were believed to have another origin—but
working far more deeply than into mere type.[54] And
the forces that worked most strongly in human bodies
in the far West, were, as we have already mentioned,
of a magnetic-electrical nature. This was clearly
recognised, and feared; and intercourse with America
was purposely interrupted for a time, as the legend
of Odrun suggests, and documents prove.

If we would find a term that might most nearly
describe what the Earth-forces impart, we might say
it is a kind of " nature-psyche "; not a " folk-
psychology " so much as a living atmosphere of the
Earth-depths that is breathed into the physical body
at birth and tends to oppose what is celestial in the
soul. Spontaneous innate tendencies to organic forms
of illness are its fruits;[55] but it also influences the
trend of ideas. Modern psychology " feels " after the
" Double " but does not follow it into its place of
origin—the Earth. This may sound very fantastic—
though occult science knows it well; and at least
the idea of " geographical medicine " is not un-
familiar.

The Earth wishes—if one can say so—to be regarded as a complete whole. Every one of her influences has its right place and function; one can be balanced by another. The "Double" emerges in our own time beyond the limited sphere of the body. It shows its effects in the sphere of *economics*. What has awakened it there?—Electricity!—the dominion of the Machine! The machine is the incarnated Double of man. The "counterfeiting spirit" has clothed itself in iron and steel.

But more than that; for these forces of the living Earth, meant to be balanced and harmonised by her other forces of productivity, have crept into human ideas and they reflect the mechanical. Everywhere; in every sphere of thought. They build an ominous barrier between the sons of Martha and the sons of Mary, between the Rose and the Lily.

The people of olden times respected the Earth; and knew the unpreparedness of humanity to delve into her deeper secrets. Very touching are the old fables of propitiating the Earth—of asking her for the healing she could bestow to counteract the forces of the "Double". In Ireland still, a new-born child will be carried out of doors and its head gently laid against the kindly soil. . . . Endless are the tales of the subterranean fairy hosts and endless the allusions to the healing gifts of Nature for warding them off! And in any and every folk-lore there are to be found descriptions of illnesses that are only to be healed by a loving contact with the earth, the stones, the running water. . . .

It is as though we are told in fairy-tale and legend and myth: "Do not forget!—we are here to remind you, in your hour of darkness, of the mystery and wonder of your existence! Three children had the great Mother Ceridwen!—the daughter of vision, the child of utter darkness, and the son of serenity!— *Redeem the darkness through your vision, that ye may become the serene sons of the Dawn!* "

So we have come to the end—which is no end but a beginning—of our " ancient Mystery ". A jumble, you may say; a fantastic mixture of legend and superstition and pseudo-history. But perhaps, here and there, the innocent beauty of some old tale may have stirred your heart so that you had to say, " It is true."

The world magician has woven a beautiful tapestry and leaves the threads of it in our hands so that we may complete it; and in the centre a space is left for us in which to weave that Figure Whose Face and Form elude us still, though we have held the threads to fashion them with for two thousand years.

The perfume of the Rose is wafted to us, so cunningly has the world-magician woven it there; and the Lily gleams above it, and the letters that are worked into the borders I will write for you here:

" I will be as the dew unto Israel: he shall grow as the Lily, and cast forth his roots as Lebanon.

" His branches shall spread, and his beauty shall be as the olive tree, and his smell as Lebanon. . . . They that dwell under his shadow shall return: they shall revive as the corn and grow as the vine; the scent thereof shall be as the wine of Lebanon."

NOTES ON CHAPTERS

1. See " The Present Age ", quarterly magazine, in an article " Christmas Through the Ages ", Vol. I, 2 .

2. There was a second Zoroaster, 600 B.C. The first Zoroaster referred to above lived 6000 B.C., and the content of his teaching appears in the teaching of the second Zoroaster, in the " Zend-Avesta " . .

3. " Die Ægyptischen Pyramiden als Zeugen vergangener Mysterienweisheit ", by Ernst Bindel. (Publishing Company of the Free Waldorf School, Stuttgart) . . . . . .

4. A light of " Soul "; and so according to esotericism, connected with the Moon rather than the Sun .

5. " The Mission of the Folk-Souls in connection with Germanic and Norse Mythology ". Eleven lectures by Rudolf Steiner. (Anthroposophical Publishing Company) . . . . .

6. The " summer country " has been interpreted by some as referring to a South-Eastern region of Europe or Asia Minor, whence the Cymry are supposed to have come . . . . .

7. " The Secret of the West ". By Dmitri Merezhkovsky. English translation . . . . . .

8. See Rudolf Steiner's " Universe, Earth and Man "; " The Gospel of St. John ", and other works. (Anthroposophical Publishing Company) . .

9. The following is a fragment from a Celtic tale told in " Voyage dans le Finisterre " (1794):
" The Prince is carried up into the vortex of the moon. Here millions of souls traverse vast plains of ice, where they lose all perception but that of simple existence. They forget the course of the adventures

in which they have been engaged, and which they
are now to recommence. On long tubes of darkness,
caused by an eclipse, they return to earth. They are
revived by a particle of light from the sun, whose
emanations quicken all sublunary things. They
begin anew the career of life."

" Towards the disk of the sun, the young Prince
approaches, at first with awful dread; but presently,
with inconceivable rapture and delight. This
glorious body consists of an " assemblage of pure
souls ", swimming in an ocean of bliss. It is the
abode of the blessed—of the sages—of the friends
of mankind."

" The happy souls, when ' thrice ' purified in the sun,
ascend to a succession of still higher spheres, from
whence they can no more descend, to traverse the
circle of those globes and stars which float in a less
pure atmosphere." .　　.　　.　　.　　.

10. These remarks only apply to the Bardism of very
early pre-Christian times .　　.　　.　　.　　.

11. In the remote past death had no terrors; it was regarded only as a transformation within the continuity of existence .　　.　　.　　.　　.

12. The Welsh Triads speak of the " stones of Gwyddon
and Ganhebon on which were read the arts and
sciences of the world ".　　.　　.　　.　　.

13. W. B. Yeats' " Later Poems ", 1924. The original (?)
legend is given in the Ancient " Book of Leinster " .

14. In the last decade researches by Frau Dr. Kolisko
(Stuttgart) have proved definitely the influences of
all the planets of our system, and of the Sun, upon
metals and plant growth, varying according to their
position and relation to one another. See Biblio-
graphy .　　.　　.　　.　　.　　.

15. See an article in " The Present Age ", Vols. I, II, and
III by Eugen Kolisko, M.D. Also Gerbert Groh-
mann's " Die Pflanze ". And Rudolf Steiner's
" Das Rätsel des Menschen ", etc. .　　.　　.

16. NOTE: This fourth " sphere " might be intended to represent what, according to occultism in general, is the first " supersensible " region of the inner part of the Earth-globe itself, into which the Moon sends its influences, but in a phantom-like way. The Earth can be regarded as a mirror, sending back into space a " reflection " of the cosmic " rays ". The reflection of the Moon-sphere proper could then well be called the " habitation of dwellers in Paradise ". But it is the region of " ghosts " .   .

17. " Beyond the North Wind ": a suggestion that those who dwell " beyond " it are those who are " behind it "—that is, know the other side of the secrets of Apollo—the secrets of Cronos. The North was regarded by the ancients as the " birth-place of Time " .   .   .   .

18. " Makrokosmos and Makrokosmos ". (Philosophisch-Anthroposophisch Verlag, Switzerland.)   .   .

19. Or alternatively, as a historical study, seeking to trace the localities throughout the world where the seven planetary oracle-sanctuaries were established after Atlantis .   .   .   .

20. Summarised from " Eurhythmy as Visible Speech ", by Rudolf Steiner   .   .   .   .   .   .

21. In the " Pistis Sophia " it is recorded that: " This is the name of the immortal: a a a, ō ō ō; and this is the name of the voice for the sake of which the Perfect Man hath set himself in motion: i i i." So, A, O, I. (G. R. S. Mead's translation)   .   .

22. Compare the " twelve Nidanas " of Buddhism, which are the twelve causes that bring the spiritual being of man into earthly incarnation, and " fetter " him.

23. "Anthroposophy "; a quarterly review. Vol. 4, No. 3. Anthroposophical Publishing Company, London .

24. " World History in the Light of the Holy Grail ". By Dr. W. J. Stein. (Orient-Occident Publishing Company)   .   .   .   .

25. See the Gospel of St. Luke, xi, 29. " the sign of the prophet Jonah ". Three days and nights in the belly of the whale refers to the mystical death of initiation   .   .   .   .

26. In the Triads (Triad of Wisdom) the Teacher tells the Disciple that " there are five elements: calas, or earth; water; breath; uvel—which is fire; and " nwyvre "; and every one of them is dead except the nwyvre which is God, from Whom comes all life." Nwyvre is described as " a fine ætherial fluid "—the " quint-essence " of the alchemists.

Much could be discovered in this connection if one could be sure of the accuracy of the naming of the plants enumerated in Taliesin's list. It is generally said that " five " plants were used.   .   .   .

27. "An end to eternal knowledge! The Sages no longer announce their wisdom to the world ".   .   .

28. There is a Persian legend which tells how Huschenk, Prince of Persia, found and tamed a " twelve-legged " horse, and in riding it overcame the Titans   .   .   .   .

29. The difficult question of reincarnation plays a most important part in the correct understanding of these things. But the question cannot be dealt with in this book   .   .   .   .

30. Selected from a MS. collection by Llywelyn Sion, about the year 1560, some of them being of great antiquity   .   .   .   .

31. " Hibernian-Druid " is not intended to be taken as " Irish Druid ", but in the sense of the whole range of influence of the Hibernian Mysteries which spread far and wide   .   .   .   .

32. For a full account of these legends see " The Arthurian Legend ", by John Rhys. (Clarendon Press).   .

33. " Die Aegyptischen Pyramiden ". By E. Bindel. There this question is fully discussed. For a suggestive description of the Egyptian initiation see Edouard Schuré's " The Great Initiates "   .   .

34. Physical experiments carried out for several years in the Biological Institute of the Goetheanum, Stuttgart, by Frau L. Kolisko have definitely proved the effects on mineral and plant substances of cosmic radiations. The results are published in a series of pamphlets, "Sternewirken in Erdenstoffen". (Orient-Occident Publishing Company, Stuttgart)   .   .

35. Many of the priestly mummies (or their cases) are inscribed as those of " Divine Fathers ". Some are to be seen in the British Museum . . .

36. A charming book on this subject is James Baikie's "Amarna Age ". (Black) . . . . .

37. We have already spoken of the connection of the " Bull " with moisture . . . . .

38. For this account I am indebted to lectures on Summer and Winter Mysteries given by Rudolf Steiner . . . .

39. In Greek mythology, after the flood caused by Zeus, Deucalion and his wife Pyrrha were the only mortals saved, and consulted the sanctuary of Themis as to how the race of men might be restored. " The goddess bade them cover their heads and throw the bones of their mother behind them. After some doubts as to the meaning of this command, they agreed in interpreting the bones of their mother to mean the stones of the earth. They accordingly threw stones behind them, and from those thrown by Deucalion there sprang up men, and from those thrown by Pyrrha women." (Classical Dictionary) .

40. But in every such case it was not the mystery of " death " that was important but the mystery of immortality. To the ancients birth and death were relatively unimportant crises in the progress of existence . . . .

41. What is said here briefly about the " shadow-soul " or " Double " touches upon a very wide sphere of knowledge which for centuries was in the possession of many secret brotherhoods. It is only recently that Science, investigating the question of electricity in the human nervous system, has begun to touch the fringes of this knowledge; and this may be a reason why the " occult " side of it is no longer strictly reserved. It should eventually become, one would imagine, an essential factor in the study of geographical medicine, once it is fully recognised what part the " Earth itself " plays in the mental and physical life of man . . . . .

42. The literature of olden times abounds with descriptions of how this " light of initiation " was seen by clairvoyant persons .   .   .   .   .

43. Many students of the Gospels have had a feeling that Lazarus and John, the " disciple whom Jesus loved", are identical.   The most exhaustive investigation into this matter has been made by Rudolf Steiner. It is quite briefly but most convincingly summarised in his book " Christianity as Mystical Fact ", and should be read by anyone interested in this question. Other works by this author deal with the subjects in greater detail   .   .   .   .   .   .

44. That only two of the Gospels are mentioned here is only for the reason that these studies must be strictly limited in scope.   Naturally the others also play a no less important part in the whole question of the relation between the ancient Mysteries and esoteric Christianity .   .   .   .   .   .

45. See figure in Chapter XIV   .   .   .   .   .

46. An English version, edited by Taylor (Clarendon Press) appeared in the thirteenth century; but the legend originated in the eighth century.   .   .

47. This from the version of Konrad Fleck   .   .   .

48. " Das Wunder von Chartres ".   By Karl Heyer. (Rudolf Geering, Basle)   .   .   .   .

49. Giraldus Cambrensis: " Speculum Ecclesiasticum ". Also Vol. II Collinson's " Somersetshire ";   and Camden's " Britain " refers to Giraldus and gives a detailed account   .   .   .   .   .

50. J. Rhys: " The Arthurian Legend "   .   .   .

51. " Sons of God " is an expression formerly used to denote the initiated .   .   .   .   .   .

52. The Bible is an occult Book and full of secrets; but how few people would agree to applying that adjective to it!   .   .   .   .

53. " Das Mysterum der Europäischen Mitte ", by Ludwig Graf Polzer-Hoditz.   (Orient-Occident Publishing Company)   .   .   .   .

54. " Man is not the mere product of the earth on which he stands. The character of a people can quite well be opposed to the forces rising from the Earth." (Steiner) .   .   .   .

55. Modern medicine is beginning to investigate the idea that certain illnesses are connected with electrical forces   .   .   .   .

INDEX

301